BLACKS IN THE NEW WORLD

August Meier, Series Editor

BOOKS IN THE SERIES

Before the Ghetto: Black Detroit in the Nineteenth Century
    David M. Katzman

Black Business in the New South: A Social History of the North Carolina Mutual Life Insurance Company
    Walter B. Weare

The Search for a Black Nationality: Black Colonization and Emigration, 1787–1863
    Floyd J. Miller

Black Americans and the White Man's Burden, 1898–1903
    Willard B. Gatewood, Jr.

Slavery and the Numbers Game: A Critique of *Time on the Cross*
    Herbert G. Gutman

A Ghetto Takes Shape: Black Cleveland, 1870–1930
    Kenneth L. Kusmer

Freedmen, Philanthropy, and Fraud: A History of the Freedman's Savings Bank
    Carl R. Osthaus

The Democratic Party and the Negro: Northern and National Politics, 1868–92
    Lawrence Grossman

Black Ohio and the Color Line, 1860–1915
    David A. Gerber

Along the Color Line: Explorations in the Black Experience
    August Meier and Elliott Rudwick

Black over White: Negro Political Leadership in South Carolina during Reconstruction
    Thomas Holt

Abolitionism: The Brazilian Antislavery Struggle
    Joaquim Nabuco, translated and edited by Robert Conrad

Keeping the Faith: A. Philip Randolph, Milton P. Webster, and the Brotherhood of Sleeping Car Porters, 1925–37
    William H. Harris

Black Georgia in the Progressive Era, 1900–1920
    John Dittmer

Black Georgia
in the Progressive Era
1900 – 1920

John Dittmer

UNIVERSITY OF ILLINOIS PRESS

Urbana   Chicago   London

Library of Congress Cataloging in Publication Data

Dittmer, John, 1939–
  Black Georgia in the Progressive Era, 1900–1920.

  (Blacks in the New World)
  Bibliography: p.
  Includes index.
    1. Afro-Americans—Georgia—History. 2. Racism—
Georgia. 3. Georgia—Race relations. I. Title.
II. Series.
E185.93.G4D57   957.8′004′96073   77-24249
ISBN 0-252-00306-3

For Ellen

Contents

Preface   xi

Introduction   1

Jim Crow Georgia   8

Working   23

Community   50

The New Slavery   72

Racial Politics   90

Race and Reform   110

Race Violence   123

The Politics of Education   141

Black Thought   163

The War Years   181

Aftermath   203

Bibliographical Note   212

Index   225

Preface

THE TERM "progressive era" has not served well to define the United States during the early twentieth century. The initial view of a period marked by governmental reform, trust-busting, and moral uplift is, upon closer scrutiny, giving way to a more realistic picture of a time when progressive change was often more cosmetic than real. Where black America is concerned, however, there remains a consensus that the progressive era was "for whites only." Race violence, urban ghettos, and Jim Crow laws, along with continuing economic exploitation and deprivation, made this the nadir of Afro-American history. This study will not challenge these assumptions; indeed, it will provide ample documentation for them. But this hypothesis, standing alone, can lead to the conclusion that black people were one-dimensional, little more than passive victims of white supremacy.

A closer look at black life in a large southern state will reveal a situation far more complex. The history of black Georgia in the progressive era is the struggle of men and women to develop their own institutions, improve their economic conditions, educate their children, gain political rights, and maintain a sense of dignity. They were the victims of white oppression, but they also fought back on all levels, attempting to take charge of their destiny.

Throughout the course of my research the directors and staffs of the following libraries and institutions were most helpful: the Trevor B. Arnett Library, Atlanta University; the Interdenominational Theological Seminary Library; the Robert W. Woodruff

Library, Emory University; the Georgia Department of Archives and History; the Southern Labor Archives, Georgia State University; the Atlanta Public Library; the Atlanta Historical Society; the Federal Records Center, East Point, Georgia; the University of Georgia Library; the Georgia State Historical Society; the Fisk University Library; the Tougaloo College Library; the Southern Collection, University of North Carolina Library; the Manuscript Division, Library of Congress; the National Archives; the Moorland Collection, Howard University Library; and the Schomburg Library.

Among the many individuals who assisted me in this study are professors Clarence A. Bacote, Robert H. Ferrell, Joseph A. Herzenberg, and James W. Silver. My debt to the late Chase C. Mooney goes far beyond the scope of this book. I am grateful to Lee Alexander, Donna and Richard Barnes, Sarah and Barclay Brown, Melba and Avery Dittmer, David B. Grace II, John A. Griffin, and George A. Owens. My special thanks to a former student, Henry Williams, who spent a summer interviewing interesting people in South Georgia.

Editor Richard L. Wentworth and assistant editor Ann Lowry Weir of the University of Illinois Press have been both patient and helpful. My debt to series editor August Meier is immense. I have profited from his guidance, criticism, and encouragement at every stage of my work.

Ellen Tobey Dittmer edited each draft of the manuscript. She is a perceptive, demanding critic—and my best friend. This book is for her.

—J. D.

Tougaloo, Mississippi
June, 1977

Introduction

NEW YEAR'S DAY 1900 dawned cold and bright over Savannah. A freak winter storm had struck the port city the day before, and residents awoke to sun shining on ice-clad trees and snowy landscapes, a rare sight in this Deep South community. Freezing temperatures and harsh winds did not stop white Savannahans from celebrating the start of a new year. The Military Rifle Association held a turkey shoot at Avondale Range, the high school football team took on the Lawton Cadets, and sixty devoted golfers braved the elements to test the new nine-hole course. For indoor sports, the New Year's attraction at the Savannah Theatre was "The Little Minister," a play adapted from a James M. Barrie story; large crowds attended both matinee and evening performances. While such activities were underway, Savannah's black citizens were commemorating an event of historical importance to them. January 1, 1900, was the thirty-seventh anniversary of the signing of the Emancipation Proclamation.[1]

Savannah's "grandest celebration of Emancipation Day" began at eleven o'clock with a parade, formed at Liberty and East Broad streets, led by the black First Battalion Infantry of the Georgia Volunteers. The neat uniforms, precision marching, and weapons flashing in the sunlight impressed crowds lining the streets, recalling a time in Georgia when black troops had more than a ceremonial function. Following the battalion were the Robert G. Shaw Post of the Grand Army of the Republic and the Georgia Artillery. Then came the civilians, led by the march-

1. Savannah *Morning News*, Jan. 1, 2, 1900.

1

ing band from nearby Georgia State Industrial College. Community leaders and members of civic clubs riding in carriages filled out the ranks of the parade, which ended at the Second Baptist Church; there the literary "exercises" commenced. The audience heard Harper B. Jefferson read Lincoln's Proclamation and joined in several songs, including "John Brown's Body."

Featured speaker was Captain J. J. Durham, D.D., battalion chaplain. Dressed in full military uniform and looking "every inch a soldier," Captain Durham was in a positive frame of mind as he reminded his listeners of their accomplishments since emancipation. His reflection on those years of struggle noted that subjection of Negroes had cost this country "more blood and treasure than it took to establish its independence." Durham advised black people to work hard and acquire wealth, seeking "by all honorable means" to live on terms of peace and good will with their white neighbors.[2]

Similar celebrations took place throughout black Georgia each New Year's Day. But despite the ceremony, marching bands, and military display, much Emancipation Day oratory had a hollow ring, for the history of the Afro-American in Georgia had been one of enslavement and repression. While blacks could be justly proud of achievements made in the face of such adversity, a ruling class dedicated to white supremacy stood as a barrier to their progress.

Nearly 12 percent of the nation's blacks lived in Georgia in 1900, and these million citizens made up over 46 percent of the state's population. Over half of them lived in the black belt, the agricultural center of the state extending across middle and southwest Georgia. Blacks were a majority in these counties, where cotton was the staple. They also outnumbered whites in the six coastal counties where, in addition to cotton and corn, blacks cultivated rice and engaged in oystering and fishing.[3]

2. Savannah *Tribune*, Jan. 6, 1900.
3. Robert Preston Brooks, *The Agrarian Revolution in Georgia, 1865–1912* (Madison, Wis., 1914), 69, 108; Bureau of the Census, *Negro Population in the United States, 1790–1915* (Washington, 1918), 36, 43 (hereafter cited as *Negro Population*); Monroe Work, "The Negroes of Warsaw, Georgia," *Southern Workman*, 37 (Jan., 1908), 29–30. For more on black life on the coastal islands, see Writers' Program, *Drums and Shadows, Survival Studies Among the Georgia Coastal Negroes* (Athens, Ga., 1940).

Between the coast and the black belt in southeast Georgia lay the wiregrass section, part of the coastal plain, with sandy soil and vast pine forests carpeted with wiregrass. Blacks began to settle here in the late nineteenth century, when use of commercial fertilizers made the land more productive. By 1910 their population had risen to nearly 40 percent in this area.[4]

The mountainous region along the northern border attracted few blacks.[5] Where the southernmost extremities of the Appalachian and Blue Ridge chains spill over into north Georgia, the rugged terrain is not conducive to farming or heavy industry. South of the mountains and north of the black belt lies the upper piedmont, a region of farms and plantations settled by whites before the Civil War. This section, containing Atlanta, was the state's wealthiest, and it became the center of Georgia's industrial development. The early decades of the twentieth century would witness considerable black migration, first to the larger cities in Georgia, and later to the metropolises of the North.[6]

W. E. B. Du Bois once observed that Georgia was not only the geographical focus of America's black population, "but in many other respects, both now and yesterday, the Negro problems have seemed to be centered in this state."[7] Georgia was in the heart of the cotton kingdom, with slavery its dominant institution before the Civil War. That conflict left much of the state in ruins. White supremacy, however, was not to be a casualty, outliving both slavery and the war to become the only "just" basis for dealing with freedmen.

The brief postwar Reconstruction did not satisfy Georgia's half-million newly freed slaves. The peculiar institution died hard there, and the federal government's failure to provide economic compensation for years of forced labor often put blacks at the mercy of former masters. After meeting all congressional require-

4. Brooks, *Agrarian Revolution*, 102–3, 127.

5. *Ibid.*, 127. Blacks composed less than 10 percent of the total mountain population in 1910.

6. *Ibid.*, 71–72, 127; Thomas M. Deaton, "Atlanta During the Progressive Era" (Ph.D. dissertation, University of Georgia, 1969), 166. In 1900 30 percent of the piedmont population was black.

7. W. E. B. Du Bois, *The Souls of Black Folk, Essays and Sketches* (Chicago, 1903), 111.

The Five Sections of Georgia, with Percentage Blacks Formed of Total Population, 1910.

Source: Based on Robert Preston Brooks, *The Agrarian Revolution in Georgia, 1865–1912* (Madison, Wis., 1914), 127.

ments, including Negro enfranchisement, Georgia rejoined the Union in July, 1868. Two months later the Georgia House of Representatives, evenly divided between Democrats and Republicans, expelled twenty-five black members. Shortly thereafter the predominantly Republican Senate removed two black members, including Henry McNeal Turner. In protesting the dismissal, young Turner warned that "white men are not to be trusted. They will betray you. . . . This thing means revolution."[8]

Failure of House and Senate Republicans, many indebted to Negro voters, to defend their black colleagues indicated the prevailing attitude toward blacks. Freedmen risked death to vote for Ulysses S. Grant in 1868, a year when Ku Klux Klan terrorism killed scores of Georgia blacks.[9] When the legislature refused to ratify the Fifteenth Amendment in 1869, Congress again placed Georgia under military rule. The state was readmitted to the Union for a second time the following year, and thereafter the federal government adopted a "hands off" policy toward Georgia.[10]

The end of Reconstruction in Georgia marked the decline of black political participation for a time. Business interests took over the state in the 1870s and either eliminated or controlled the black vote.[11] Opposition to these "New South" conservatives arose among thousands of poor white farmers frustrated by lack of money and credit and by falling farm prices. The crop lien system, where supplies advanced by a merchant were secured by the farmer's crop, converted the state's economic system into a "huge pawnshop."[12] Farmer demands for redress eventually led to the rise of the Populists and brought the black man back into the political spotlight.

Populism in Georgia meant Tom Watson. Red-haired, freckle-faced, of slight stature and youthful appearance, Watson was a fiery orator who began his agrarian crusade in the 1880s. Elected

8. Edwin S. Redkey, *Black Exodus, Black Nationalist and Back-to-Africa Movements, 1890–1910* (New Haven, 1969), 27; Alan Conway, *The Reconstruction of Georgia* (Minneapolis, 1966), 52, 55–56, 138, 165–67; *Atlanta Constitution*, Sept. 4, 1868. The third black senator, A. A. Bradley, resigned under pressure earlier in the session.

9. Conway, *Reconstruction of Georgia*, 174–75.

10. *Ibid.*, 185, 223.

11. Alex M. Arnett, *The Populist Movement in Georgia* (New York, 1922), 32, 42.

12. *Ibid.*, 64.

to Congress in 1890 as a Democrat, Watson bolted the party to run as a Populist in 1892 and 1894. He viewed Georgia politics in terms of class struggle, and his uncompromising attacks on unjust privilege won him the enmity of leading politicians, industrialists, and editors. Campaigning for reelection in 1892, Watson addressed the race issue: he shared platforms with black speakers before integrated audiences, denounced lynching and the convict lease system, and hammered at the theme that white and black farmers faced the same problems.[13] Democrats defeated Watson's reelection bids by employing tactics of terror and fraud which had been perfected during Reconstruction. Populists fared better statewide, making a respectable showing in the 1892 elections and gathering nearly 45 percent of the vote two years later.[14] But the election of 1896, which saw the Populists nominate Democrat William Jennings Bryan for President, marked the decline of the Populist party in Georgia as well as nationally.[15]

The race question led to Populism's defeat in Georgia. Watson and his poor white farmers never saw blacks as social equals; rather, they advocated interracial cooperation only to strengthen the movement (just as a decade later for the same reason Watson would call for black disfranchisement).[16] Blacks supported the Populists to further their own political and economic interests. As it turned out, Democrats used race to keep other Democrats in the fold and to divide white Populists. Accusing Watson and his "communist" followers of plotting a return to "Negro rule," Democratic politicians steered their campaigns clear of economic issues and kept the Populists on the defensive. Democrats skillfully used the Negro issue to get white votes, while obtaining black votes through coercion and bribery.[17]

13. C. Vann Woodward, *Tom Watson, Agrarian Rebel* (New York, 1938), 221. See also Charles Crowe, "Tom Watson, Populists, and Blacks Reconsidered," *Journal of Negro History*, 55 (Apr., 1970), 99–116. Crowe's view of the possibilities of the white-black Populist coalition is less optimistic than Woodward's.

14. Woodward, *Tom Watson*, 234–41, 261.

15. Clarence A. Bacote, "The Negro in Georgia Politics, 1880–1908" (Ph.D. dissertation, University of Chicago, 1955), 209; Horace Calvin Wingo, "Race Relations in Georgia, 1872–1908" (Ph.D. dissertation, University of Georgia, 1969), 85–86.

16. Francis M. Wilhoit, "An Interpretation of Populism's Impact on the Georgia Negro," *Journal of Negro History*, 52 (Apr., 1967), 124.

17. Bacote, "Negro in Georgia Politics," 207–8; Woodward, *Tom Watson*, 234.

Failure of the Populist experiment in interracial politics, then, was due largely to efforts of conservative Democrats—wealthy, educated, "respectable"—who exploited racial tensions to preserve their power. They destroyed a class movement and kept the Negro in place. White Populists then made the black man scapegoat for their defeat, placing racial feeling above economic welfare and thus insuring white supremacy in Georgia.[18] Blacks would not again be a factor in state elections for over half a century. Populism's failure heightened tensions between poor whites and blacks and increased race violence and proscription. Twentieth-century Georgia inherited the legacy of the 1890s, and, in the area of race relations, at least, did not profit from its mistakes.

18. Theodore Saloutos, *Farmer Movements in the South, 1865–1933* (Berkeley, 1960), 135; Robert Sanders, "Southern Populists and the Negro, 1893–1905," *Journal of Negro History,* 54 (July, 1969), 255.

Jim Crow Georgia

THE BROAD PATTERN of racial segregation in Georgia did not take shape immediately after the Civil War. It is true that two distinct societies, one black and one white, had existed since slavery, and social custom and practice had always circumscribed black freedom. Postwar legislatures did pass laws segregating public schools, prohibiting interracial marriage, and separating black and white convicts, while most local governments legislated against blacks being buried in white cemeteries. Still, blacks had more freedom of movement in Georgia in the 1870s and 1880s than they would enjoy again until the 1960s. Blacks and whites sat next to each other on streetcars and trains, shared the same public recreational facilities, and shopped in integrated business districts.[1] At the turn of the century black professionals were still renting space in "white" office buildings, and black businessmen were operating stores for a racially mixed clientele in the white business district. Although the courts were in the hands of white men, as late as 1902 blacks occasionally served on juries.[2] All this was to change.

Although segregation was to become a way of life throughout Georgia, the battle over Jim Crow would be waged in the cities. In the years after emancipation the city increasingly became the center of black intellectual life, political protest, social activity,

1. John Hammond Moore, "Jim Crow in Georgia," *South Atlantic Quarterly*, 66 (Fall, 1967), 556; Wingo, "Race Relations in Georgia," 272; H. M. Turner, *The Laws and Judicial Decisions Affecting the Colored People of the State of Georgia* (Atlanta, 1906), 17, 36–38.
2. City directories for Atlanta, Savannah, Augusta, Macon, 1900–1905. A black juror in Augusta made news because his color prevented the sequestered jury from eating in a Jim Crow restaurant. Augusta *Chronicle*, Apr. 20, 1902.

business enterprise, and religious and fraternal organization. Yet black migration was matched and surpassed by that of whites, many of whom were poor illiterates just off the farm. This biracial influx upset the old balance between paternalistic aristocrats and Negroes who kept their place, and when white urbanites began to demand legalized segregation, blacks protested vigorously in major cities.

Nearly a third of Georgia cities had black majorities in 1900, yet almost half the urban black population lived in Atlanta, Savannah, and Augusta.[3] These cities housed much of the black middle class, the important intellectual and political leaders, and all the four-year colleges. They were also home to thousands of impoverished people who existed in ·slums much worse than today's ghettos. A look at residential patterns in these three cities will shed light on the urban condition of blacks and demonstrate Jim Crow's increasing presence in Georgia cities.

Savannah is Georgia's oldest and proudest city. The many parks, public squares, monuments, and charming old homes convey a sense of history and genteel aristocracy, an image Savannahans have long cultivated. Savannah looked to Charleston, not to Atlanta, for inspiration, and like its Carolina counterpart took pride in a reputation for racial paternalism which went back to the days of slavery. Before the Civil War blacks lived in all parts of Savannah, in small cabins behind their masters' residences or in their owners' homes. Well into the 1870s black and white laborers shared modest neighborhoods while wealthier blacks lived in affluent white areas, causing historian John Blassingame to conclude that "Residential segregation during this period appears to have been based as much on class and economic status as on race." As late as the turn of the century a good number of the old house-servant class were still living beside the sons of their former masters, but racially identifiable neighborhoods were becoming the rule.[4]

3. Bureau of the Census, *Negroes in the United States, 1920–1932* (Washington, 1933), 96 (hereafter cited as *Negroes in the U.S.*).
4. John W. Blassingame, "Before the Ghetto: The Making of the Black Community in Savannah, Georgia, 1865–1880," *Journal of Social History*, 6 (Summer, 1973), 481; W. E. B. Du Bois, ed., *Some Notes on Negro Crime, Particularly in Georgia*, Atlanta University *Publications*, No. 9 (Atlanta, 1904), 52; Savannah

Savannah's residential pattern in the early twentieth century contrasts with more recent urban trends, for in Savannah the central city was predominantly white (including the wealthiest whites) and the outlying sections were largely black. Twenty-eight thousand blacks lived in Savannah in 1900, comprising 51.8 percent of the population. Du Bois saw the distribution of population resembling a great 0, with the whites in the center and the blacks in the surrounding circle. While this is a simplified picture, Savannah's whites were in danger of becoming trapped in their own ghetto by the city's black majority.[5] Part of official Savannah's response to this dilemma involved an early urban renewal project, with Negro removal its primary objective. Confined on the north by the Savannah River and on the west by a large black slum, whites wanted to expand to the southeast, where there were large tracts of undeveloped land. A lower-class black neighborhood named Sunnyside had blocked access to this outlying area, but in 1909 city fathers decided to eliminate the community, which "has long retarded the growth of the city in that section." Since blacks did not own the shacks and tenements there, they were powerless to protest once white landlords and officials agreed to level the area.[6] What resulted was "a beautiful restricted residential development," with paved streets and sidewalks and modern sanitation and water facilities. Reflecting on this progress, Mayor George W. Tiedman concluded that Savannah "should stand ready to undertake any similar work in any locality within the city limits, upon like conditions."[7]

By the end of World War I Savannah showed a more segregated housing pattern than it had in 1900. Poor rural blacks moved into city slums which produced one of the highest death rates in the country. The black middle class escaped these conditions as

City Directory, 1900. This examination of residential patterns is based upon studies of city directories, especially in Savannah, Augusta, and Atlanta, for the period 1900–1920. County tax digests were helpful in determining relative wealth of black and white citizens. Unless otherwise noted, these are the sources for the following analysis of urban housing patterns.

5. W. E. B. Du Bois, "The Negro South and North," *Bibliotheca Sacra*, 62 (July, 1905), 504; *Negro Population*, 93.

6. Savannah *Municipal Reports*, 1909, p. 14; *Negro Population*, 471. Only 6 percent of Savannah blacks owned homes.

7. Savannah *Municipal Reports*, 1912, p. 34.

best it could, with a number of families moving from their old homes in the "integrated" central city into a new black neighborhood on the east side. Yet there remained many racially integrated streets, and more effective residential segregation in Savannah would not come until years later.[8]

Augusta lies on the banks of the Savannah River 130 miles northwest of the port city, drawing energy for its cotton mills from the river as it runs through the piedmont down toward the coastal plain. At first glance the "Lowell of the South" appeared much different from Georgia's oldest city, but Augusta and Savannah had much in common. Both were old communities, home to aristocratic white families who looked down on the "rednecks" of the rest of the state.[9] Like Savannah, Augusta contained a sizable segment of the state's small free black population before the war, and it produced outstanding black leaders.

As late as 1900 blacks lived in most areas of Augusta, including the exclusive white section near Greene Street. But as one former black resident recalled, blacks "who had lived in the center of town were finding it convenient to move out." While white workers rented homes in the mill district in northwest Augusta, most blacks lived on the southern outskirts of town. A self-contained black community called the "Terri" developed there, and became the center of black business, educational, and social life.[10] If its middle class lived in comparative comfort, most of black Augusta shared the fate of nearly all urban poor: streets were unpaved, water and sewage lines unavailable, drainage bad, and lighting poor. This was a breeding ground for disease.[11] Local officials used residential segregation to deprive blacks of essential city services, while red light districts, saloons, and gambling dens were located in black areas away from the white

8. *Negroes in the U.S.*, 452; Savannah *City Directory*, 1918; John Finney, "The Human Ecology of Savannah, Georgia: A Spatial Analysis of Racial Segregation, 1940–1970" (Master's thesis, Atlanta University, 1972).

9. W. E. B. Du Bois, "Georgia, Invisible Empire State," in Ernest Gruening, ed., *These United States, A Symposium* (New York, 1924), 323; E. Franklin Frazier, *The Negro Family in the United States* (Chicago, 1966), 151–53.

10. Richard R. Wright, Jr., *87 Years Behind the Black Curtain: An Autobiography* (Philadelphia, 1965), 60; *Official Reports, City of Augusta, Georgia*, 1901, pp. 30–31; Augusta *City Directory*, 1902, 1910, 1919.

11. Augusta Department of Public Health, *Report*, 1914, p. 7; Augusta *Official Reports*, 1901, p. 202.

middle class. Black Augustans could neither compel nor convince
city officials to respond to their needs. Ironically, these same
public servants often cited squalid living conditions as evidence
of black depravity.[12]

In the foothills of north Georgia, Atlanta stands in sharp contrast to Augusta, Savannah, and the rest of the state. By the turn
of the century Atlanta was a boom town, rapidly becoming the
commercial center of the South. Although it had established white
families, the postwar aristocracy here rested on new wealth. Atlanta's muse was Henry Grady, not Jefferson Davis. To be sure,
there was much parlor talk of the Old South and the Lost Cause,
and white Atlantans never forgave General Sherman. But the
emphasis was on the future, and the smell of money in the air
lured people from throughout the South. The bulk of the new
migrants were mountain whites from north Georgia and blacks
up from plantations and small towns. These two groups shared
a common poverty, provincialism, lack of education, and mutual
distrust. Each came to the city hoping for good jobs, decent
housing, and education for their children. Given prevailing racial
attitudes, it was natural that poor whites and blacks would come
into conflict while struggling to better their lots. If the Atlanta
race riot of 1906 was not inevitable, it was certainly predictable.

Atlanta's residential patterns reflected its history. The city was
home to few blacks during the war, so there was no antebellum
tradition of house servants and free blacks living in respectable
white neighborhoods.[13] The war devastated Atlanta, and when it
was rebuilt, black migrants moved in where they could. Du Bois
saw the black population of Atlanta "stretched like a great dumb-
bell across the city, with one great center in the east and a smaller
one in the west, connected by a narrow belt." Black settlement
began in the center of the city, where there was less resistance.
When immigrants tried to expand first to the east and later to the
west, their efforts met strong white opposition.[14]

Black population more than doubled from 1890 to 1920, when

12. Augusta *Official Reports*, 1900–1920.
13. Franklin M. Garrett, *Atlanta and Environs: A Chronicle of the People and
Events*, I (New York, 1954), 740. Only seven free blacks were listed as living
in Atlanta in 1860.
14. Du Bois, "Negro South and North," 505; Dorothy Slade, "The Evolution
of Negro Areas in the City of Atlanta" (Master's thesis, Atlanta University, 1946),
30, 33.

nearly 63,000 blacks lived in the capital city. Most of these immigrants were unskilled or semi-skilled and had to settle in slum-
infested valleys and bottoms. (Whites usually occupied the ridges
and hilltops.[15]) The worst slums were on the west side, between
the Georgia Railroad and Atlanta University. Neglected by the
city, streets were full of holes, mud, and debris. There were no
sanitation facilities in these crowded neighborhoods, which were
centers of prostitution and bootlegging. Except for the Atlanta
University vicinity, middle-class blacks avoided west Atlanta during the early part of the century; instead, they bought homes in
the old fourth ward just east of downtown. Here was the heart of
the Negro business district, and black doctors, dentists, clergymen,
civil servants, and businessmen lived in close proximity. Decatur
Street, one of the earliest main thoroughfares in black Atlanta, for
a time housed the majority of black businesses and resorts. Later
Auburn Avenue, also in the fourth ward, would emerge as the
center of black enterprise.[16]

Although blacks concentrated in the east and west sides near
downtown Atlanta, they also lived in most other sections. Despite
the variety of housing patterns, Atlanta in 1900 was more segregated than older communities like Savannah and Augusta, and
pressures to keep blacks in their defined sections grew with the
continuing flow of immigrants seeking housing. It is not surprising
that Atlanta was the first Georgia city to attempt residential segregation by law.[17]

The Atlanta segregation ordinance of 1913, patterned after
Baltimore's, established white and black neighborhoods and stated
that an occupant of a house in a mixed block could legally object
to a person of another color moving in next door.[18] The first case

15. *Negroes in the U.S.*, 57; Garrett, *Atlanta and Environs*, I, 740. Atlanta's
white population grew even faster than its black population during this thirty-
year period.

16. Slade, "Evolution of Negro Areas," 24; Louie Davis Shivery, "The Neighborhood Union," *Phylon: The Atlanta University Review of Race and Culture*, 3
(Second Quarter, 1942), 151. For an informative description of the development
of black Atlanta, see Dan Durett and Dana F. White, *An-Other Atlanta: The
Black Heritage* (Atlanta, 1975).

17. Slade, "Evolution of Negro Areas," 25; Atlanta *City Directory*, 1900–1920;
Fulton County *Tax Digest*, 1900, 1910, 1920.

18. Roger L. Rice, "Residential Segregation by Law, 1910–1917," *Journal of
Southern History*, 34 (May, 1968), 181. See also Gilbert T. Stephenson, "The
Segregation of the White and Negro Races in Cities," *South Atlantic Quarterly*,
13 (Jan., 1914), 1–18.

tried under the law involved a white man brought to court by a group of black tenants and owners. The judge ordered him to move from the Negro neighborhood within thirty days. This law was so arbitrary that the Georgia Supreme Court struck it down in 1915.[19] While extralegal pressures prevented blacks from encroaching into white areas, the city council passed a second ordinance stipulating that no Negro could occupy a residence in a block with a white majority. Atlanta blacks challenged this law's constitutionality, but the Georgia courts ruled it legal. A year later, in a landmark decision, the Supreme Court in *Buchanan* v. *Warley* held that laws interfering with a person's right to buy or sell property were in violation of the Fourteenth Amendment.[20] Several Georgia cities ignored the decision and passed new residential ordinances. More effective were tactics of coercion, ranging from restrictive covenants to Klan-type terrorism. Ultimately, blacks could move only into undeveloped areas or residential sections that whites no longer found desirable.[21]

Examination of residential patterns in representative Georgia cities leads to several conclusions.[22] First, racial separation in housing during the early twentieth century was not simply an "other side of the tracks" phenomenon. Although there were places like Albany, where a line drawn through the center of town divided nine-tenths of the whites from nine-tenths of the blacks, other cities had more complex patterns.[23] Larger communities like Atlanta, Savannah, and Augusta had black sections scattered throughout the city, with many streets having a checkerboard appearance. Some blocks were divided racially, often by a vacant lot or store. Totally black areas were more common than all-white sections. A familiar sight in older, wealthier white areas was an alley behind a row of homes. Here lived the families of black domestics. Newer, exclusive white addresses such as West

---

19. Atlanta *Constitution*, Feb. 8, 1914; *Cary* v. *City of Atlanta*, 143 Ga. 192, 845 E. 456 (1915).

20. *Buchanan* v. *Warley*, 245 U.S. 81 (1917); Savannah *Tribune*, Nov. 10, 1917; Atlanta *Constitution*, July 26, 1916; Sept. 1, 1917.

21. Moore, "Jim Crow in Georgia," 558.

22. In addition to Savannah, Augusta, and Atlanta, which were examined in detail, city directories and tax digests for Columbus, Macon, Albany, and Rome were checked, as was a special census taken in 1911 in Milledgeville, available in the Georgia Department of Archives and History, Atlanta.

23. Du Bois, "Negro South and North," 504.

Peachtree Street in Atlanta and Walton Way in Augusta had no black alleys, nor did these residences list black help as "living in." The decline of the master-servant relation contributed to segregation of upper-class neighborhoods.

Middle-class blacks led the drive for better housing, and in the early twentieth century many resided on the same streets with whites. Here black ministers, teachers, and businessmen lived next door to lower-middle-class whites. Mrs. Cecilia Carter Rogers, daughter of a prominent black Atlanta clergyman, recalls that when she was a child white people "lived in front of us, and all the way down on both sides." Across the street was a white policeman, whose two daughters "would come over to our house to practice their music lessons. We had a little pony and cart and on Sundays they used the cart."[24] Black business and professional people lived peaceably with whites of lower occupational but similar economic status in Georgia's major cities. These whites moved out into newer subdivisions between 1900 and 1920, and transitional areas turned black. By the time young Cecilia Carter entered college, no whites remained on her street.

Blacks had as their primary goal decent housing, not racial integration. Certainly there were no status gains for the black physician who lived next door to a white soft-drink salesman in an integrated block. Paved streets, curbs, and sidewalks, along with street lighting, and water and sewer mains, were no doubt of more importance to the doctor. And after World War I, when real estate men began developing middle-class housing for blacks, complete with modern facilities, blacks responded enthusiastically, building homes in their segregated neighborhoods which were the envy of many whites.

The pattern of racially segregated housing evolved gradually in Georgia cities during the half-century following the Civil War. While poor blacks had always found themselves packed together in shanties in disease-ridden slums, the black middle class for a

24. Interview with Mrs. Cecilia Carter Rogers, July 13, 1973, Atlanta. Reverend E. R. Carter was pastor of Friendship Baptist Church for sixty-two years, and was author of *The Black Side of Atlanta* (Atlanta, 1894). The term "middle class" as used here refers to all blacks living above the poverty level, from skilled artisans to business and professional people. Few blacks had the wealth to be designated "upper class," although this term will be used later in connection with social stratification within the black community.

time had no geographical "place" on the city map. By the 1890s the complementary philosophies of "scientific" racism and Social Darwinism were creating pressures in the white community, not only for totally segregated neighborhoods, but also for Jim Crow regulations further proscribing the freedom of all blacks.

The first major test came in 1891, when the General Assembly passed legislation permitting Georgia cities to separate the races on streetcars. This statute was vague, leaving implementation to the transit lines. Company officials, who thought the law a nuisance, yielded to black boycotts in Atlanta, Augusta, and Savannah in the 1890s.[25] But by 1900 increasing segregationist sentiment led Augusta and other cities to pass municipal ordinances segregating trolleys.[26] Most local laws did not designate seats for black and white passengers; instead, they provided only that whites should sit from front to rear and blacks from the back forward. Eager to move blacks to the rear, conductors were not so zealous in asking whites to move forward, forcing many black passengers to stand when plenty of front seats were available. Violence, even death resulted from feuds over territorial prerogatives. Humiliation was a daily occurrence for black riders, who had to remain passive while white conductors and passengers ordered them about.[27] Blacks resisted new regulations in cities all over the South, with Georgia boycotts in Atlanta, Augusta, and Rome in 1900, and Savannah in 1906–7.[28]

Trouble in Atlanta began when the city chartered a second streetcar line pledged to separate the races. When blacks boycotted the new company and continued to patronize the original line, the city council enacted an ordinance segregating all trolleys.[29] Blacks then boycotted both lines in the spring of 1900, with

25. *Acts and Resolutions of the General Assembly of the State of Georgia*, 1891, pp. 157–58 (hereafter cited as *Georgia Laws*); August Meier and Elliott Rudwick, "The Boycott Movement against Jim Crow Streetcars in the South, 1900–1906," *Journal of American History*, 55 (Mar., 1969), 756; George Baldwin to Thomas Webster, May 22, 1905, George Johnson Baldwin Papers, Southern History Collection, University of North Carolina Library, Chapel Hill.

26. Moore, "Jim Crow in Georgia," 557; Meier and Rudwick, "The Boycott Movement," 756–58.

27. Atlanta *Independent*, May 25, 1907.

28. Meier and Rudwick, "The Boycott Movement," 758–59.

29. Du Bois, "Negro South and North," 509.

some initial success. Grace Towns Hamilton remembers that her father, George A. Towns, and a black lawyer named Peyton Allen "just both bought bicycles and refused to subject themselves to segregation." Despite such acts of defiance, the companies held firm. Eventually the inconveniences proved too great, and the boycott collapsed. A similar fate met efforts in Rome.[30]

The Augusta city council passed a Jim Crow law after a socially prominent white man was shot to death by a black man following an altercation over seating arrangements. The next day a mob lynched the alleged killer, William Wilson.[31] Three weeks after the shooting, black editor William Jefferson White of the *Georgia Baptist* reprinted an article from the Washington *Bee* which referred to Wilson as "a martyr in defense of female virtue." Two hundred enraged whites marched on White's office, threatening to burn the building and lynch the editor. Blacks surrounded the office to prevent the mob from doing its work, and passions subsided only after White publicly apologized for reprinting the article.[32]

In this atmosphere of racial tension Augusta blacks organized a boycott to protest streetcar segregation. Initially they were successful in keeping blacks off the cars. But whites were determined to make the new law stick, and because blacks had no alternative form of mass transit they eventually accommodated to the new law.[33]

This initial wave of Jim Crow sentiment did not hit Savannah, where conservative whites took pride in their patronizing approach toward blacks. A coalition of leading whites and the streetcar officials joined blacks in 1902 to convince the city council to defeat a segregation ordinance. Yet popular support developed among whites for segregated streetcars, and in 1906 the council unanimously passed a Jim Crow ordinance. Angered by this setback, Savannah blacks agreed not to ride the streetcars. The black community acted with solidarity. There were even attempts to

30. Interview with Mrs. Grace Towns Hamilton, Mar. 18, 1974, Atlanta; Meier and Rudwick, "The Boycott Movement," 768, 775.
31. Augusta *Chronicle*, May 14, 15, 1900.
32. *Ibid.*, June 3, 4, 1900.
33. *Ibid.*, May 17, 23, 24, June 4, 1900. Another factor working against the boycott was that streetcar ridership was overwhelmingly white, so the owners of the line were not financially crippled by the boycott. *Ibid.*, May 23, 1900.

organize black transit lines.[34] Black hackmen charged boycotters reduced rates, and enforcers stationed at streetcar stops helped dissuade potential passengers.

White Savannah was surprised by the boycott's success. Both city officials and the streetcar company failed to break it, although police intimidated boycotters and arrested unlicensed hackmen.[35] The Savannah Electric Company, which owned the line, worked behind the scenes to persuade blacks to ride the cars. Its president, George Johnson Baldwin, was also head of five railway companies outside Georgia, active in local civic and charitable organizations, and president of the Savannah Board of Trade. To end an earlier boycott against his Jacksonville, Florida, line, Baldwin had bribed influential Negro ministers to exhort their flocks to ride the streetcars, and he may have done the same in Savannah.[36]

Black ministers, instrumental in organizing the boycott, had in their ranks a few white-designated "leaders" who did the establishment's bidding in return for small favors. Such a man was Reverend E. Johnson Nelson, author of an anonymous letter to the Savannah *Press* denouncing the "uncalled for agitation against the streetcar company." Nelson did not sign the letter for fear of being called a "white man's nigger," and further confided to George Baldwin that boycott leaders were "immoral scamps . . . many of whom, because they are of a lighter hue from the masses, hold themselves 'as good as the white people.' . . ."[37]

Divided leadership was a factor in the decline of the boycott's effectiveness in the spring of 1907. Many lost heart when instructors at the state industrial school started to ride the cars again, for, as one man put it, "what can be expected of the less informed ones when men of their ilk will Jim Crow?"[38] The boy-

---

34. Savannah *Tribune*, Sept. 1, 8, 15, 22, 29, 1906; Meier and Rudwick, "The Boycott Movement," 760, 763–64. See also August Meier and Elliott Rudwick, "A Strange Chapter in the Career of Jim Crow," in August Meier and Elliott Rudwick, eds., *The Making of Black America, Essays in Negro Life and History*, II (New York, 1969), 14–19.

35. Savannah *Tribune*, Sept. 22, 1906; Meier and Rudwick, "The Boycott Movement," 763–64.

36. Baldwin to Webster, May 22, 1905, Baldwin Papers; Savannah *Tribune*, Mar. 16, 1907.

37. E. Jonathan Nelson to Baldwin, Dec. 15, 19, 1906, Baldwin Papers; Savannah *Press*, Dec. 17, 1906; Savannah *Tribune*, Mar. 16, 1907.

38. Savannah *Tribune*, Mar. 16, 1907.

cott had hurt the streetcar company, costing $50,000 in lost revenues over a two-year period and decreasing earning power to a point where the company sought tax relief from the city. But economic pressure was not enough to change a policy demanded by whites.[39] Despite failure, boycott leaders in Savannah and other cities—the ministers, businessmen, and professionals— did unite their communities for a time against a trend toward total segregation. Their leadership was a model for those who, years later, would dismantle the Jim Crow system.

Railroads and steamship companies also drew the color line. Boycotting railroads was impractical, so blacks limited protests to challenges of the 1891 law segregating races on trains and an 1899 statute segregating sleeping cars. Du Bois, J. W. E. Bowen, and the Reverend H. H. Proctor protested the Pullman car law, which failed to require trains to furnish sleeping-car facilities for black passengers. Booker T. Washington secretly encouraged these efforts. As late as 1904 Washington and Du Bois were planning court action against the Pullman Company, but the suit did not materialize.[40] Five bishops of the A.M.E. Church, including Henry McNeal Turner, filed a complaint before the Interstate Commerce Commission, charging several southern railroads and the Pullman Company with furnishing inferior first-class accommodations for blacks. The Commission dismissed the complaint on grounds that "undue discrimination or prejudice was not shown."[41] On the Atlantic coast the Beaufort-Savannah steamship line began to segregate ships during the summer tourist season of 1912, forcing black passengers to ride on the lower deck amidst freight, boilers, and engines. A boycott the next year discouraged black organizations from booking excursions (which were not Jim Crowed), but after a few months black excursionists resumed their voyages.[42]

Protests failed to stop the march of Jim Crow through Georgia.

39. Baldwin to Mayor and Aldermen, Mar. 24, 1908, Baldwin Papers; Meier and Rudwick, "The Boycott Movement," 763; Savannah *Tribune*, July 4, 1908.

40. *Georgia Laws*, 1899, p. 66; Savannah *Tribune*, Dec. 30, 1899; Booker T. Washington to W. E. B. Du Bois, Jan. 27, Feb. 27, 1904; Emmett J. Scott to Richard W. Thompson, Feb. 10, 1905, Booker T. Washington Papers, Manuscript Division, Library of Congress; Louis R. Harlan, "The Secret Life of Booker T. Washington," *Journal of Southern History*, 37 (Aug., 1971), 399–400.

41. Atlanta *Constitution*, Feb. 27, 1908; June 30, 1909.

42. Savannah *Tribune*, July 13, 1912; Feb. 15, Mar. 5, Apr. 5, June 7, 1913.

Although blacks had never shared equal access to public accommodations, laws separating the races had not appeared with
any frequency until the 1890s. The *Plessy* v. *Ferguson* decision of
1896 gave federal sanction to "separate but equal" facilities.
Whether by law or custom, urban blacks in the early twentieth
century found themselves increasingly segregated.[43] Canton, with
less than a thousand inhabitants, prohibited any blacks except
nurses in charge of white children from "passing upon or loitering
in the park of the town." Violators were subject to a hundred-
dollar fine or sixty days on the chain gang, or both. Other towns
excluded blacks from most parks, either legally or through intimidation. In the early twentieth century Savannah had five playgrounds for white children, none for blacks. These recreational
areas had facilities and equipment for baseball, basketball, tennis,
soccer, volleyball, and gymnastics, all paid for in part by black
Savannahans who could not even set foot on the playgrounds as
spectators.[44]

By the second decade of the twentieth century nearly all larger
cities required racial separation in restaurants, usually by parti-
tion. Theatres, lectures, concerts, and athletic events were either
closed to blacks or open only on a Jim Crow basis. Swimming
pools were exclusively for whites. When the Southern Bank of
Savannah established separate deposit windows in 1903, most
black patrons withdrew their accounts—but the separate windows
remained.[45]

Despite its "New South" image, Atlanta was also a Jim Crow
city. Bars and restaurants were open to only one race, and barber
shops also had to designate whether they served black or white
patrons. Jim Crow trains were becoming the rule in the South, yet
Atlanta even refused blacks permission to enter and leave by the
front door of the terminal. The city council passed an ordinance in
1903 prohibiting black college athletes from playing football

43. Wingo, "Race Relations in Georgia," 118–20; Moore, "Jim Crow in
Georgia," 557.
44. Moore, "Jim Crow in Georgia," 559; W. E. B. Du Bois, "Looking Seventy-
five Years Backward," *Phylon*, 3 (Second Quarter, 1942), 243; Savannah *Municipal Reports*, 1915, pp. 343–55.
45. Moore, "Jim Crow in Georgia," 558; Arthur F. Raper, *Tenants of the
Almighty* (New York, 1943), 140; Savannah *Tribune*, Apr. 11, 1903; City of
Macon, *Code*, 1914, pp. 459–60. Macon permitted Negro nurses and their white
charges to enter white motion picture theaters, but forbade the women from
taking white children into a black theater.

games in Brisbane Park, black prisoners rode to the stockade in separate vehicles, and black witnesses swore on Jim Crow Bibles in Atlanta courts.[46] As in other cities, black customers received shabby treatment in Atlanta stores. A clerk in a local haberdashery told a college graduate that he might "buy but not try on" a hat, while clerks in other stores would not fit gloves or shoes on black women. By the 1900s nearly all office building elevators were labeled "For White People Only," or "For Colored People, Freight, Etc."[47] All of Atlanta's twenty parks were segregated, including the zoo area at Grant Park. There each race followed its separate passage through the grounds. Separation of the races became so complete that when a black man first bought an automobile a white Atlantan asked him, "Whose road are you going to drive it on?"[48]

Blacks could not even visit public libraries. Du Bois led an Atlanta delegation into the newly dedicated Carnegie Library in 1902 to ask trustees to open the building to all people, arguing that a public library should benefit both races and pointing out the illegality of using tax money to support library facilities for whites only. The chairman responded: "Do you not think that allowing whites and negroes to use this library would be fatal to its usefulness?" As the delegation left, the trustees promised a separate library for blacks would soon be forthcoming. Nineteen years later the Negro public library branch opened its doors.[49] The officials who denied intellectual opportunities to blacks could not have been unaware that the decision was yet another step toward a permanent caste system.

During the first two decades of the twentieth century, segregation in Georgia reached a new plateau: the color line gave way to a color wall, thick, high, almost impenetrable.[50] Whether *de jure*

46. Moore, "Jim Crow in Georgia," 558; Atlanta *Independent*, June 17, 1905; Clarence A. Bacote, *The Story of Atlanta University* (Atlanta, 1969), 228; Deaton, "Atlanta During the Progressive Era," 327; C. Vann Woodward, *The Strange Career of Jim Crow* (New York, 1955), 87.

47. *Voice of the Negro*, 3 (Dec., 1905), 18; (Sept., 1906), 653.

48. *Scroll*, 7 (May, 1903), 92 (the *Scroll* was the Atlanta University student newspaper); Rayford W. Logan, *The Betrayal of the Negro, from Rutherford B. Hayes to Woodrow Wilson* (New York, 1965), 336–37.

49. W. E. B. Du Bois, "The Opening of the Library," *Independent*, 54 (Apr. 3, 1902), 809–10.

50. Wingo, "Race Relations in Georgia," 118.

or *de facto*, blacks found themselves Jim Crowed at every turn. Separation of the races was essential to white supremacy, and white supremacy was necessary for survival of the white southern way of life. Belief that theirs was the superior race no doubt caused some whites to demand segregation. W. E. B. Du Bois maintained that Jim Crow laws and other segregationist practices were not designed primarily to brand blacks as inferior, but to "flatter white labor to accept public testimony of its superiority instead of higher wages and social legislation." The white worker could

> not only follow the old aristocrats into the front entrances of railway stations; and go with them to the best theatres and movies; but in all places he could sit above and apart from "niggers.". . . He had a right to the title of "Mister." . . . He could sit in "public" parks and enter "public" libraries where no Negro could enter, he need seldom fear to get the worst of a streetcar altercation, or to lose a court case against a Negro. . . . He grew to love those proofs of superiority.[51]

As for Georgia blacks, they dealt with the caste system in different ways. Theoretically, many forms of protest were open, but in fact choices were few, limited by the very system they were fighting. Petitions to the city council, court suits, lobbying influential whites, and selective boycotts were tactics endorsed by most leaders. Later many would accept the status quo as a necessary evil. Fathers who never rode streetcars or sat in Jim Crow theatres looked on as their children boarded the segregated trolley en route to the "peanut gallery" of the local white moviehouse. Other blacks "arranged their lives so that they touched as few raw edges as possible," avoiding contact with the white world by withdrawing into their own society. Yet some men and women saw potential for racial advancement in Jim Crow Georgia, and they dreamed of a separate and independent community built on the bedrock of a self-sustaining black economy.[52]

51. Du Bois, "Georgia, Invisible Empire State," 331. For a moving personal account of segregation and its effects in Atlanta during the 1920s, see Benjamin E. Mays, *Born to Rebel* (New York, 1971), 66–98.
52. Interview with Mrs. Grace Towns Hamilton, Mar. 18, 1974, Atlanta; *The Reminiscences of W. E. B. Du Bois* (1963), 166, in the Oral History Collection of Columbia University (hereafter cited as Du Bois, OHC).

Working

AFTER THE CIVIL WAR most black people followed the same line of work they had engaged in during slavery. Antebellum house servants became caterers, barbers, maids, and cooks, while slave carpenters, blacksmiths, and brick masons sold their own services after freedom. The legacy of the field slave was strongest, for despite urbanization Georgia remained dependent upon agriculture, especially cotton. Farmers and farm workers were 60 percent of the state work force in 1900, and of this number over half were black. Of the approximately quarter-million black farmers and farm workers, over two-thirds were wage laborers, the lowest economic class. Another 70,000 were tenants and cash renters, and fewer than 10,000 owned their farms. While half of the white farm operators were owners in 1900, the figure for blacks was but 12 percent.[1]

The agricultural heartland was the black belt, where a disproportionate share of Georgia's poorest citizens tilled some of the South's richest farmland. Most blacks there were farm laborers, with wages in 1900 ranging from a minimum of two dollars a month with furnishings to fifteen dollars without them.[2] Few black farm operators in this area were owners; many were tenants farming someone else's land for a share of the crop. The plight of Georgia's sharecroppers differed little from that of other croppers throughout the South. The operator did not control his farm-

1. *Twelfth Census, Special Report, Occupations,* 154–57; *Negro Population,* 609; W. E. B. Du Bois, "Georgia Negroes and Their Fifty Millions of Savings," *World's Work,* 18 (1909), 11,550–54.
2. Arthur F. Raper, *Preface to Peasantry: A Tale of Two Black Belt Counties* (Chapel Hill, 1936), 3; Edward A. Gaston, "A History of the Negro Wage Earner in Georgia, 1890–1940" (Ph.D. dissertation, Emory University, 1957), 117.

land, could not choose his crops, and usually found himself in debt to the landowner or merchant. The crop lien system, with its high interest rates and cotton economy basis, limited the farmer's freedom by tying him to fluctuations of the depressed cotton market.[3]

Dougherty County in southwest Georgia exemplified the problems facing black belt farmers. Outnumbering whites five to one in 1900, blacks held only 5 percent of the county's acreage and aggregate property. White farmer F. F. Putney, with his 60 farms and 13,000 acres, owned 20 percent more land than all of Dougherty's 11,000 blacks![4] An 1898 study showed that only 81 black families owned any farmland at all, while the overwhelming majority of black men and women barely survived as farm laborers and sharecroppers.[5] Most tenants lived in old slave quarters or in "newer" cabins built along antebellum lines:

> All over the face of the land is the one-room cabin—now standing in the shadow of the Big House, now staring at the dusty road, now rising dark and somber amid the green of the cotton fields. It is nearly always old and bare, built of rough boards, and neither plastered nor ceiled. Light and ventilation are supplied by the single door and by the square hole in the wall with its wooden shutter. There is no glass, porch, or ornamentation without. Within is a fireplace, black, smoky, usually unsteady with age. A bed or two, a table, a wooden chest, and a few chairs compose the furniture; while a stray showbill or a newspaper makes up the decorations for the walls. Now and then one may find such a cabin kept scrupulously neat, with merry steaming fireplace and hospitable door, but the majority are dirty and dilapidated, smelling of eating and sleeping, poorly ventilated, and anything but homes.[6]

Above all, the cabins were crowded. An investigator in Dougherty County met many families of eight or more living in a single room.

---

3. Brooks, *Agrarian Revolution*, 87. For a fascinating account of the life of an Alabama sharecropper during this era, see Theodore Rosengarten, *All God's Dangers: The Life of Nate Shaw* (New York, 1974).

4. Dougherty County *Tax Digest*, 1900.

5. W. E. B. Du Bois, "The Negro as He Really Is," in Donald B. De Nevi and Doris A. Holmes, *Racism at the Turn of the Century, Documentary Perspectives 1870–1910* (San Rafael, Calif., 1973), 126–28.

6. Du Bois, *Souls of Black Folk*, 106–7.

Bath facilities were poor or nonexistent, beds were filled with vermin, and cabins were hot in summer and cold or overheated in winter, making dwellers susceptible to tuberculosis and pneumonia.[7]

A few farm families managed to escape poverty. Dougherty's most prosperous black, Deal Jackson, owned 2,000 acres of rich farmland and for thirteen consecutive years marketed the first bale of cotton east of the Mississippi. His land alone was worth $50,000, and he also owned much equipment and livestock. Whites spoke highly of Jackson's farming skill and praised his public attitude of deference and humility.[8] Another successful black landowner was Bartow Powell, who owned several farms in Dougherty and Baker counties. He also operated a cotton gin and a store to serve his black tenants, whom he treated well. Powell was struck down in his prime by an unknown assailant as he was driving his carriage through Albany. Local blacks believed the killer to be an envious white man.[9]

More blacks owned land outside the black belt in the wiregrass and coastal regions, where the soil was less productive and whites would sell to anybody. In 1910 in Lowndes County (on the Florida border) 281 blacks owned over 25,000 acres. (Dougherty County, with an equal black population, had by then only 43 blacks owning about 7,000 acres.[10]) Along the Atlantic coast in McIntosh County an astonishing 87 percent of black farm operators owned their land outright in 1910, compared with a 2 percent figure in Dougherty. However, the average black farm in McIntosh was only 40 acres, with some land assessed as low as fifty cents an acre. Whites had long since given up on this land, which produced some corn and little cotton.[11]

Farming in the rich piedmont area was a different matter. In

7. W. E. B. Du Bois, ed., *The Negro American Family*, Atlanta University *Publications* No. 13 (Atlanta, 1908) 53, 129; W. B. Hill, *Rural Survey of Clarke County, Georgia, With Special Reference to Negroes*, Phelps-Stokes Fellowship *Studies* No. 2 (Athens, Ga., 1915), 53–54.

8. Savannah *Tribune*, Apr. 22, 1911; Dougherty County *Tax Digest*, 1910.

9. Dougherty County *Tax Digest*, 1900; interview between Mr. Henry Williams and Mrs. Ethel Wright, Aug. 14, 1973, Newton. Mrs. Wright's father was a tenant on one of Powell's farms.

10. *Negro Population*, 712; Lowndes County *Tax Digest*, 1910; Dougherty County *Tax Digest*, 1910.

11. *Negro Population*, 712–15; McIntosh County *Tax Digest*, 1900, 1910.

the northern half of Georgia the white majority increased each year, and was generally unwilling to see black farmers move in and prosper. Established black farmers did well as long as they were left alone. But the upper piedmont was a volatile area, and whites sometimes forced blacks to flee their land, leaving all possessions behind. This practice of whitecapping was directed mainly against successful black farmers, but occasionally whites terrorized the entire black population of a county. In the piedmont county of Forsyth some whites, enraged by stories of alleged rapes, flooded the countryside with printed circulars demanding that all blacks get out. These vigilantes threatened whites who did not dismiss black tenants, and they drove hundreds of "good, peaceable, hardworking blacks" from the county.[12]

So, in addition to dealing with economic problems facing all farmers, the black farmer had to contend with racism. In settling accounts the tenant was at the landowner's mercy, for the majority of black farmers were illiterate, kept no records, and could only hope for fair treatment from owners or merchants. Blacks rarely challenged settlement terms in a time when tenants were killed over money disputes. Repeated injustices led Du Bois to conclude that white landlords had withheld three-fourths of the wages earned by black farmers since emancipation.[13] Blacks were also charged higher interest rates. In a sample taken in 1913, black farm renters paid an average annual rate of 18.6 percent on bank loans, compared with 8.8 percent for white renters. Similar discrepancies existed between black and white owners seeking loans.[14]

Agriculture provided the livelihood of a great majority of black Georgia families during the first two decades of this century, but most barely scratched a living from the land. Farm workers

12. *Negro Population*, 712–15; Floyd County *Tax Digest*, 1900, 1910, 1920; Atlanta *Constitution*, Oct. 3, 1912; William J. Northen, "Christianity and the Negro," p. 11, pamphlet in the William J. Northen Collection, Georgia Department of Archives and History, Atlanta.

13. Gaston, "Negro Wage Earner," 95. The relationship of the courts and laws to peonage will receive attention in the chapter on "The New Slavery." W. E. B. Du Bois and A. G. Dill, eds., *The Negro American Artisan*, Atlanta University *Publications* No. 17 (Atlanta, 1912), 135.

14. Arthur N. Moore *et al.*, *Credit Problems of Georgia Cotton Farmers*, Georgia Experiment Station *Bulletin* No. 153 (Experiment, Ga., 1929), 21, 26.

received subsistence wages, and black sharecroppers were trapped in a system designed to keep them impoverished. Black farm owners did not fare much better. Their farms averaged only sixty-three acres, nearly a third were under ten acres, and half were worth less than a hundred dollars. And although the number of black farm owners at first increased slightly, by 1930 there were fewer black owners than in 1900, and their acreage had decreased by over a quarter-million acres.[15] Some owners were reduced to sharecropping; others migrated to urban areas. The unstable cotton economy forced the black farmer in Georgia to be constantly on the move. He sought to better his condition first within the rural South, and later in the cities of the South and North, where his future appeared more promising.[16]

The lure of the city was strong and irreversible. Booker T. Washington might extoll the virtues of the peasant life, but each day blacks in rural Georgia put down their plows and hoes, gathered their few belongings, and headed for Macon or Columbus, Savannah or Atlanta, or any of the nearly fifty communities that census takers designated "city." At the turn of the century 160,000 Georgia blacks lived in urban areas; that figure would rise to over a quarter-million by 1920.[17] The city offered blacks society, entertainment, churches, and schools. It also provided employment, though the jobs were usually low-paying and the work often demeaning.

Nearly a third of the state's black labor force worked in domestic and personal services, the largest area of employment next to agriculture.[18] Some blacks were janitors, porters, and waiters, but most worked in and around the homes of whites. Here, where the

15. W. E. B. Du Bois, "The Savings of Black Georgia," *Outlook*, 69 (Sept., 1901), 130; Gaston, "Negro Wage Earner," 54; *Negro Population*, 109; *Fifteenth Census, Agriculture*, II, 524.

16. The great northern migration of the World War I years will receive attention in the chapter on "The War Years."

17. *Negroes in the U.S.*, 53; *Negro Population*, 91–92, 155–56, 272, 289–90, 464. Women were predominant in all Georgia cities. In Atlanta, for example, 58 percent of the black population in 1900 was female, while the sexual ratio was more evenly divided in the country. A lower percentage of urban blacks were married, and birth rates were lower in cities than on farms. Throughout the South the average family size was decreasing, from 5.4 persons per black family in 1890 to 4.6 in 1910. *Ibid.*

18. *Negro Population*, 92; *Twelfth Census, Occupations*, 254–56.

greatest amount of social contact between the races occurred, racial stereotypes were perpetuated. A favorite complaint of employers was lack of competent, reliable domestic help. Many whites based their racial views on empirical observation of maids and cooks, concluding from such scientific sampling that Negroes had regressed since the days of slavery and the magnificent, sainted black mammy![19] No doubt the quality of service had declined some since slavery, when working in the big house gave prestige. But master-slave relations carried over into many white households after the war, with servants frequently overworked, exploited, and underpaid. (As late as 1912 the average weekly wage for cooks in Athens was $2.72, and for maids, $2.34.[20]) Commenting on the many disadvantages of domestic work, Du Bois concluded that "so long as the conditions under which domestic service is done involve social stigma, material discomfort, and moral danger, American girls are going to avoid it whenever they can; and this is not because they are white or black, but because they are human."[21]

If economic necessity drove black women into white kitchens, prospects for the unskilled black man were no better. He might work as a yard man, as a janitor or garbage worker, or in an industry which hired blacks to do back-breaking labor. In Savannah black longshoremen constituted 95 percent of the total force. These dockworkers organized a union, staged several strikes, and occasionally won grudging concessions from the shipping companies.[22] Railroads employed 11,000 blacks by 1910, and though most were common laborers on section gangs, they comprised a majority of firemen and brakemen until the Great Depression and held a monopoly on jobs as porters, dining-car waiters, and cooks. Lumber and turpentine industries in the wiregrass region, as well

19. Thomas J. Woofter, *The Negroes of Athens, Georgia,* Phelps-Stokes Fellowship *Studies* No. 1 (Athens, Ga., 1913), 47; Ruth Reed, *The Negro Women of Gainesville, Georgia,* Phelps-Stokes Fellowship *Studies* No. 6 (Athens, Ga., 1921), 5.

20. Reed, *Negro Women of Gainesville,* 25–27.

21. "Conversation between W. E. B. Du Bois and Rev. C. B. Wilmer," p. 9, transcribed in late 1906, MS in Ray Stannard Baker Papers, Manuscript Division, Library of Congress.

22. Mercer G. Evans, "A History of the Organized Labor Movement in Georgia" (Ph.D. dissertation, University of Chicago, 1929), 186–90; *Thirteenth Census, Population,* IV, 450.

as furniture manufacturing and ceramics industries, foundries, and general repair shops hired a high percentage of blacks.[23]

Blacks at first achieved their biggest gains in the skilled trades. Blacksmithing had been an important slave craft, and as late as 1890 41 percent of the state's blacksmiths were Negroes. The building trades offered promise. In the 1890s blacks were 37 percent of Georgia's 10,000 carpenters, two-thirds of the 2,000 brick and stone masons, and three-fourths of the 600 plasterers and cement finishers.[24] These artisans did not get rich—before World War I few made over $800 a year—but they supported their families, educated their children, and some managed to build small savings accounts.[25]

This group of skilled workers, numbering less than 20,000 in the 1890s, formed a promising base for expansion. The black artisan had proven his ability, and a growing urban economy should have brought him prosperity. Instead, the twentieth century marked the decline of Georgia's black craftsmen. The report of a Savannah editor was typical: "Years ago colored carpenters, brick layers, etc. had the call in the building operations in this city. Today there is a change; the white mechanics are in the ascendancy."[26] Technology reduced demand for skills like blacksmithing and opened new fields like electronics, where blacks had little experience or apprenticeship opportunity.[27] Inadequate industrial training schools offered courses in obsolete trades like shoemaking and wheelmaking because funds were not available to purchase modern machinery for instructional purposes.[28] If black workers had received the best training with the newest equipment they still would have faced serious problems, for it was race, not competence, that increasingly controlled employment conditions.

Racial friction among skilled tradesmen took root in the slave system, where free whites competed with slave artisans. Tensions

23. *Thirteenth Census, Population,* IV, 449–50; *Sixteenth Census, Population,* III, 729–30; Gaston, "Negro Wage Earner," 456, 214–16, 220.

24. *Eleventh Census, Population,* I, pt. 2, 548.

25. Du Bois, ed., *Negro American Family,* 116–18, 148–51.

26. Savannah *Tribune,* Apr. 10, 1915.

27. Gaston, "Negro Wage Earner," 470. There were never more than fifty black electricians in Georgia at any one time until World War II.

28. Du Bois and Dill, eds., *Negro American Artisan,* 120–22.

continued throughout the late nineteenth century, and while as late as 1900 black and white carpenters, brick-layers and plasterers worked on the same projects in outward harmony, mutual fear and distrust lay beneath the surface.[29] Racism among white craftsmen was apparent in the practices of Georgia's trade unions, which generally excluded black workers. The Georgia Federation of Labor did not bar racially mixed unions, but it refused to stand for worker solidarity across the color line and thus condoned the racial exclusiveness of most locals. Georgia labor leaders as a whole were conservative, Protestant, Democratic, and Ku Klux Klannish.[30] More enlightened than the state political leaders on issues like disfranchisement, usury, and child labor, union spokesmen never seriously attempted to repudiate the basic assumptions of white supremacy. During the bloody 1906 race riot, for example, the Atlanta *Journal of Labor* kept silent on the atrocities, but praised the daily newspapers whose racist editorials had incited the riot.[31]

Trade union locals at times set up watchdog committees to investigate reports of black economic encroachment. The International Association of Machinists' Atlanta branch instructed its business agent to check out a rumor that a Negro engineer had been employed at Grady hospital, and another Atlanta local appointed a group to "look into the matter" of the employment of a black machinist at a factory. At one union meeting "Bro. Riley made a red hot speech about negroes being allowed to do machinist work" at a shop, and "emphatically stated it had to stop." A union officer was instructed to call on members of the Atlanta Sanitation Commission, urging them to continue to hire white workers. Conversely, the Savannah Trades and Labor Assembly censored Mayor W. L. Pierpont for employing blacks in his factory, a practice "not conducive to the advancement of white labor in the community."[32]

29. W. E. B. Du Bois, ed., *The Negro Artisan*, Atlanta University *Publications* No. 7 (Atlanta, 1902), 102.
30. *Ibid.*, 92; Evans, "Organized Labor Movement in Georgia," 215.
31. Evans, "Organized Labor Movement in Georgia," 212–15, 229, 250; *Journal of Labor*, Oct. 19, 1906.
32. Minutes, International Association of Machinists Contract Lodge 43, Atlanta, Feb. 23, 1915, in Alfred G. Kuetner Collection, 1902–16, Southern Labor Archives, Georgia State University, Atlanta; Minutes, International Association of

Despite such union hostility, some blacks participated in the labor movement. Independent all-black craft unions were rare, and these were usually just social organizations. Separate but affiliated black locals formed in several cities, with white and black leaders meeting periodically to coordinate union affairs. Segregated locals almost always put blacks in inferior bargaining positions. In a few instances blacks so dominated a trade that they controlled integrated unions. Most prosperous was the International Association of Plasterers and Cement Finishers local organized in Atlanta in 1900. All officers were black, and they exercised complete authority, including the all-important assignment of jobs. The predominantly black National Association of Letter Carriers local saw blacks maintain power by limiting white membership.[33]

Occasionally blacks were invited to join white unions, but with no guarantee of equal benefits. The brick masons' local in Atlanta charged blacks higher initiation fees, yet provided them lower sickness and death benefits. White union members got the best jobs in mixed-local contracts. Most often white organizers scorned black workers on grounds that they were not loyal unionists, would work for less than scale, and would cross picket lines to break strikes. Black artisans, aware that the white working class was unsympathetic, distrusted white-dominated unions.[34] The labor union itself was suspect, particularly in the South, and the black union member had to bear the double stigma of race and alleged radicalism. Few blacks belonged to unions in Georgia at any time before World War II, for racist unionists and capitalists combined to keep the black artisan subservient.[35] One student

Machinists Lodge 1, Atlanta, June 9, 1904, in Machinists Lodge No. 1 Records, 1893–1971, Southern Labor Archives; Minutes, Machinists Lodge No. 1, Mar. 23, 1905; Minutes, Contract Lodge 43, June 15, 1915; Crisis, 12 (Aug., 1916), 187. The International maintained a "whites only" membership policy until 1948.

33. Leonard H. James, "Policies of Organized Labor in Relation to Negro Workers in Atlanta, 1869–1937" (Master's thesis, Atlanta University, 1937), 56–59; Du Bois, ed., Negro Artisan, 102; John Michael Matthews, "Studies in Race Relations in Georgia, 1890–1930" (Ph.D. dissertation, Duke University, 1970), 222.

34. Du Bois, ed., Negro Artisan, 102; James, "Policies of Organized Labor," 58; Deaton, "Atlanta during the Progressive Era," 137.

35. In Atlanta, Georgia's biggest union town, fewer than 10 percent of the black artisans belonged to any union at the turn of the century. See Du Bois, ed., Negro Artisan, 120.

of the southern labor movement has concluded that throughout the first three decades of this century southern trade unionism was "in good measure a protective device for the march of white artisans into places held by Negroes."[36] Denied apprenticeship and union recognition, the black craftsman had to work long hours at lower pay to compete against white workers, a situation which depressed wages generally and benefited only employers.

Identical problems occurred among unskilled workers. Great numbers of poor whites moved down from the hill counties to the cities after the Civil War. These uneducated and unskilled migrants poured into the cotton mills, where they dominated the labor market and moved over into what had been classified as "Negro jobs." Struggle for positions on the bottom rung of the economic ladder led to demands upon public and private employers to substitute white labor for black. After retiring an aged Negro messenger on full pay, the Macon Western Union office summarily dismissed all other black employees. In 1915 a Savannah organization called the Silent Brotherhood persuaded the city administration to fire some black workers to make room for whites. About the same time the head of Atlanta's sanitation department suggested that whites replace the city's 500 black garbage workers at a 30 percent pay increase.[37] As the white southerner's distaste for working with his hands decreased, so did unskilled jobs available to blacks.

Though interracial competition among unskilled workers continued well into the twentieth century, the battle for the cotton mill had ended by the early 1900s. A confrontation over employment opportunity in Georgia's most important industry occurred in 1897 at Atlanta's Fulton Bag and Cotton Mill, when 1,400 white workers walked off their jobs to protest the hiring of 20 black women to work alongside white women as spinners. Management capitulated after only one day, agreeing to fire all Negro spinners. But whites pressed further, insisting on removal of all black workers except janitors and scrubbers. After another day-long

36. George S. Mitchell, "The Negro in Southern Trade Unionism," *Southern Economic Journal*, 2 (1935–36), 27, quoted in George B. Tindall, *The Emergence of the New South 1913–1945* (Baton Rouge, 1967), 163.

37. Atlanta *Constitution*, Apr. 24, 1911; Savannah *Tribune*, Apr. 10, 1915; Atlanta *Independent*, Jan. 16, 1915; Gaston, "Negro Wage Earner," 286. The black garbage workers kept their jobs.

strike, owners resolved the issue by segregating remaining black employees. A similar walkout in a Rome mill resulted in dismissal of all black operatives, and in Barnesville white women led a five-day strike which forced mill owners to fire all blacks.[38] A fifth of all Georgia's cotton mill operatives in 1890 had been black. A decade later the figure had fallen to just 3 percent, or 282 black operatives, and by 1910 even this token number had been cut in half.[39] Though whites drove blacks from the mills, their economic grievances went unanswered. Mill owners who gave in easily on racial issues drew the line over questions of wages, working conditions, and child labor. Ironically, owners would use black scab labor to break future strikes over economic issues.[40] Exclusion of blacks was a Pyrrhic victory for the white mill worker, for the cost of white supremacy was high, and he could least afford to pay it.

Race prejudice hurt white workers in other areas, such as the railroad industry. The Georgia Railroad strike of 1909 was precipitated when an official replaced ten white firemen, paid $1.75 a day, with ten blacks at $1.25. The white Brotherhood of Locomotive Firemen then struck, shutting down the railroad for two weeks. Strikers claimed the railroad hired black firemen because they would always be paid less than whites. Management conceded the point, defending its policy as good business. Moreover, since only whites could become engineers, black firemen who were denied promotion built up seniority for good runs, thus gaining advantage over young white firemen. A union spokesman attacked the system, stating that it was no good if it meant Negroes getting priority over whites.[41]

Race became the dominant issue in the strike, as whites demanded total elimination of black firemen. Union members testified that blacks were incompetent and complained that the white fireman resented "sitting on the same seat, putting his

38. Evans, "Organized Labor Movement in Georgia," 84–85, 89; Atlanta *Constitution,* Aug. 5–8, 1897; Matthews, "Studies in Race Relations," 218.

39. *Eleventh Census, Population,* I, pt. 2, 548; *Twelfth Census, Special Report, Occupations,* 254–56; *Thirteenth Census,* IV, 449–50; Gaston, "Negro Wage Earner," 471.

40. Macon *Telegraph,* Sept. 9–25, 1919.

41. Atlanta *Constitution,* May 17, 30, 1909; Sterling D. Spero and Abram L. Harris, *The Black Worker: The Negro and the Labor Movement* (New York, 1931), 210.

clothes in the same box and using the same utensils as the Negro."
Under cross-examination whites admitted that "some" blacks
were good firemen.[42] Support for strikers came from whites along
the route of the Georgia Railroad, which ran from Atlanta to
Macon and Augusta. Communities held mass meetings, vowing to
do without mail and to haul food in wagons before permitting
black men back into the cabs. Violence erupted along the line
when the company attempted to break the strike by sending out
freight trains fired by blacks, who were stoned and beaten by
mobs. The company asked Governor Hoke Smith to call out the
militia to protect the trains, but the governor sympathized with
the strikers and refused to act.[43]

After two weeks of disrupted service and sporadic violence
both sides agreed to arbitration, with each appointing a man
favorable to its interests. Key figure was the third arbiter, University of Georgia chancellor David C. Barrow, a racial moderate.
The compromise settlement left strikers dissatisfied. Black firemen
remained on trains and the seniority system was preserved, with
some modification enabling engineers-in-training to gain road
experience. One of the union's few "victories"—equal pay for
black and white firemen—was of immediate benefit to blacks. The
union believed that forced adherence to a single salary scale
would cause the company to hire whites over blacks, but blacks
would remain as firemen until the 1930s.[44] The Georgia Railroad
strike of 1909 was the first of several attempts by white brother-
hoods to exclude blacks from the fireman's craft, and was symbolic
of the many racial barriers blocking the progress of the black
worker in Georgia.

Georgia's small black business and professional class also met
white competition and opposition, but here the problems—and
opportunities—were different. Black workers depended primarily

42. Spero and Harris, *Black Worker*, 290; Atlanta *Constitution*, May 17, 1909;
"Arbitration Between Georgia Railroad and Its White Firemen Under the
'Erdman Act' June 21–26, 1909," pp. 10, 14 (copy of report at Georgia State
Library, Atlanta). See also John Michael Matthews, "The Georgia 'Race Strike'
of 1909," *Journal of Southern History*, 40 (Nov., 1974), 613–30.

43. Atlanta *Constitution*, May 23, 1909.

44. *Ibid.*, June 27, 1909; *Fourteenth Census, Population*, IV, 904–5; *Fifteenth
Census, Population*, IV, 388–89; Spero and Harris, *Black Worker*, 292–93.

on white employers; in contrast, black doctors, lawyers, and busi-nessmen relied on black patronage. There were exceptions. Throughout the late nineteenth century a few grocers catered to a white clientele, and black barbers and hackmen made a good living providing personal services for white people. And there was the black dentist with his office on Peachtree Street and waiting room full of white patients, or the successful black contractor who built homes for fashionable whites.[45] By the turn of the century even these exceptions were becoming rarer, thanks to the growth of Jim Crow thought and white competition. Now the black businessman and professional had to win the patronage of his race to survive, a formidable and at times frustrating task.

Atop the professional class stood the physician. His rise to social and economic prominence in black Georgia was a twentieth-century development, for black doctors were rare in post–Civil War years. At first young black physicians met suspicion, if not hostility, from sizable segments of their community. A resident recalled that when the first two black doctors came to Atlanta in the 1890s "Our folk did not have too much confidence in them." One of Atlanta's most distinguished physicians, Dr. Homer E. Nash, remembers that when he hung out his shingle in 1910 "the cooks and maids and poor people looked at me and said, 'Ain't no Negro doctor gonna give me no medicine!'"[46] Doubts were not confined to the uneducated. The black professor who took it for granted that he should educate the youth of his race would often patronize a white physician. Many blacks who could afford white doctors went to them.[47] But as black doctors became more com-mon and proved themselves competent, their prestige and prac-tices grew. Patronage of black physicians would eventually become a test of race loyalty, and during World War I Atlanta University investigators reported that in some areas a black family going to a white doctor risked social ostracism.[48]

The number of black physicians remained small, and they were

45. Matthews, "Studies in Race Relations," 271.
46. Interview with Mrs. M. G. Wartman, Mar. 19, 1974, Atlanta; interview with Dr. Homer E. Nash, July 4, 1972, Atlanta. At the time of this interview Dr. Nash had maintained an active practice in Atlanta for sixty-two years.
47. Interview with Dr. Homer Nash, July 4, 1972; Asa H. Gordon, *The Geor-gia Negro, A History* (Ann Arbor, 1937), 277–78.
48. Du Bois and Dill, eds., *Negro American Artisan*, 133.

concentrated in larger cities. In 1914, 145 black doctors were practicing in Georgia, an increase of almost a hundred since the turn of the century. Still, eighty-eight counties had no black doctors, and a third of the physicians practiced in the five largest cities where only about 10 percent of the black population lived.[49] This shortage resulted from both economic and racial factors. The state provided a medical school to train white doctors, but had no facilities for blacks. A spokesman for the Medical Department of the University of Georgia put it bluntly: "There are no niggers in this school and there never have been and there never will be as long as one stone of this building remains upon another."[50] Few young blacks had the money to enroll in out-of-state schools like Meharry or Howard, nor did the Georgia public school system prepare them for such rigorous advanced training.

Medical school graduates who established themselves professionally lived comfortably. Dr. G. S. Burruss of Augusta established Burruss Sanitarium, the most complete hospital for blacks in the South, with twenty-seven rooms, modern equipment, a staff of twelve black physicians, and a training department for nurses. Quiet and unassuming, Dr. Burruss had a net worth of over $50,000. A number of physicians served as directors of black banks and accumulated considerable real estate holdings.[51] They were usually at the center of the community's intellectual and social life. Educated and relatively independent of white control, black physicians became both the pride and envy of the communities which supported them.

Black doctors outnumbered dentists almost six to one. Twenty-six black dentists practiced in eighteen Georgia counties in 1914; their numbers did not increase until after the war.[52] Demand for dental services was less than for medical treatment, since an aching tooth could usually be extracted by someone without a diploma on his wall. Most dentists practiced in urban areas and, like physicians, were respected community leaders.[53]

49. *Report of the Comptroller-General, State of Georgia*, 1914, pp. 234–37; *Negro Population*, 768.
50. W. E. B. Du Bois, ed., *The Health and Physique of the Negro American*, Atlanta University *Publications* No. 11 (Atlanta, 1906), 98.
51. *Voice of the Negro*, 3 (Apr., 1906), 339–41; A. B. Caldwell, *History of the American Negro, Georgia Edition*, II (Atlanta, 1920), 106, 174, 198.
52. Georgia Comptroller General, *Report*, 1914–20.
53. City directories for Atlanta and Savannah; Gordon, *Negro in Georgia*, 278.

No black professional was more adversely affected by racism than the attorney. While a black doctor or dentist could treat his patients without outside interference, the lawyer had to confront the white power structure in order to deliver for his client. Since Georgia justice was the monopoly of white men, blacks were reluctant to employ attorneys of their race, particularly in litigation against a white person. According to the comptroller general, fewer than ten black lawyers were practicing in Georgia in any year before World War I.[54] These attorneys depended almost entirely on black patronage and made a modest living dealing in real estate, insurance, and claims collections. They were the most political of the professionals, with men like Henry Lincoln ("Linc") Johnson of Atlanta and Judson Lyons of Augusta exerting some influence in the national councils of the Republican party.[55]

For the small group of black businessmen in Georgia, the period 1890–1920 brought dramatic change. As noted, during the nineteenth century most successful black entrepreneurs performed some service for whites. Before the Civil War several free blacks owned grocery stores that catered primarily to white customers. Solomon Humphries, a prosperous Macon grocer in the 1830s, had more credit than any other merchant in town. And when Atlanta was rising from its ashes James Tate, the father of black business in that city, was already doing a thriving grocery trade with whites which made him a wealthy man.[56]

Blacks dominated the barbering trade, outnumbering whites ten to one in 1890.[57] Most were small-time operators, but occasionally a man like Alonzo F. Herndon combined tonsorial skill with a flair for promotion to achieve remarkable results. Born a slave in North Carolina, Herndon arrived penniless in Atlanta in 1882,

54. As late as 1934 only fourteen black attorneys worked in Georgia, and half of these lived in Atlanta.
55. August Meier, "Negro Racial Thought in the Age of Booker T. Washington, Circa 1880–1915" (Ph.D. dissertation, Columbia University, 1957), 764–65; Georgia Comptroller General, *Report*, 1900–1920. Black ministers and educators, who may also be identified as professionals, will be discussed in the next chapter and the chapter on "The Politics of Education" respectively.
56. John Henry Harmon, Arnett G. Lindsay, and Carter G. Woodson, *The Negro as a Business Man* (College Park, Md., 1929), 3, 9; Carter, *The Black Side of Atlanta*, 20.
57. *Eleventh Census, Population*, I, pt. 2, 548. There were 899 black barbers, 86 whites.

but he soon established himself as the city's premier barber. His shop at 66 Peachtree Street was a regular stopping place for state supreme court judges, influential lawyers, planters, ministers, and politicians from every Georgia community. When Herndon enlarged his shop in 1913, it gained a reputation as the largest and finest in the South. The new shop had twenty-three chairs, was finished in white marble and equipped with bronze electric chandeliers. The sixteen-foot front doors of solid mahogany and beveled plate glass were copies of a pair Herndon had seen in Paris. Downstairs were bath and shower facilities.[58] All of Herndon's barbers were black, and his customers, white. The most successful example of black exploitation of a white market, Herndon's operation prospered long after other black barbers had lost their white customers.

The black barber's loss of white clients typified the fate of black service operations. The ten-to-one black monopoly in 1890 gave way to a two-to-one white majority by 1920, when most black barbers had only black customers; the internal combustion engine changed the nature of the local transportation industry, forcing black hackmen off the roads; and changing residential patterns and growing segregationist sentiment eliminated the black grocer from competition for white trade.[59] Technological innovation, then, along with white competition and harassment, shifted the focus of black business in twentieth-century Georgia, as entrepreneurs turned inward to the black community for support.

The movement to establish a viable black economy met with little philosophical opposition, drawing support from all segments of the black intellectual community. Though the percentage of nineteenth-century black businessmen relying on white trade was large, their absolute number was small, and blacks entering the modern business world did so with an eye to the needs of the growing urban black populace. Nor was there much debate on the "evils" of economic separatism. If whites had decreed that segregation would be the law in Georgia, then blacks would make the best of it. Doctrines of race pride, self-help, and economic self-sufficiency may not have originated in Jim Crow Georgia, but

58. Garrett, *Atlanta and Environs*, I, 609.
59. *Fourteenth Census, Population*, IV, 904–5.

white supremacist attitudes encouraged development of black identity and purpose.[60]

As early as 1899 at the Fourth Annual Atlanta University Conference, W. E. B. Du Bois and conference members resolved that "Negroes ought to enter business life in increasing numbers . . . the growth of a class of merchants among us would be a far-sighted measure of self-defense, and would make for wealth and mutual cooperation." The conference went on to urge "the mass of Negroes . . . to patronize business enterprises conducted by their own race, even at some slight disadvantage. We *must* cooperate or we are lost."[61] These sentiments echoed in black pulpits and newspapers across the state, cutting across ideological lines. Significantly, when the Atlanta University Conference under Du Bois suggested formation of Negro businessmen's leagues, it was Booker T. Washington who set organizational machinery in motion.[62]

Founded in Boston in August 1900, the National Negro Business League had as its goals stimulating development of local Negro enterprise and informing the nation of progress made by blacks in business. Sixteen local leagues were functioning in Georgia by 1915, with the strongest chapter in Savannah.[63] The League never caught on in Atlanta, where leading black businessmen formed the Board of Trade. Although its dominant force was editor Benjamin Davis, normally a Washington ally, the Board of Trade pursued an independent course and was even hostile to the NNBL.[64] Aside from propagandizing and lending moral support to businessmen, the NNBL appeared to accomplish little, either in Georgia or nationally. Realities of the business world seldom came through in the annual meetings, which were a combination of Horatio Alger and black Babbittry. In frustration, the black Louisville *News* complained: "What does the Business League do but exaggerate and pretend? The tales of hardship overcome and wealth made 'in the sweat of their brows,' as told by some

60. See the chapter on "Black Thought" for more on black nationalism.
61. W. E. B. Du Bois, ed., *The Negro in Business,* Atlanta University *Publications* No. 4 (Atlanta, 1899), 50.
62. *Ibid.*
63. "Resolutions and Recommendations Adopted by the National Negro Business League at Its First Meeting Held in Boston, August 23 and 24, 1900," p. 2, Washington Papers; Scott to O. V. Everett, Jan. 15, 1916, *ibid.*
64. R. W. Tyler to Washington, Jan. 14, 19, 1913, *ibid.*

members of the Business League, would make Ananias blush for
shame. . . ."[65]

The annual tub-thumping at NNBL meetings could not hide the
fact that most black businesses were small, shoestring operations.
A high failure rate was inevitable, given the combination of nega-
tive factors facing the black entrepreneur. To begin with, American blacks lacked a business tradition. Slaveowners did not teach
their property the intricacies of the free enterprise system, and
capitalism remained the domain of the white man after freedom.
Blacks criticized some of their businessmen for "the too prevalent
haphazard method of conducting business, and the lack of regard
for neatness and cleanliness in business places." Two black
investigators concluded that "Negro merchants have yet to learn
the values of politeness and cheer. They carry all of their dis-
appointments and family life into the business."[66] There was little
reason for the average black businessman to be cheerful. Black
scholars Monroe Work and Asa Gordon toured Georgia during
World War I, finding that in almost all the small towns "the
Negro business is pushed off on side streets and back alleys, and
of course the general run-down condition of the segregated Negro
business section increases the tendency toward the untidy and
unsightly business house." They learned that in some towns any
sign of success in a black business "is taken as a notice that the
business should be crippled or destroyed." In one community
Gordon was told it was customary for white city officers to revoke
the license or charter of any Negro business doing too well.[67]

Lack of capital was the black entrepreneur's most important
problem. Georgia blacks had little money for investment, and
those with savings were reluctant to gamble on a new black enterprise, by definition a high risk venture. The black person starting
a business often had to borrow money from whites at exorbitant
rates. If denied loans, even at usurious rates, he would begin his
business undercapitalized, with increased chances of early failure.[68] With more capital and credit, the white businessman could

65. Quotation from Louisville News, in Crisis, 9 (Dec., 1914), 71.
66. Thomas I. Brown, ed., Economic Cooperation Among the Negroes of
Georgia, Atlanta University Publications No. 19 (Atlanta, 1917), 7; Woodson et
al., The Negro as a Business Man, 37.
67. Brown, ed., Economic Cooperation, 18.
68. Ibid., 14.

buy in volume and sell goods at a lower price. This discrepancy grew worse as the trend toward monopoly increased; ultimately some black businessmen could not buy merchandise as cheaply as white retailers could sell it. Atlanta University researchers estimated in 1917 that black Georgians were spending one hundred times as much with white businessmen as they were with blacks. While black editors and intellectuals bemoaned this racial disloyalty, there was little they could do to reverse the pattern. As one black historian put it: "While the Negroes were being taught race pride, and manifested it when it was not expensive to do so, they could not be expected to give a man ten cents for an eight-cent pound of sugar and two cents for race pride."[69]

The family grocery was the most common black enterprise, for anyone who could rent a building and scrape up two or three hundred dollars for stock could open his doors for business. Most black groceries were "Mom and Pop" stores where everybody worked long hours to keep the business afloat. When these stores survived, it was because of convenience of location, good management, and loyal patronage by neighborhood blacks. These grocers also benefited from dishonest business practices in some white-owned stores serving black areas.[70]

As black urban populations grew, so did recreation areas. Each big town had at least one black-owned pool hall or saloon, and larger cities had black vaudeville houses or movie theatres. Savannah was the first city to have a black-owned hotel, although all cities had Negro boarding and lodging houses. Restaurants and lunch counters were popular businesses, partly because they required little capital outlay.[71]

Despite the growing number of black physicians—and a more than adequate supply of patients—until the 1890s Georgia had no black pharmacy. That changed when the ownership of Gate City Drug Store passed from white to blacks hands. Key figure in

69. Woodson *et al.*, *Negro as a Business Man*, 16; Brown, ed., *Economic Cooperation*, 22.

70. A group of black women investigated white-owned grocery stores in Atlanta and found that some owners weighed sacks of flour with rocks and short-weighed sugar and meat. See Louie Davis Shivery, "The History of Organized Social Work Among Atlanta Negroes, 1890–1935" (Master's thesis, Atlanta University, 1936), 54.

71. City directories for Atlanta, Macon, Savannah, Columbus, Augusta.

the transaction was Moses Amos, who for years had been running the store for its white owners. Born in Haynesville, Georgia, Amos moved to Atlanta in 1876; there he quickly caught the eye of a white pharmacist, who hired and trained him. Thirteen years later Amos and two black doctors bought the store, which for years was one of the most successful black enterprises in the South.[72] Amos's nephew, Dr. Miles Amos, himself a well-known Atlanta pharmacist, remembers that his uncle's store was the gathering point for many Atlanta blacks, and that distinguished visitors to the town "would break for Butler and Auburn Avenue." Booker T. Washington was a frequent guest; his friendship with Moses Amos began long before the Tuskegean became famous.[73]

The Gate City Drug Store was a pleasant place to relax. Glass-topped tables and wrought iron chairs surrounded a circular, marble-topped fountain which dispensed sodas, ice cream, and of course Coca-Cola. Part of the store was a post office substation, making it more of a community center. Amos's policy was "All articles under all circumstances cash!"[74] To compete with whites, most black businessmen had to extend credit, and at first the Gate City Drug Store was no exception. After uncollected debts nearly drove Moses Amos out of business, he "came down to a cash basis. We trust no one, and since then we have been doing well." Soon other blacks opened drug stores, and by World War I larger cities had at least one black-operated pharmacy.[75]

A successful and ambitious pharmacist was M. O. Lee of Albany, who opened the Artesian Drug Store in 1902. His business prospered so that he established a wholesale department for his own line of drug preparations. Lee promised "to furnish pure drugs and reliable remedies (instead of quack medicines and harmful nostrums)," but, as with most drug manufacturers in the days before stringent federal regulation, Lee made strong claims for some of his products. For example, LEE'S LATEST was a remedy for "sexual weakness," and LEE'S LUCKY NO. 13 (GONORRHOEA GUARANTEE) "will cure any ordinary case."[76]

72. Ray Stannard Baker, *Following the Color Line, American Negro Citizenship in the Progressive Era* (New York, 1908; Harper Torchbook edition, 1964), p. 42.

73. Interview with Dr. Miles Amos, Mar. 20, 1974, Atlanta.

74. *Ibid.*, advertisement in Atlanta *Constitution,* Oct. 23, 1912.

75. Baker, *Following the Color Line,* 43.

76. Clippings in Box 1094, Washington Papers.

Growth of the black urban middle class meant increased demand for building construction. While several Negro contractors operated in the state, Atlanta provided the best opportunity. One early contractor was Alexander Hamilton, who with his son and an integrated work force constructed buildings for black and white clients.[77] The leading black contractor was R. E. Pharrow. Born in Washington, Georgia, in 1868, Pharrow mastered the brick mason's trade in Augusta before moving to Atlanta. His Sale Hall at Morehouse College was the first building constructed there by a black contractor. Pharrow also built the First Congregational Church and designed and erected the five-story Odd Fellows building on Auburn Avenue.[78]

A black businessman least concerned about white competition was the mortician: white undertakers preferred a Caucasian clientele. Blacks in the trade made a good living, for black people believed in giving loved ones a proper burial. The leading black mortician was David T. Howard of Atlanta. Of dark complexion, Howard was the son of a white lawyer, as well as the half-brother of a congressman. A generous man and community leader, Howard had considerable real estate holdings and acquired substantial wealth.[79]

While most black businesses were small, single-owner enterprises, the idea of economic cooperation found favor among some leaders. In Clarke County near Athens Mrs. Judia C. Harris organized a group of farmers, none of whom owned land or homes, into the Mutual Benefit Society. Pooling resources, the group bought land, erected homes, built a school, sawmill, cotton gin, and threshing machine, and generally prospered. Black farmers formed land-buying clubs in other parts of the state; though some enjoyed success, the cooperative idea did not catch on, partly because of white opposition in the countryside.[80]

77. Du Bois and Dill, eds., *Negro American Artisan*, 102–3; Deaton, "Atlanta during the Progressive Era," 169. Hamilton and other black contractors were often frustrated by their failure to land contracts at the white-run black colleges. Atlanta University hired white southern firms to construct its buildings, even when Hamilton submitted a low bid. See Atlanta *Independent*, Apr. 30, May 21, 1904.

78. W. B. Matthews, ed., *The Negro Business Directory and Commercial Guide of Atlanta* (Atlanta, 1911), 122; Atlanta *Constitution*, Oct. 23, 1912.

79. Caldwell, ed., *History of the Negro, Georgia Edition*, II, 192; interview with Mrs. M. G. Wartman, Mar. 19, 1974, Atlanta; interview with Mr. J. B. Blayton, Mar. 19, 1974, Atlanta; Woodson *et al.*, *Negro as a Business Man*, 14.

80. Hill, *Rural Survey of Clarke County*, 56–57; Gaston, "Negro Wage Earner," 67.

In the cities land-buying cooperatives were the basis for black entry into the real estate business. The first agency, the Georgia Real Estate Loan and Trust Company, started in Atlanta in 1890, and within the decade most large towns had black agencies. By the end of World War I Savannah had four firms "doing business on a large scale." Foremost was the G. H. Bowen agency, owned by one of Savannah's wealthiest blacks. (Bowen's modest slogan was "I Sell the Earth.") He also organized the Union Development Company to buy business property in downtown Savannah. A few realtors branched out into land development, opening tracts for construction of black housing. The most ambitious was Atlanta's Heman Perry, whose companies handled every aspect, from land purchase to housing construction and financing.[81]

Georgia blacks owned a few manufacturing concerns, including a mattress factory in Savannah, a chair factory in Moultrie, a broom factory in Macon, and a beverage company in Atlanta. One group of blacks from the south Georgia community of Waycross bought a casket company from whites in 1919 and employed fifty workmen.[82] But examples of black industry were rare, for few blacks had capital to risk in ambitious manufacturing ventures with little chance to compete against white firms.

Inability to raise capital in a white business world led blacks in several cities to pool resources and start banks. White bankers usually took a dim view of black entrepreneurship, charging extremely high interest rates when they did agree to loan money. The black bank incorporated race pride, self-help, and economic cooperation. Black banks opened in Georgia's five major cities during the first twenty years of this century, with Savannah, not Atlanta, the black banking capital.[83] Just why that port city with a smaller and poorer black population dominated is not totally clear, but Savannah did possess a strong group of black leaders from old, distinguished families. Their stability and financial expertise were favorable factors.

    81. Brochure in Container 9, Washington Papers; Matthews, "Studies in Race Relations," 274.
    82. Matthews, "Studies in Race Relations," 274–75; Gaston, "Negro Wage Earner," 34; Brown, ed., *Economic Cooperation*, 18–19; Savannah *Press*, Feb. 17, 1919; Savannah *Tribune*, Oct. 11, 1919.
    83. The cities are Atlanta, Savannah, Macon, Columbus, and Augusta. Between 1904 and 1916 thirteen banks were founded in these cities. See Gaston, "Negro Wage Earner," 33.

Georgia's major black bank was the Wage Earner's Savings Bank, organized in 1900 by a group of blacks who claimed to have been inspired by a Booker T. Washington speech in Savannah.[84] Starting with capital of $102, assets reached the million-dollar mark in 1920. At one time there were about 18,000 depositors, mostly agricultural and industrial workers. About half the loans were of the short-term commercial type, falling due in three months. The Wage Earner's Bank expanded as assets increased, moving into a new building in 1915 and buying an entire block in downtown Savannah in 1919. This was part of a half-million-dollar plan to develop new black businesses, including a hotel and department store.[85] The Wage Earner's Bank would not survive the Great Depression, but for over a quarter-century it was a symbol of black economic power and potential.

The best example of economic success through racial cooperation was the insurance business. Black insurance companies began developing in the early twentieth century, but blacks had been insuring themselves against sickness, accidents, and death since just after the Civil War. The most popular insuring agent then was the lodge or fraternal order. Between 1870 and 1920 Georgia blacks paid in about $16.5 million to lodges, and the greater part of this amount went out in death benefit payments. Not all lodge treasurers were honest or able, and many failures of fraternal societies resulted from insolvencies in their insurance departments. But for some time lodges filled the need for insurance among blacks, and they laid the foundation for the more reliable and scientifically operated old-line legal reserve insurance companies.[86]

At first, young Georgia companies like the Pilgrim Health and Life Insurance Company of Augusta sold only industrial insurance, collecting small weekly payments, providing funds when workers were sick or injured, and paying out death benefits. These companies were undercapitalized and some were actuarily unsound. In any year economic depression or a high death rate could sink a company. Competition from white firms was also a

84. L. E. Williams to Washington, Dec. 12, 1905, Washington Papers.
85. Woodson *et al.*, *Negro as a Business Man*, 67–68; Savannah *Tribune*, July 9, 1919; Aug. 7, 1920.
86. M. S. Stuart, *An Economic Detour: A History of Insurance in the Lives of American Negroes* (New York, 1940), 8, 20–21. The lodge will be discussed in more detail in the next chapter.

problem. Although the largest white insurance companies were generally not interested in selling policies to poor southern blacks, certain firms competed fiercely with fledgling black concerns. The Afro-American Life Insurance Company, for example, was a white-owned business employing only white agents. This company did much of its Georgia business by paying agent commissions to county school commissioners, who persuaded black teachers to take out policies—a form of job insurance, perhaps.[87] Insensitivity of white agents often helped black companies, whose salesmen were quick to point out examples of white racism to prospective customers.[88]

Between 1900 and 1910 the number of black insurance companies gradually increased, and then in 1912 an extraordinary experiment in black enterprise began when the Standard Life Insurance Company opened its offices in Atlanta. In less than a dozen years Standard Life would become the largest Negro insurance company in the world, a position gained through the talents of its president and founder, Heman Perry. Perry shocked the Georgia business community by starting Standard Life as an old-line, legal reserve organization instead of as a mutual company. To do so he needed to raise $100,000 in two years for a state charter. When his first attempt fell $30,000 short, Perry returned all money to subscribers with 4 percent interest. His second effort was successful, and within three years Perry had nearly two hundred agents working nine southern states.[89]

Enthusiasm at Standard's home office on Auburn Avenue was infectious, spreading to the backwoods areas of the Deep South. "The whole race of Ten Million of our folks is waiting to be sold to," proclaimed Secretary-Treasurer Harry Pace in his monthly report to agents in the field. When Standard Life paid its first large death claim, Pace trumpeted, "This [$2,000] check makes history. No colored company has ever before paid as large a sum as this. There is no one operating that can do it. You have a fine piece of canvassing material in that claim. Use it for all it is worth." Each agent received a picture of the cancelled check made out to the widow of the insured.[90]

87. Harry Pace to W. P. Burrell, July 28, 1915, Washington Papers.
88. Stuart, *Economic Detour*, 37.
89. *Crisis*, 13 (Mar., 1917), 240.
90. Circulars in Standard Life Folder, Washington Papers.

As Standard Life's assets grew, so did its founder's reputation. Born in Texas and possessing only a seventh-grade education, Heman Perry was an excellent organizer who knew the insurance business inside out. "A combination of sterling integrity, youthful vigor and enthusiasm, forceful personality, broad vision, and unselfish service," read the description of Perry in the Standard Life *Year Book*. The eulogist might have added that Perry was a teetotaler, a non-smoker, a bachelor, and a hard-driving man who expected total dedication from subordinates. He could be arrogant; he was stubborn and dictatorial. Above all, Heman Perry was an adventurer and a dreamer, and these human qualities would lead to his downfall.[91]

Not content with running one of the leading insurance companies, Perry expanded operations during and after World War I. He started by chartering the Service Company and establishing a thriving laundry in Augusta. Spurred by this success, Perry extended his interests to include more laundries, groceries, drug stores, farms, printing concerns, and a bank. His most ambitious venture was real estate. The Service Realty Company bought $600,000 worth of land on Atlanta's west side and built and financed homes there for middle-income blacks.[92] To help run this fledgling empire Perry imported "as intelligent and promising a galaxy of trained young Negroes as have ever moved into any community. . . ."[93] But Perry often ignored their expertise and disregarded their advice. J. B. Blayton, who was later to become the nation's first black certified public accountant, began his career with Perry. He recalls that once, after becoming concerned about a service company's financial situation, he took the balance sheets to Perry, who "read the assets sheet and threw the statement of liabilities into the wastebasket."[94] By the early 1920s Perry was overextended. His buccaneering tactics led him to take huge risks, watering stock of service companies and speculating with funds of Standard Life, the parent company. This, and perhaps a conspiracy headed by the Georgia Ku Klux Klan, brought Perry's

---

91. Comradge L. Henton, "Heman E. Perry: Documentary Materials for the Life History of a Business Man" (Master's thesis, Atlanta University, 1948), 66, 272, 274.

92. "Memorandum from J. B. Blayton to W. E. B. Du Bois," *ibid.*, 234.

93. Ira De A. Reid, "Research Memorandum of the Negro in the Economic System," *ibid.*, 254.

94. Interview with Mr. J. B. Blayton, Mar. 19, 1974, Atlanta.

downfall in 1924. Standard Life passed first into the hands of a white insurance company, and then in 1927 became part of a black company which folded during the Depression.[95]

Heman Perry was a magnificent failure. Like Marcus Garvey, whose meteoric career coincided with his, Perry had a dream which lay beyond his grasp. Perry's "black empire" was to be in the United States, and he was one of the first to put the rhetoric of black economic nationalism into large-scale practice. Though his grand design did not succeed, Perry left his imprint on Atlanta's west side, where he made it possible for hundreds of blacks to live together in respectable surroundings, and in the city's business community, where the talented young men he recruited stayed on to play a major role in making Atlanta one of the nation's centers of black enterprise.

While Perry was vaulting to the top of the business world, Alonzo F. Herndon, founder and president of the Atlanta Mutual Life Insurance Company, was rising, too, but more slowly—and surely. There was something of the tortoise-hare relationship between the two. Where Perry was an ascetic, hard-driving entrepreneur who ate and slept business, Herndon was "a good local citizen who liked to play checkers and to make talks in church meetings and things of that sort." A friend of the family remembers Herndon as a jolly, approachable person who "told jokes all the time." But behind the pleasant smile was the mind of a shrewd businessman.[96]

Like John Merrick, a founder of the North Carolina Mutual Life Insurance Company, Alonzo Herndon came to the insurance business by way of barbering. Herndon took the profits from his shop and wisely invested them. In 1905 he took over a handful of small black insurance companies whose directors could not meet the new law calling for a $5,000 deposit with the state for protection of policyholders. The Atlanta Mutual Life Insurance Company started with a clerk, two agents, one branch office, and fifty dollars' worth of insurance outstanding.[97] A half-dozen years later Atlanta Mutual boasted 70,000 policyholders in Georgia and

95. Walter B. Weare, *Black Business in the New South: A Social History of the North Carolina Mutual Life Insurance Company* (Urbana, 1973), 104, 124. Reid, "Research Memorandum," 254.

96. Interview with Mr. J. B. Blayton, Mar. 19, 1974; interview with Mrs. M. G. Wartman, Mar. 19, 1974, Atlanta.

97. Gordon, *The Georgia Negro*, 411.

Alabama, with eighty-four branch offices. By 1915 Herndon's company was one of the "Big Four" in black insurance.[98]

Though business rivals, Herndon and Perry at first cooperated, with Herndon serving as a director of the upstart Standard Life. The two men fell out after Perry took measures adversely affecting Atlanta Mutual without consulting Herndon. Herndon angrily resigned from the board, confiding to Emmett J. Scott that since Perry had "used me . . . I thought it would be well to let them catch another sucker."[99] After the break between the two black capitalists Standard Life grew more rapidly than Atlanta Mutual, but the latter made sound, steady progress under Herndon's conservative leadership.

In the end, of course, Herndon would win out. The Atlanta Life Insurance Company today is a strong black enterprise and its principal stockholder, Herndon's son Norris, is one of the wealthiest blacks in America. A millionaire himself before he died in 1927, Alonzo Herndon was for many blacks the personification of the American dream. He married one of the most beautiful women in Georgia, an accomplished actress who taught dramatics at Atlanta University. He built a mansion near the A.U. campus which would have been the envy of any antebellum planter. A proud man, Herndon supported the radical views of his friend Du Bois and was one of the "Original Twenty-nine" who attended the founding meeting of the Niagara Movement.[100]

Alonzo Herndon also represented the change in direction taken by the black business community in the late nineteenth and early twentieth centuries. The young man who began by cutting white men's hair and accepting their small tips ended his years as head of a wealthy black institution entirely supported by black men and women. The philosophy of race pride, self-help, and economic nationalism gained ascendancy during his career, and though his success was atypical, Herndon symbolized the economic possibilities inherent in the black community.

98. The other companies were North Carolina Mutual, Standard Life, and National Benefit Life (with home offices in Washington, D.C.). See Weare, *Black Business*, 103.

99. A. F. Herndon to Scott, Jan. 18, 1915, Washington Papers.

100. Du Bois, OHC, 190; Herbert Aptheker, ed., *The Correspondence of W. E. B. Du Bois: Volume I, Selections 1877–1934* (Amherst, 1973), 89.

Community

TO BE BLACK in Georgia was to fall victim to white oppression, to live each day in the shadow of violence. White supremacy prevailed, but it did not destroy the spirit of the black community. Blacks built their own institutions behind the walls of segregation, preaching race pride and practicing self-help. Just as lynchings, whitecappings, and race riots were facts of life in black Georgia, so were church picnics, baseball games, and Saturday night "frolics." The history of the black community defies easy generalization. It is the complex story of men and women struggling to build their own society within a hostile environment.

W. E. B. Du Bois pointed to the black church as "the only social institution of the Negroes which started in the African forest and survived slavery."[1] In Georgia it began with the founding of Baptist churches in Savannah and Augusta during the American Revolution. Growth was slow during slavery, in part because plantation owners did not want slaves assembling in their own places of worship. After the Civil War the black church expanded rapidly, and by the early twentieth century there were a half-million members.[2]

Next to the family, the church was the most important institution, the religious and social center of Negro life. Here parish-

1. W. E. B. Du Bois, ed., *Some Efforts of American Negroes for Their Own Social Betterment*, Atlanta University *Publications* No. 3 (Atlanta, 1898), 4.
2. W. E. B. Du Bois, ed., *The Negro Church*, Atlanta University *Publications* No. 8 (Atlanta, 1903), 30; Special Report of the Bureau of the Census, *Religious Bodies, 1906*, pt. 1 (Washington, 1910), 546.

ioners learned the price of cotton or the date of the next circus.
They wore their most fashionable clothes and heard about up-
coming elections. (Before disfranchisement, white office-seekers
would begin their campaigns for black votes in the church, if
possible with the minister's endorsement.[3]) Weddings, funerals,
summer revivals, church suppers, and bazaars provided much
of the community social life, and youth groups, women's missionary societies, and meetings of deacons and elders gave blacks
the opportunity of self-government denied them in the greater
society.

While denominational creeds varied, the black church was
basically fundamentalist in theology and otherwordly in its
interests.[4] With notable exceptions, the Sunday service was
emotional enough to bring a dramatic response from the congregation. Ministers used imaginative descriptions of hell, heaven,
and Christ's crucifixion to bring parishioners to their knees. This
type of service, so widespread in the countryside, was also popular
in smaller urban Baptist and Methodist churches. It somewhat
resembled the service of the fundamentalist white church.[5]

The head of the church, the minister was the most controversial
of all black leaders. Each denomination had in its pulpits men of
high caliber, religious scholars and self-educated preachers who
by teaching and example uplifted and inspired their flocks. At
the other extreme were the religious hustlers, men on the move
who lacked education and religious training but who had "heard
the call" to preach the gospel. White editors delighted in reporting incidents which involved Negro preachers in brawls and even
shoot-outs, but strongest criticism came from black intellectuals,
including church leaders. At its 1913 meeting the General State
Baptist Convention of Georgia denounced "the habits of many
ministers in taking whiskey and other liquors to our Sunday
School convention grounds and to our associations, and there
drink and are sometimes far from sober when they make

3. W. H. Holloway, "A Black Belt County in Georgia," in Du Bois, ed., *The Negro Church*, 57; McClure P. McCombs, "Pittsburg: A Sociological Study of a Natural Area" (Master's thesis, Atlanta University, 1951), 45. The disfranchise-ment amendment to the Georgia constitution passed in 1908. (See pp. 97–101.)

4. Gordon, *The Georgia Negro*, 117.

5. Wright, *87 Years Behind the Black Curtain*, 76–77; William H. Pipes, *Say Amen, Brother* (New York, 1951), 155; Du Bois, ed., *The Negro Church*, 76.

motions."[6] The Savannah *Tribune* berated ministers who failed
to support race enterprises, and Ben Davis of the Atlanta *Independent* kept up a running battle with the black clergy, quoting
approvingly Bishop Turner's statement that "The average Negro
preacher is a curse to his race."[7]

While supporting the church's position as "the most powerful
agency in the moral development and social reform of 9,000,000
Americans of Negro blood," the Atlanta University Conference
of 1903 resolved that the church needed "cleansing, reviving,
and inspiring."[8] A decade later a Georgia correspondent reported
that black ministers in his community "seem to have the idea
that their only mission in life outside of making a loud noise in
church service is to raise money for themselves," and the 1913
conference body concluded that "The majority of Negro churches
remain however financial institutions catering to a doubtful round
of semi-social activities."[9] Critical of certain church practices and
preachers, black intellectuals did not deny the importance of the
church to most black Georgians.

By far the largest black denomination was the Baptist Church.
Boasting a third of a million communicants in 1906, Georgia
Baptists went over the 400,000 mark a decade later. Female
members outnumbered men almost two to one.[10] The 2,500 congregations had a great deal of autonomy, for Baptists had no
ecclesiastical hierarchy. Each member had a voice in church
policy, and therein lay denominational weakness as well as
strength. Democracy on the congregational level made it easy
for church bodies to divide, and throughout this period local
Baptists were plagued by splits and factions. Baptists produced
few national figures, for without a church hierarchy most clerics
had little visibility outside the parish.[11] Georgia Baptists did,

6. "Minutes of the Twenty-first Annual Session of the General State Baptist
Convention of Georgia" (Atlanta, 1913), 69, copy in Interdenominational Theological Center Library, Atlanta.

7. Savannah *Tribune*, Jan. 28, 1905; Atlanta *Independent*, July 15, 1905.

8. Du Bois, ed., *The Negro Church*, 208.

9. W. E. B. Du Bois and A. G. Dill, eds., *Manners and Morals Among Negro Americans*, Atlanta University *Publications* No. 18 (Atlanta, 1913), 110, 7.

10. *Religious Bodies, 1906*, 546; Special Report of the Bureau of the Census, *Religious Bodies, 1916*, pt. 1 (Washington, 1920), 562. Women were a majority in all black denominations in Georgia.

11. Benjamin Brawley, *Negro Builders and Heroes* (Chapel Hill, 1937), 199–200.

however, have powerful clergymen who presided over large, strong congregations. Probably the best known was Reverend Charles T. Walker of Augusta, called the "Black Spurgeon" because of his oratorical ability. Pastor of the 1,700-member Tabernacle Baptist Church (and also for a time of Mount Olivet Baptist Church in New York City), Walker was conservative in theology and politics, a follower and friend of Booker T. Washington.[12] Other Baptist leaders included Reverend E. K. Love of Savannah, who until his death in 1900 was pastor of the oldest black church, the First African Baptist; and Reverend E. R. Carter, the minister and author who for many years presided over Friendship Baptist Church in Atlanta, the birthplace of Spelman College.[13]

The African Methodist Episcopal Church was next in size and influence, claiming about 90,000 members during the 1900-1920 period. Founded in 1816 by Richard Allen of Philadelphia and other blacks who resented imposition of segregation in the Methodist Church, the A.M.E. denomination was an outspoken foe of racism. Conservative theologically, the church tolerated a variety of political views, including the Back-to-Africa program of its senior bishop, Henry McNeal Turner. While railing against the "card table, the theatre, and the modern dance," A.M.E. delegates to the Georgia Conference also denounced racist politicians like Hoke Smith and Thomas M. Hardwick. The *A.M.E. Church Review* featured articles on race pride and African migration, while denouncing American imperialism.[14]

Two of the most important African Methodists lived in Georgia. Bishop Wesley J. Gaines was born in slavery in Wilkes County, joined the A.M.E. Church in 1865, and became a bishop in 1885. He led the drive to found Morris Brown College and was the guiding force behind the building of the famed Big Bethel A.M.E. Church in Atlanta. Best known for his black nationalist views, Bishop Henry McNeal Turner also worked hard to advance African Methodism. As senior bishop of the denomination

12. Silas X. Floyd, *The Life of Charles T. Walker* (Nashville, 1902).
13. Atlanta *Constitution*, Oct. 23, 1912.
14. "Speeches Delivered at the Golden Jubilee Rally" (Macon, 1916), 108, pamphlet in ITC Library; A.M.E. Church Annual Conference, *Georgia Conference Minutes*, 51st sess., Nov. 22–26, 1916, p. 52; *A.M.E. Church Review*, 16 (Jan. 1, 1900).

Turner wielded tremendous power, and the church bore his stamp until his death in 1915.[15]

Two smaller branches had ties with white Methodists. The Colored Methodist Episcopal Church organized in 1870 with assistance from the parent body, the Methodist Episcopal (South) Church. They cooperated during the late nineteenth century, jointly founding Paine College in Augusta, which for many years had white southern Methodists as presidents. C.M.E. leaders were defensive about ties with whites, conceding that a number of blacks opposed this relationship. Church rules limited membership to blacks.[16] Leading light of the Colored Methodists in Georgia and nationally was the church's senior bishop, Lucius H. Holsey. Born into Georgia slavery, Holsey was elected bishop for the Southwest before he reached thirty. Tall, slender, and dignified in appearance, he was chief founder of Paine College, the Holsey Normal and Industrial Academy in Cordele, and a string of C.M.E. churches in a dozen Georgia cities. Holsey was a prolific writer who favored unification of all black Methodists, and later in life championed black separatism in the United States.[17]

The 25,000 Georgia blacks in the Methodist Episcopal Church were part of a northern white denomination. Money from northern congregations helped found Clark College and the well-endowed Gammon Theological Seminary in Atlanta, but blacks felt they lacked a voice in both church and school affairs. Black Methodist Episcopalians wanted their own bishop; their candidate was the scholarly J. W. E. Bowen, once president of Gammon and professor of historical theology there. In 1896 he received a plurality of votes at the church conference but fell short of the necessary two-thirds majority. Bowen never did become a bishop, and membership in the black congregations of the M.E. Church declined slightly in Georgia during the first two decades of the

15. Cornelius V. Troup, *Distinguished Negro Georgians* (Atlanta, 1962), 186; M. M. Ponton, *Life and Times of Henry M. Turner* (Atlanta, 1917). Bishop Turner's career will be examined more thoroughly in the chapter on "Black Thought."

16. J. A. Bray, C.M.E., "Speech to the General Conference, A.M.E. Church," in *Journal* of the General Conference, A.M.E. Church, 1908, pp. 179–80; Du Bois, ed., *The Negro Church*, 47.

17. John B. Cade, *Holsey The Incomparable* (New York, 1963), 71–74, 153–54. For discussion of Holsey's separatist views, see the chapter on "Black Thought."

century.[18] Other white denominations had black churches in
Georgia, including the high-status Episcopalians, Congregationalists, and Presbyterians. None could claim as many as 3,000
members, but the number of black leaders belonging to these
denominations gave them greater influence in the community
than membership figures indicate.[19]

The lodge, or secret society, challenged the church as the most
important social organization for black men. Ministers believed
the fraternal orders to be less important than the church and were
dubious about the quasi-religious nature of lodges. They resented
the popularity of the fraternal orders, particularly when lodge
activities competed with church affairs. A church official reported
that weeknight church meetings and socials died out in one part
of the state when parishioners became involved in lodge festiv-
ities, feeling "duty-bound only to attend the worship of God on
Sunday."[20] Competition between church and lodge became so
intense in one area that A.M.E. bishop Charles Spencer Smith
prohibited ministers in his district from serving as lodge officers.[21]
The Masons, Knights of Pythias, and Odd Fellows were the
leading national fraternal orders in Georgia. The prestigious
Masons traced their origin to the mother lodge in England in the
late eighteenth century. The Grand Lodge for Georgia organized
in 1870 and grew to over 10,000 members by 1910. A decade later
the figure rose to 28,000 members in nearly 500 Georgia cities
and villages, with property valued at $500,000. The Order of the
Eastern Star for wives and female relatives of Masons had 350
state chapters by 1920. Active in community affairs, Masons
maintained an orphans' home in Macon in addition to contributing
to other self-help projects. The Masons were particular about

18. A.M.E. Church Review, 17 (July, 1900), 85; Meier, "Negro Racial
Thought," 725. In 1912 Bowen wrote An Appeal for Negro Bishops, But No
Separation (New York, 1912), where he argued that blacks belonging to the
M.E. Church should not be segregated into a black conference district, as some
whites had suggested, but that two black bishops should be assigned to the South
under existing church structure. His appeal went unheeded.
19. Religious Bodies, 1906, 546; Religious Bodies, 1916, 562.
20. "Speeches Delivered at the Golden Jubilee Rally," 111; Voice of the
People, Jan. 1, 1903.
21. A.M.E. Church, Annual Conference, Georgia Conference Minutes (n.p.,
1908), 27.

membership; they had on their rolls representatives of such aristocratic black families as the Deveaux and Toomers, as well as men of influence like Bishop Turner, Savannah editor Sol C. Johnson, Atlanta's John Wesley Dobbs, and their long-time leader, Dr. H. R. Butler.[22]

Less wealthy and selective than the Masons, the Colored Knights of Pythias recorded over 15,000 members in the years before World War I and more than doubled that number by 1920.[23] During the early part of the century the Colored Knights struggled for survival against two onslaughts, first from the white Knights and later from the Georgia legislature. The white Knights secured a permanent injunction in 1906 against the Colored Knights of Fulton County to keep the blacks from using the same name, regalia, and ritual as the white lodge. Blacks took the case to court, losing at the state level but winning a U.S. Supreme Court ruling in 1912.[24] Meanwhile Georgia legislators schemed to destroy black secret orders through a 1909 bill placing all black lodges under prohibitive bond. The attempt failed, but Governor Joseph Brown did sign an act forbidding "the use by Negro Secret Societies of the insignia, ritualistic work, grips, etc. of orders composed of whites," aimed at the black K of P and Elks lodges in particular. These groups avoided prosecution by making slight changes in ritual.[25]

Georgia whites did not appreciate the idea of black men using the same names, rituals, and uniforms, but their opposition to black lodges went much deeper. From days of slavery whites had distrusted groups of black men meeting behind closed doors, fearing anti-white conspiracy. When legal attempts to outlaw black fraternal orders failed, white vigilantes launched their own campaigns of bombing and burning. In one Early County episode

22. William H. Grimshaw, *Official History of Freemasonry among the Colored People of North America* (Montreal, 1903), vii, 67, 265; H. R. Butler, *The History of Freemasonry Among Colored Men in Georgia* (Atlanta, 1911), 12–13, in Schomburg Collection, New York Public Library; Sol C. Johnson, "History of the Grand Lodge," 4, 9, printed MS in Schomburg Collection; Mrs. E. E. Burnett, "The Real Status of the Eastern Star," 17, undated MS in Schomburg Collection.
23. *History and Manual of the Colored Knights of Pythias N.A., S.A., E.A., A. and A.* (Nashville, 1917), 376, 837–38; Caldwell, ed., *History of the Negro, Georgia Edition*, II, 11.
24. *Colored Knights of Pythias*, 371; Atlanta *Constitution*, June 15, 1912; Matthews, "Studies in Race Relations," 264.
25. *Colored Knights of Pythias*, 281–82; Atlanta *Constitution*, Aug. 12, 15, 18, 1909; Atlanta *Independent*, Aug. 21, 1909.

several blacks were killed and all but one lodge hall burned after a rumor circulated that a Negro lodge had delegated a member to kill a white farmer. Black fraternal leaders defended their groups as neither political nor anti-white, and white editors condemned the mobs, but acts of violence against black lodge halls and members continued.[26]

The strengths and shortcomings of the fraternal movement came together in the Grand United Order of Odd Fellows and its controversial Georgia leader, Benjamin Davis. The state's largest and wealthiest black fraternal order expanded rapidly in the early twentieth century; by 1916 it counted 1,100 lodges and 33,000 members, with assets close to a million dollars. Several years earlier officers had purchased nearly an entire block on Atlanta's Auburn Avenue and erected a large office building and auditorium, paid for in advance from the Odd Fellows treasury. Committed to development of black enterprise, the Odd Fellows established a sinking fund of $300,000 to finance loans for purchasing businesses, farms, and homes.[27]

The driving force behind the Odd Fellows was Benjamin Davis. Born to humble parents on a farm in Dawson, Georgia, Davis was an ambitious young man who moved to Atlanta, where he became active in fraternal and political affairs. Shortly after the turn of the century he launched a black weekly newspaper, the Atlanta Independent; filling its columns with lodge news, he promoted his own interests in the process. One contemporary remembers Davis as "a wheeler and a dealer," and several times Davis found himself in court on the wrong end of a lawsuit. But he had a loyal following, especially among Georgia Odd Fellows, and in 1912 they were confident of electing him National Grand Master. The thousands of members who poured into Atlanta from all over the country for the national convention were welcomed by white government officials who opened segregated parks and gave permission for a parade through city streets.[28]

26. Atlanta *Constitution*, Jan. 1–3, 1916; Atlanta *Journal*, Sept. 9, 1904, Jan. 27, 1907; Savannah *Tribune*, Dec. 28, 1907.

27. Stuart, *Economic Detour*, 23; Grand United Order of Odd Fellows in America, *Proceedings of the 18th B.M.C.* (n.p., 1916), 26–27; *Crisis*, 8 (June, 1913), 63; Atlanta *Constitution*, Apr. 2, 1913; Matthews, "Studies in Race Relations," 263; Atlanta *Independent*, Apr. 18, 1914.

28. Interview with Dr. Miles Amos, Mar. 20, 1974, Atlanta; *Crisis*, 4 (Oct., 1912), 270.

What followed was lodge-hall politics at its worst. Long prominent in national fraternal affairs, Davis believed he had insured his nomination by a "gentleman's agreement" with Grand Master E. H. Morris. Though Davis thought the latter would not seek re-election, the Grand Master had other ideas. By engaging in tactics of filibuster and delay (which included polling each of 12,000 delegates) Morris prevented completion of balloting, thereby, according to the by-laws, giving himself another two-year term. Davis was infuriated at what he saw as a double-cross. He began a feud with Morris which split the Odd Fellows into warring factions, eventually leading to Davis's suspension and removal of the Georgia lodge's charter.[29] Then came a series of court fights over control of the Georgia chapter's considerable assets, with Davis contending that his faction represented the interests of Odd Fellows in Georgia. His lodge went into receivership in 1916. Few resources remained by the time all claims were paid six years later, and the Odd Fellows Grand Lodge and Benefit Association of Georgia was dissolved.[30] Decline of the Georgia Odd Fellows preceded the collapse of the Standard Life Insurance Company, and failure of two of the most successful examples of economic cooperation was a blow to race pride and black enterprise.

Flamboyant costumes and display, elaborate ritual, and scheming politicians were facts of life in black lodges, just as they were in white lodges. Still, there remains something to be said for black fraternal orders. Secret societies sprang from the need for fellowship, association, and status. Lodge membership gave blacks a sense of "belonging," of "being somebody."[31] It provided training in leadership, teamwork, and institutional government for a race excluded from participation in the affairs of the total

29. A sample of Davis's anti-Morris rhetoric: "The Kaiser in Germany is no more heartless and wicked, is no more desparate in his efforts to destroy the peace of the world and enslave all mankind, than Ed Morris is in his desparation to destroy the property rights of Odd Fellows in this country and to reduce them to serfs." Atlanta *Independent*, June 23, 1917.
30. *Proceedings of the 16th B.M.C.* (n.p., 1912); Stuart, *Economic Detour*, 23–25; Atlanta *Constitution*, Jan. 17, 30, 1917.
31. Charles H. Wesley, *History of the Improved Benevolent and Protective Order of Elks of the World, 1898–1954* (Washington, 1955), 19; Clarence A. Bacote, "Some Aspects of Negro Life in Georgia, 1880–1908," *Journal of Negro History*, 43 (1958), 199.

community. Thousands of members and their families received millions of dollars in sickness and death benefits from lodge insurance programs. And beneath all the ritual and regalia, the black fraternal order stressed the need for racial unity. If at worst it was but a pale copy of its white counterpart, at its best the Negro lodge gave strength and direction to the black community.

Georgia blacks were divided into socioeconomic classes. While stratification was not rigid, each major city had its small black elite, a large group of poor, unskilled workers, and a middle class between the extremes of relative wealth and absolute poverty. Ancestry, education, and color were all criteria, but occupation was the major determinant of social position.[32] In rural areas the farm owner commanded greatest respect, followed by the renter, sharecropper, and wage laborer. The situation in the cities, with a wider choice of careers, was more complex. In the late nineteenth century upper-class Atlanta blacks were primarily ex-slaves of mixed ancestry and their descendants; they were the leading grocers, barbers, doctors, and realtors. A minister, a lawyer, a contractor, and several postal employees and college teachers completed the elite roster. A number of upper-class businessmen catered to a white clientele. This would change in the first thirty years of the twentieth century, when an entrepreneurial class developed which served blacks exclusively and espoused doctrines of race pride and economic chauvinism. Two students of the subject have concluded that in time this new business group "came to constitute not only the economic elite, but the social elite as well."[33] Augusta and Savannah, with relatively large numbers of antebellum free blacks, had a more firmly entrenched Negro aristocracy. Ancestry appears to have influenced status there more than in most Georgia cities.

Social class in black Georgia was reflected in membership rolls of churches, lodges, and social clubs, as well as in college alumni rosters. As noted, the Masons were the most exclusive fraternal

32. See August Meier, "Negro Class Structure and Ideology in the Age of Booker T. Washington," *Phylon*, 23 (Fall, 1962), 258–66.
33. August Meier and David Lewis, "History of the Negro Upper Class in Atlanta, Georgia, 1890–1958," *Journal of Negro Education*, 28 (Spring, 1959), 129–30; Meier, "Negro Class Structure," 260–62.

order, and the Odd Fellows had the greatest mass appeal. There
was some overlapping membership, as some blacks belonged to
two or three different lodges. Upper-class urban blacks usually
preferred churches which also enjoyed high prestige in the white
community, particularly the Congregational and Episcopal denominations. St. Stephen's Episcopal Church attracted many
upper-class blacks in Savannah, while Atlanta's black aristocracy
centered around the First Congregational Church, with its close
ties to Atlanta University.[34] Generally, Methodists were middle
and lower-middle class, while the black masses filled the ranks
of the Baptists. Methodists and Baptists did have members of
high position, like entrepreneur David T. Howard and Morehouse
College president John Hope. The individual church more often
determined status than the denominational label alone. Higher
education was a status symbol, if only because it was available
to so few. The handful of black professionals educated in eastern
universities received greatest esteem. Of Georgia's black colleges
Atlanta University was the most prestigious, followed by Morehouse, Clark, and Spelman.

The pinnacle of society was the exclusive social club. Blacks on
all social levels belonged to clubs, a favorite form of entertainment; however, each Georgia city had at least one or two select
groups where wealth, education, and proper religious affiliation
did not in themselves guarantee entry. Membership was kept
small, with new members initiated only when vacancies occurred.
Atlanta's Chautauqua Circle was one of the most highly regarded
of these clubs. Founded in 1913 by a small group of educated
women, the Circle limited membership to fifteen. (During its
first twenty-three years there was a total of only thirty members.) With their slogan "Keep Moving: A Standing Pool Becomes Stagnant," members prepared and discussed papers on
topics ranging from civil rights, politics, and international relations to art, literature, and religion. What began as an organization of talented young women broadening their intellectual

34. Meier and Lewis, "History of the Negro Upper Class," 130–31; James
Perdue, *The Negro in Savannah, 1865–1900* (New York, 1973), 91. Atlanta
University was founded by the Congregationalists' American Missionary Associa-
tion.

horizons became a status symbol, and even today membership in the Chautauqua Circle is an envied distinction.[35]

Correlation between skin color and social status is difficult to assess, but pigmentation was undeniably a factor. Color caste was strongest in Savannah in the late nineteenth century. As early as 1872, St. Stephen's Episcopal Church split after the body's near-white vestrymen tried to exclude dark-skinned Negroes. Angered blacks walked out and formed their own church.[36] Robert Abbott, crusading editor of the Chicago *Defender,* bore scars from his youth, for color-conscious students and teachers at Savannah's Beach Institute ostracized him. In his study of black Savannah historian James Perdue concludes, "The lighter-skinned Negroes were clannish and constituted a colored aristocracy that had little in common with blacks."[37]

Color was not so important in black Atlanta, which had no ante-bellum mulatto aristocracy, but here too a light skin stood out. Atlanta University's most exclusive fraternity, the Owls, chose members "on color and financial status"—and this in an institution already referred to by some blacks as "that half-white school."[38] Walter White, an A.U. graduate who later gained attention by passing for white while investigating lynchings for the NAACP, admitted that some blacks showed "resentment against us because we occupied a slightly more comfortable and better kept home and were less dark than they."[39]

The champion mulatto-baiter was Ben Davis. Not himself of pure African descent, neither was he part of upper-class black society. In his editorial columns he railed against what he perceived as a light-skinned aristocracy led by the likes of Collector of Internal Revenue Henry L. Rucker and Congregationalist minister H. H. Proctor. Accusing the two of "having exclusive mulattoes in their society and for their associates," Davis went

35. Material on the Chautauqua Circle is from the organization's scrapbook, "Chautauqua Circle, 1913–1963," Chautauqua Circle Collection, Negro Collection, Trevor Arnett Library, Atlanta University.

36. Perdue, *Negro in Savannah,* 90.

37. *Ibid.,* 91; Roi Ottley, *The Lonely Warrior: The Life and Times of Robert S. Abbott* (Chicago, 1955), 61–62.

38. Bacote, *Story of Atlanta University,* 243; interview with Mr. J. B. Blayton, Mar. 19, 1974, Atlanta.

39. Walter White, *A Man Called White* (New York, 1948), 21.

on to charge that Proctor's church preferred mulatto members.[40] Sensitive to color distinctions in the fraternal world, Davis stated that "The dances in the Odd Fellows Roof Garden are as moral and decent as the dances where Henry Rucker's daughters and Proctor's daughters dance. . . . The men and women who attend the roof garden are not mulattoes as are those who attend the dances that Rucker's and Proctor's families participate in, but they are just as moral."[41] Another time Davis charged the Tri-State Medical Association, whose annual convention was meeting in Atlanta, with inviting only light-skinned Atlanta Negroes to their dance. The offended editor was appalled that the all-black medical association had become "so struck with the color line that they actually had a white orchestra."[42]

Davis no doubt exaggerated the importance of a light complexion in determining status. The record is full of black Negroes who through education or occupation achieved leadership and respect in their communities. Yet mulattoes as a group had economic and educational advantages dating back to slavery, when they made up a disproportionately large percentage of house servants and free blacks. As sons and daughters of slaveholders they often received special training and privileges, including at times emancipation. Subsequent economic success enabled them to educate their own children, who in turn became doctors, teachers, and business leaders. Light skin color was thus the symbol and not (as whites commonly believed) the biological cause of success.[43] The light-complexioned Negro remained atop the black socioeconomic pyramid into the twentieth century, but an increasingly rigid Jim Crow mentality, opposed by a black ideology of racial pride and unity, would reduce the social significance of skin color in Georgia.

Aware that white officials ignored the range of problems facing their communities, blacks put the principle of self-help into prac-

40. Atlanta *Independent,* Oct. 23, 1915.
41. *Ibid.,* May 30, 1914.
42. *Ibid.*
43. Edward B. Reuter, *The Mulatto in the United States* (reprinted, New York, 1969), 180. Newspaper ads often specified that the employer wanted a mulatto to fill a position. See Mary White Ovington to Ray Stannard Baker, Apr. 13, 1907, Ray Stannard Baker Papers, Manuscript Division, Library of Congress.

tice. The most critical area demanding cooperation was prevention and control of disease in the cities. Affluent blacks might live in comfortable, well-furnished homes, but they were never far from slums like the one in Atlanta which contained "Human beings packed like sardines in a box, without the slightest effort for any provision of modern sanitation, and kept in that condition by the greed of the landlord."[44] These ghettos created such health hazards that as late as 1917 the average life span for blacks was but thirty-five years, with high mortality rates due to tuberculosis, pneumonia, and infant deaths—causes directly related to environment.[45] Often sanitation officials ignored disease-breeding conditions in black settlements and refused to force landlords to upgrade wretched housing.[46]

Black civic organizations took the lead in attacking health-related problems. In Macon the Organized Charities and Civic Settlement League concentrated on upgrading housing and sanitation facilities. The Negro Civic Improvement League of Savannah sponsored "Clean Up" days in slum areas. Young children learned personal hygiene in the Gate City Free Kindergarten in Atlanta, which began in two poverty districts in 1905 and soon expanded into other neighborhoods. The Savannah Urban League gave special attention to the problems of the aged, and across the state churches and fraternal organizations operated schools, orphanages, and day care centers, assisting those unable to care for themselves.[47]

No religious or fraternal organization was more active than Atlanta's First Congregational Church. Under the leadership of Henry Hugh Proctor, graduate of Yale Divinity School, this upper-class congregation became the first black institutional church in the South, providing neighborhood social service pro-

44. Brown, ed., *Economic Cooperation*, 33; Du Bois, ed., *Negro American Family*, 58–59; Woofter, *Negroes of Athens*, 13–16, 18.

45. Brown, ed., *Economic Cooperation*, 25; Deaton, "Atlanta During the Progressive Era," 171. Reverend E. R. Carter admitted, "We have to keep two separate communion sets in my church because of tuberculous Negroes." Carter, letter to Atlanta *Constitution*, Feb. 5, 1914.

46. Atlanta *Constitution*, Oct. 4, 1904; Woofter, *Negroes of Athens*, 13.

47. *Crisis*, 9 (Apr., 1915), 270; Savannah *Tribune*, May 11, 1912; Dec. 6, 1913; July 11, 1914; Shivery, "Neighborhood Union," 149; W. E. B. Du Bois, ed., *Efforts for Social Betterment Among Negro Americans*, Atlanta University *Publications* No. 14 (Atlanta, 1910), 72, 77, 81–96, 126–27.

grams in a non-sectarian community center. Remodeled before 1910, First Church had an auditorium, gymnasium, library, and reading room, along with a kitchen and shower. Close by was the church-run home for black working girls, the first of its kind. The church operated business and cooking schools, a kindergarten, and an employment bureau; it also helped support the Carrie Steele Orphanage and carried on mission work in the slums.[48]

The most ambitious self-help agency was the Neighborhood Union, a pioneer effort in community organization begun in 1908 by Mrs. Lugenia Hope, the wife of the Morehouse president. Starting with a house-by-house survey to determine the needs and grievances of black residents of Atlanta's west end, the organization quickly established a health clinic which also served as a community center, combining educational, social, and political activities. The Union was child-oriented, providing vocational classes for children and a boys' club and girls' club. Union leaders were active lobbyists who frequently appeared before the city council to denounce inadequate or non-existent public facilities in black areas. The group also went to the school board, requesting more black schools and higher pay for teachers. By 1911 the Neighborhood Union covered five black sections, and four years later expanded its services to the entire city.[49]

Organizers of the Neighborhood Union were educated, dedicated women who displayed a singleness of purpose and adopted a no-nonsense approach to their work. Union organizers lived in or near the areas they served and experienced community problems directly. They rented a Neighborhood House on a street lined with saloons and cheap eating joints, and made spirited attempts to rid their blocks of prostitution and gambling dens.[50]

The force behind the Neighborhood Union was its founder. Lugenia Hope was a soft-spoken woman who associated herself

48. Henry Hugh Proctor, *Between Black and White, Autobiographical Sketches* (Boston, 1925), 106, 111; Atlanta *Constitution*, Dec. 13, 1908; David A. Russell, Jr., "The Institutional Church in Transition: A Study of the First Congregational Church of Atlanta" (Master's thesis, Atlanta University, 1971), 1–3, 13.

49. Neighborhood Union, *Minute Book, 1908–1921,* Neighborhood Union Collection, Negro Collection, Trevor Arnett Library, Atlanta University; Shivery, "History of Organized Social Work," 44, 47, 52, 100; Shivery, "Neighborhood Union," 149–55.

50. Mrs. Hattie R. Watson, "Work of the Neighborhood Union," Spelman *Messenger*, Nov., 1916, p. 6; Neighborhood Union, *Minute Book,* 38–40, 66, 84.

with "the struggle of the poor to preserve their independence and self-respect."[51] A patient, tireless worker, Mrs. Hope knew first-hand the frustrations of community organization:

> Did it ever occur to you how difficult it is to get all of this work started—how many years it takes to get enough folks together to accomplish anything? *Why?* We have to work to get people together who have nothing in *common* and then to get them sufficiently acquainted with each other to be able to work together. Then we see each other only once or twice per month and really there is very little accomplished.[52]

Under Mrs. Hope's firm hand the organization served well. In its first twelve years the Neighborhood Union provided direct aid for needy families; pressured city fathers into improving roads, lighting, and sanitation facilities in black neighborhoods; secured appointment of a black probation officer for juveniles; and lobbied successfully for increased support for black education—all in addition to the regular on-going programs of health care, education, and recreation in black areas. The work of the Neighborhood Union cut across social and economic lines; it was perhaps the best example of self-help through community action in the South.[53]

Life was not all work, struggle, and sacrifice. Recreation and amusement facilities were more available in cities than in the country, but farm families found opportunities for relaxation and pleasure. The isolation and monotony of country life caused rural folk to get together as often as possible. The Saturday excursion to town was more than a marketing trip; it was a holiday where friends met to swap stories and unwind. Sunday church was also a social event where people gathered early in the morning and stayed until late afternoon. Revivals, usually held in the fall after the crops were laid by, brought large crowds to emotional nightly

51. Mrs. Lugenia Hope, pencil draft of speech, Neighborhood Union Collection.
52. Mrs. Lugenia Hope, "Memoranda," Mar. 20, 1921, MS in Neighborhood Union Collection.
53. Undated brochure in Neighborhood Union Collection listing achievements of the Neighborhood Union; Louie D. Shivery, "Atlanta Health Campaign," Jan. 12, 1914, MS in Neighborhood Union Collection; "Survey S. B. Brooks," 1914, MS in Neighborhood Union Collection.

meetings. Weddings, special days like the Fourth of July, and funerals were major social occasions, as was the "frolic," where neighbors gathered at the host's cabin for an evening of gossip, dancing, food, and drink. The week beginning with Christmas and ending with New Year's Day was the most festive period for country blacks; this holiday tradition dated back to slavery, when the master gave slaves time off for recreation. Many honest, hard-working, sober men got drunk "religiously and regularly" every Christmas.[54]

The city offered social diversions ranging from church bazaars to houses of prostitution. Black editors and ministers deplored a lack of "wholesome" recreational activities, condemning those—especially the young—who frequented dives, poolrooms, and dance halls.[55] Singled out for attack were railroad and steamboat excursions, which attracted both seamy characters and families who had saved all year for an outing. Violence, always played up by the white press, was not uncommon. One railroad excursion from Atlanta to Griffin, a seventy-five mile trip, reached its destination with over a dozen dead and scores wounded. Many had been injured jumping from the train to escape the brawl.[56] Railroad and steamboat officials turned their backs on law and order on these trips, since hoodlums were their best customers and victims of the outbursts were almost always black.

The theater provided entertainment in larger cities, usually at the price of Jim Crow accommodations. Black leaders urged citizens to avoid these theaters, where they normally had to enter through a dark alley and climb back stairs to a "peanut gallery."[57] If some blacks accepted their "place" in the balcony, they did not always keep it during a performance. Atlanta blacks attending Thomas Dixon's racist play *The Clansman* (later made into the movie *The Birth of a Nation*) cheered actors portraying blacks and expressed enthusiasm in places unanticipated by the playwright. As a black villain came to trial, cries of "Lynch him!" from whites in the audience drew hisses and taunts from the balcony. The situation became so tense that the management

54. Du Bois, ed., *Negro American Family*, 130–31.
55. Atlanta *Constitution*, Oct. 1, 1917; Savannah *Tribune*, Dec. 31, 1904.
56. *Voice of the Negro*, 2 (Aug., 1905), 530–31.
57. Atlanta *Independent*, Sept. 16, 1905.

kept house lights on throughout the performance and stopped
soda-pop sales early to avoid a rain of bottles onto the stage and
orchestra seats. Police eventually responded by storming the
balcony and making arrests.[58] In Atlanta and Savannah black-
owned theaters featured black vaudeville talent in addition to
motion pictures. The manager of the Pekin Theater in Savannah
proclaimed: "The pictures are hand-colored, the performers, the
patrons and the proprietor are so by nature. Glad of it, aren't
you."[59]

Whether in the theater or church, in the dance hall or cotton
field, music was essential to black life. Musical tastes varied.
Upper-class Negroes were suspicious of black music, accepting
spirituals but scorning the blues and ragtime, music of the masses.
This rejection of black music stemmed in part from its origins in
the cotton fields and barrooms; but also significant was white
exploitation of blacks in music, first in minstrel shows and then
in the 1890s in the popular "coon songs," where songwriters employed racial stereotypes in such classics as "All Coons Look
Alike to Me" and "The Coon's Trademark: A Watermelon, Razor,
Chicken and Coon." Sheet music covers duplicated in picture
form the offensive caricature of the lyrics. When the first piano
rags became popular at the turn of the century, their sheet music
covers bore the same unflattering stereotypes.[60] Music like Scott
Joplin's "Maple Leaf Rag" was miles away from the "coon song"
socially and aesthetically, but many blacks linked the two. An
Atlanta University student called on black composers to "lead
Negro music away from the detestable ragtime and coon-song
quagmire into which it has recently been thrown," and black
editors denounced ragtime "songs and dance which are nothing
shorter than the grossest vulgarity and obscenity."[61]

Musical training on black college campuses emphasized European classical composers. As late as 1916 the music curriculum
at Atlanta University neglected black music. The many campus
recitals were heavy with works by "serious" composers, with an

58. *Ibid.*, Nov. 4, 1905.
59. Savannah *Tribune*, May 25, 1912.
60. William J. Schafer and Johannes Riedel, *The Art of Ragtime, Form and Meaning of an Original Black American Art* (Baton Rouge, 1973), 168–71.
61. *Scroll* (Dec., 1902), 15; Waycross *Gazette and Land Bulletin*, Jan. 27, 1900; Savannah *Tribune*, Feb. 21, 1914.

occasional spiritual finding its way onto the program. One such student recital featured two works by Chopin performed by a young pianist named Fletcher Henderson, later to become one of the great jazz composers and arrangers.[62]

If the community's moral and educational leaders scorned secular black music, it thrived outside church and campus walls. Georgia had no Memphis or New Orleans, but famous musicians like W. C. Handy would come to perform in Decatur Street clubs in Atlanta, and vaudeville groups took the latest music and dances to black-owned clubs in smaller cities like Macon and Savannah.[63] More important, Georgia blacks created their own music while working in plantation fields, slaving on chain gangs, and entertaining in small clubs.[64] The blues and ragtime may not have been "respectable," but along with spirituals they best expressed the sorrows, joys, and dreams of black Georgians. Respectability would come later.

Among leisure activities, sports were extremely popular. Hunting and fishing were favorite rural pastimes, while townspeople enjoyed a variety of athletic contests. Football quickly caught on, especially in Atlanta's black colleges, where large crowds watched archrivals A.U. and Morehouse compete. By far the best-loved sport was baseball, the national pastime. Black colleges had teams, and many fans gathered for pick-up games like the contest between Atlanta's black doctors and college professors for the benefit of the Neighborhood Union.[65] Blacks played ball in farm communities and cities. Most small towns fielded teams, and intercity competition was spirited. As early as 1884, clubs from Atlanta and Savannah squared off for the championship of Georgia.[66]

Larger cities had semi-professional black clubs, and local fans turned out to see some of the best players in the country. The

62. Atlanta University *Catalog*, 1915–16, p. 19; *Scroll* (May, 1917), 3.

63. Interview with Mrs. M. G. Wartman, Mar. 19, 1974; C. H. Douglas to Scott, July 10, 1916, Washington Papers; interview with Dr. Miles Amos, Mar. 20, 1974, Atlanta.

64. Atlanta *Constitution*, Nov. 1, 1916; Arthur G. Powell, *I Can Go Home Again* (Chapel Hill, 1943), 21.

65. Neighborhood Union, *Minute Book*, 1913, p. 116.

66. Atlanta *Constitution*, Sept. 6, 1914; Robert Peterson, *Only the Ball Was White* (Englewood Cliffs, N.J., 1970), 38.

legendary John "Pop" Lloyd began his professional career with the Macon Acmes in 1905. While Lloyd was dominating the Negro leagues, a youth named Josh Gibson was learning the game on the sandlots of Buena Vista, a village not far from Atlanta.[67] Men like Gibson and Lloyd would have been stars in the major leagues, but like most black professional athletes they fell victim to the color line. Until the late 1890s black jockeys competed successfully against whites, and Willie Sims of Augusta was one of the best riders of his day. Yet by the turn of the century interracial athletic competition was practically unheard of on the professional level.

An exception was prizefighting. Somehow black boxers survived the early wave of Jim Crow hysteria, and when a flamboyant black man named Jack Johnson became heavyweight champion of the world, his fight with white ex-champ Jim Jeffries grabbed the attention of blacks and whites alike. Jeffries had won the crown in 1899 and retired as champion in 1905; the son of a former slave, Johnson had become champion in 1908. Jeffries at first refused to meet Johnson, stating he would never fight a Negro, but, cast in the role of the "white hope," he yielded to pressure. After negotiations with several cities fell through, the fight was set for Reno, Nevada, on July 4, 1910.[68]

Excitement ran high in Georgia as the day drew near. Bishop Turner threw open the doors of his Atlanta tabernacle to fight fans, installing an Associated Press wire service on his pulpit. A black undertaker from Savannah bought a round-trip ticket to Reno, vowing to wager every cent he had on the black champion. Thousands of blacks bet heavily and sported buttons bearing Johnson's photograph.[69] Enthusiasm was not limited to blacks. White newspapers began coverage several weeks before the fight, and headlines heralded the day of the battle. The Savannah *Press* published a fight extra of 15,000 copies which sold out quickly. Thousands of Georgians gathered around the state to get round-by-round telegraph results. An enterprising Macon promoter

67. Peterson, *Only the Ball Was White*, 75, 161.
68. New York *Times*, July 3, 1910.
69. Augusta *Chronicle*, July 4, 1910; Savannah *Press*, July 4, 1910; Atlanta *Journal*, June 16, 1910.

rented a baseball park, installed a ring, and hired two boxers to "present the actual movements of the fighters in a vigorous manner."[70]

Jeffries climbed into the ring a solid favorite, but Johnson quickly changed all that, taunting his opponent in the ring, conversing with spectators over Jeffries's shoulder, and incidentally giving the former champion the beating of his life. When the 10,000 fans assembled at Broad and Alabama streets in Atlanta heard that Jeffries's manager had thrown in the towel in the fifteenth round, shocked whites stared as black Atlantans went wild with joy.[71]

The fight's aftermath was bloodier than the contest. Macon authorities doubled the police force in an unsuccessful attempt to prevent celebrating blacks from clashing with angry whites.[72] The first Atlanta disorder occurred at the Grand Opera House, where a racially mixed crowd heard the results. Police halted efforts by blacks to parade through the streets, averting a serious outbreak by arresting six whites who attacked a black man exercising his freedom of speech. As black Georgia celebrated its triumph, whites either suffered silently or avenged their champion's defeat as best they could. No one was killed in the state, but throughout the nation disturbances erupted in which at least a half-dozen blacks died.[73]

The day after the contest mayors in Georgia cities banned the fight films, ostensibly because they would inflame racial tensions.[74] A bill introduced in the Georgia legislature to prohibit showing of all interracial fight films drew cheers from legislators on the floor. More to the point, the chairman of the Atlanta Police Board warned: "We don't want Jack Johnson down in this part of the country. If he is wise he will not come to Atlanta."[75] The Columbus *Enquirer-Sun* believed that boxing would now be banned in America, for "throughout the country the idea of an African whipping a white man in public is distasteful, and probably will never be repeated." The Macon *Telegraph* concurred

70. Macon *Telegraph*, July 2, 1910; Savannah *Press*, July 5, 1910.
71. New York *Times*, July 5, 1910; Atlanta *Journal*, July 5, 1910.
72. New York *Times*, July 5, 1910.
73. *Ibid.*
74. Atlanta *Journal*, July 6, 1910.
75. New York *Times*, July 7, 1910.

that "effects of such encounters are too demoralizing to have them continue."[76]

The aftermath of the Johnson-Jeffries fight illustrates the problem facing the black community in twentieth-century Georgia: at some point, white people always asserted their authority. Georgia whites did not permit their supremacy to be challenged in the business world, on the plantation, or even in the boxing ring. Efforts by black leaders to build community pride and economic strength behind the Jim Crow wall were constantly being thwarted by the people who built the wall in the first place. If white racism could unite the black community, it would also intimidate it and limit its potential. And nowhere was racism and intimidation more evident than in the administration of Georgia justice.

76. Columbus *Enquirer-Sun*, July 5, 1910; Macon *Telegraph*, July 5, 1910.

The New Slavery

IN THE SUMMER of 1902 Sheriff Thomas J. Mc-
Clellan of Waycross, a small southeast Georgia town, arrested a
young black woman named Lula Frazier on an adultery charge.
At the sheriff's suggestion Mrs. Frazier retained a young white
attorney, William F. Crawley. Crawley was no help, but the city
solicitor refused to prosecute the defendant because she was
legally married to Nathan Frazier, the man named in the charge.
Instead of letting her go, the sheriff kept Mrs. Frazier in jail without charge while her attorney wired a wealthy Valdosta farmer,
Edward J. McRee, to "Come to Waycross for woman." As McRee's
brother was boarding a train for Waycross, Crawley and Sheriff
McClellan were informing their prisoner she had been found
guilty and faced either a fifty-dollar fine or a year on the county
chain gang. Penniless and fearing imprisonment, Lula Frazier
agreed to work for Edward McRee for eighteen months if he paid
her fine. Upon arriving, McRee's brother wrote Crawley a fifty-
dollar check which he cashed and, presumably, divided with
Sheriff McClellan. At the McRee plantation Mrs. Frazier was
beaten, locked up at night, and sexually assaulted. After she had
worked there nine months her husband and a new sheriff obtained
her release.[1]

Two black youths, Henry Brimmage and David Smith, were
convicted and sentenced to a month on the Ware County chain

1. Assistant U.S. Attorney Alexander Akerman to Attorney General, Dec. 2,
1903, Box 1313, folded file 3098–02, File 50, Classified Subject Files of the
General Records of the Department of Justice, Record Group 60, National Archives (hereafter cited as Justice Dept. Records); *Congressional Record*, 63rd
Cong., 3rd sess., Appendix, p. 549 (Mar. 1, 1915); Savannah *Tribune*, Jan. 13,
1903, quoting Waycross *Journal*.

gang for stealing a watermelon in August 1903. (The judge refused to fine them, speculating that someone else would pay the fee and the boys would not suffer for their crime.[2]) The day after sentencing, attorney Crawley got in touch with Edward McRee, who paid sixty-five dollars to cover Crawley's legal fees and Sheriff McClellan's jail expenses. Although the boys were in jail under commitment with no court provision for release, McClellan placed Brimmage and Smith in McRee's custody. At the jail the three men also seized Jeff Brimmage, who had come to intercede for his older brother, and took the young blacks to McRee's plantation; there they served seven months instead of the original thirty days. The older youths still faced the chain gang, for their time on McRee's farm was not legal punishment and they technically had not served their sentence.[3]

Fifteen-year-old Lula Durham, on her way from Vienna, Georgia, to White Springs, Florida, stopped at Valdosta and spent the night at a Negro boarding house run by the mother-in-law of a local Negro physician, Dr. J. M. Cobb. The next morning the doctor accused Miss Durham of immoral conduct with a young man and threatened to prosecute unless she paid him twenty-five dollars. Learning that she had no money, Dr. Cobb and his partner, George Hart, called Frank McRee and told him that a girl patient owed twenty-five dollars for a medical bill. Frightened, inexperienced, and away from home, Lula Durham agreed to work out her "debt" on the McRee plantation. She labored there for three months while her mother employed counsel to obtain release. Lula's mother had to pay McRee three-fourths of the original "purchase price" before he would free her daughter.[4]

Edward McRee was a leading Valdosta citizen and a member of the Georgia legislature. With his two brothers he operated a 22,000-acre plantation and owned a large crate factory in Lowndes County.[5] Before 1900 the McRees depended upon convicts

2. *Independent,* 55 (Dec. 29, 1903), 3080.

3. *Ibid.; Cong. Record,* 63rd Cong., 3rd sess., Appendix, p. 549 (Mar. 1, 1915).

4. Akerman to Attorney General, Dec. 2, 1903, Justice Dept. Records. Cobb and Hart later pleaded guilty to peonage charges, but each got off with a $300 fine. *United States* v. *J. M. Cobb and Geo. P. Hart,* Mar. 22, 1905, in *Minutes,* U.S. District Court, Eastern Division, South District, Georgia, 576, Federal Records Center, East Point, Ga.

5. New York *Times,* Nov. 24, 1903.

leased from the state for labor, but after investigating charges of cruel treatment the prison commission refused to send more prisoners to the McRees. Deprived of convict labor, the brothers conspired with officers of nearby cities and counties to arrest blacks on petty charges. They paid fines for those individuals found guilty and attorney's fees for those who were acquitted; they sometimes fabricated convictions to put prisoners in their debt. After signing contracts agreeing to work out debts, hand-cuffed prisoners were taken to McRee's estate and confined in the old convict stockade. Blacks attempting to escape were treated as runaway slaves, tracked by dogs and whipped when captured.[6]

The McRee brothers, attorney Crawley, ex-Sheriff McClellan, and others involved in this new slave trade were indicted by a federal grand jury on charges of peonage, compulsory service in payment of a debt. The court fined Edward McRee $1,000 after he pleaded guilty to thirteen indictments of holding citizens in peonage. (He could have drawn a $65,000 fine and a sixty-five-year jail sentence.[7]) Charged with seizing blacks and selling them to the McRees, Crawley and McClellan went to trial in March 1905 with public sentiment on their side. A recent University of Georgia graduate, Crawley was a promising member of the Georgia bar. Defense counsel was impressive: W. G. Brantley, local congressman and member of the House Judiciary Committee, contributed a brief in behalf of the defendants; the chairman of the penitentiary committee appeared for the prisoners; and the district solicitor general, charged with prosecution of such offenses, sat with the prisoners' attorneys and assisted the defense.[8] After all the evidence was heard, defense attorneys asked Judge Emory Speer for a directed verdict of not guilty. When he refused, McClellan and Crawley changed their plea to guilty on a four-count indictment. Speer sentenced each man to pay a thousand-dollar fine, but later the same day reduced the amount by half. Neither defendant served time in prison. The following day

6. Akerman to Attorney General, Aug. 10, 1903, Justice Dept. Records.
7. New York *Times*, Nov. 24, 1903; *Independent*, 55 (Dec. 29, 1903), 3079.
8. New York *Times*, Nov. 24, 1903; *United States* v. *McClellan et al.*, 127 Fed 972–73 (1904); Akerman to Attorney General, Mar. 16, 1904, Justice Dept. Records.

the judge dismissed eight other counts of peonage against the ex-sheriff.[9]

These cases were unusual, not because of the extremely light sentences but because the accused were convicted at all. Proving guilt in peonage cases was not easy, for the white public often supported the offenders, and the law was vague and subject to broad interpretation. Congress in March 1867 had approved an act "to abolish and forever prohibit the system of peonage in the territory of New Mexico and other parts of the United States"; this would presumably end peonage in New Mexico Territory, where Indians had been held for years.[10] The statute lay unnoticed for decades, although similar practices started in southern states after the Civil War.[11] When federal attorneys finally began prosecution, some jurists expressed doubts concerning the law. Federal Judge William T. Newman of Georgia's North District declared in 1899 that the peonage statute did not apply in his state, for "No such system as this ever existed in Georgia. African slavery existed, but this was ownership of Africans and persons of African descent as chattels. There could not be, therefore, in Georgia, any such thing as holding persons under this system or returning them to it."[12]

Jurists differed, but in 1905 the Supreme Court declared the 1867 anti-peonage law constitutional and applicable to all states and territories.[13] While this enabled the Justice Department to prosecute violators, it did little to end peonage in the South. The statute as written and interpreted applied only to cases involving forced labor for debt payment. Incredibly, there was no federal law against simple slavery. After investigating involuntary servitude in the South, the Immigration Commission concluded that "it is apparent that Congress has never passed a general measure

9. *United States* v. *William F. Crawley and Thomas J. McClellan*, Mar. 22, 1905, in *Minutes*, U.S. District Court, Eastern Division, Southern District, Georgia, 575–76, 580–81.

10. 14 *Stat.* 546.

11. T. H. Malone, "Peonage—Its Origins and Growth," *Voice of the Negro*, 2 (Dec., 1905), 29.

12. *United States* v. *Eberhart et al.*, 127 Fed 252 (1899).

13. *Clyatt* v. *United States*, 197 U.S. 207 (1905). Judge Speer delayed the trials of McClellan and Crawley until the Supreme Court had ruled in the *Clyatt* case.

providing for the enforcement of the Thirteenth Amendment."[14] Assistant U.S. Attorney Charles W. Russell called for a federal law "repeating the Thirteenth Amendment with appropriate penalties," but Congress failed to respond.[15]

Like most southern states, Georgia used a contract labor law to force unwilling laborers into peonage. The legislature designed the statute to prevent tenant farmers and lumber, railroad, and turpentine workers from breaking contracts. Any contract laborer quitting while in debt to his employer could be charged with "procuring money fraudulently on contract for service" and sentenced to prison. Since failure to fulfill the contract was evidence of intent to defraud, in effect the law sanctioned imprisonment for debt.[16] Advancing money or supplies to tenant farmers was common, and many tenants found themselves in debt before they began work. Plantation owners persuaded illiterate tenants to sign long-term contracts by promising benefits not appearing in the written agreement.[17] Many signed contracts giving the employer authority over their lives and found themselves virtually slaves on the master's plantation. Those tenants who escaped were usually caught and returned to their employer or put in jail, charged with intent to defraud. Threat of a long term on the chain gang was enough to make most people return. The contract labor law closed the avenue of escape to tenants and contract laborers by converting a violation of a civil contract into a penal offense.[18]

Alabama's contract labor law, almost identical to Georgia's, was declared unconstitutional by the Supreme Court in the *Alonzo Bailey* case in 1911. Bailey had contracted to work for a year as a farm laborer on an Alabama plantation for twelve dollars a month and had received a fifteen-dollar advance from the hiring company. After a month's work he quit, only to be arrested for intent to defraud. The jury found him guilty, and the judge

14. United States Immigration Commission, *Abstracts of Reports*, II, 61st Cong., 3rd sess., p. 446 (Mar. 4, 1911).

15. Department of Justice, *Annual Report of the Attorney General of the United States* (Washington, 1907), 207.

16. *Georgia Laws*, 1903, pp. 90–91.

17. G. W. Williams, report given at Tenth Annual Convention of the NAACP, 1919, NAACP Papers, Manuscript Division, Library of Congress.

18. T. H. Malone, "Peonage, 'The Five Years Contract,'" *Voice of the Negro*, 3 (Apr., 1906), 263–64.

sentenced him to 136 days at hard labor. Under Alabama law Bailey's quitting was *prima facie* evidence of intent to defraud. The state presented no other evidence, and Bailey was not allowed to testify in his own behalf.[19] When the Supreme Court heard the appeal, Chief Justice Charles Evans Hughes spoke for the majority, which ruled that "The state may impose involuntary servitude as punishment for crime, but it may not compel one man to labor for another in payment of a debt, by punishing him as a criminal if he does not perform the service or pay the debt." Concluding that the Alabama law violated the Thirteenth Amendment, the court ordered Bailey's release.[20]

Georgia courts refused to accept the *Bailey* decision as binding. In 1912 the Georgia Supreme Court declared the state contract labor law constitutional, since it differed from Alabama's statute in that no provision prevented the defendant from issuing a statement in his own behalf.[21] This reasoning was specious, for the decision in the Alabama case mentions the evidential rule only as an additional factor entering into the Court's decision. Indeed, the rule on evidence was not even part of the Alabama statute declared unconstitutional. The Georgia contract labor law remained on the books until 1942, when the Supreme Court finally laid it to rest.[22]

Peonage in Georgia was widespread in the black belt and along the Florida border in the turpentine camps, but it was also common in the eastern piedmont, where the black and white population was more evenly divided. The center of peonage in the piedmont was Oglethorpe County, about seventy-five miles east of Atlanta. Oglethorpe's reputation for peonage went back as far as the 1880s, and involuntary servitude had continued there for so long that it was a way of life.[23] This county was the home of James Monroe Smith, one of the state's wealthiest planters.

19. *Bailey* v. *Alabama*, 219 U.S. 219 (1911); Ray Stannard Baker, "A Pawn in the Struggle for Freedom," *American*, 72 (Sept., 1911), 608–9.

20. *Bailey* v. *Alabama*, 219 U.S. 250. For a detailed account of the case, see Pete Daniel, "Up from Slavery and Down to Peonage: The Alonzo Bailey Case," *Journal of American History*, 57 (Dec., 1970), 654–70, and Daniel, *The Shadow of Slavery: Peonage in the South, 1901–1969* (Urbana, 1972), pp. 65–81.

21. *Wilson* v. *State*, 138 Ga. 489 (1912).

22. Charles S. Magnum, *The Legal Status of the Negro* (Chapel Hill, 1940), 168; *Taylor* v. *Georgia*, 315 U.S. 25 (1942).

23. Malone, "Peonage—Its Origins and Growth," 27–29.

Smith's ambition to own "all the land that's next to mine" helped him acquire 20,000 acres of good farmland, with his own railroad, cotton gin, brick works, saw mill, cottonseed oil mill and refinery, guano plant, and blacksmith shop. A gray-bearded, heavy-set man with a "wen as big as a cabbage" on his neck, he was perhaps the closest thing to an antebellum slave baron that twentieth-century Georgia would see. At the height of operations he worked more than 1,000 people on his plantation at Smithonia; many were convicts in leg irons and chains whom Smith had leased from the state.[24] A state investigation in the 1880s showed that Smith's convicts were "badly managed," received whippings, and suffered from malnutrition.[25] Smith also used "free" black labor, the mainstay of his operation after the state abolished the convict lease system in 1908. Wage hands received food, clothing, and lodging, but, in the words of a former employee, "never no cash money."[26]

Smith ruled with an iron hand. Many laborers were working off debts contracted when he paid court fines, but sometimes Smith bought convicts, such as Jackson Morrison, from other planters. Convicted of selling liquor, Morrison faced a fine of a hundred dollars or a year on the chain gang. A farmer from Comer paid Morrison's fine and worked him two months before "selling" him to Smith, who agreed to free Morrison after seventeen months. Smith persuaded Morrison's wife, Mentha, to work for seven dollars a month, which she could use to reduce her husband's sentence. Mentha Morrison was never paid, nor was her husband's term shortened, and after eighteen months she quit. Smith confiscated her personal possessions. Realizing that the planter did not intend to honor their agreement, and sensing that he might be held in bondage for life, Jackson Morrison escaped; but two months later the sheriff of Oglethorpe County found him, arrested him on another charge, and carried him back to Smith's. When a Justice Department official arrived to question

24. Charles R. Koch, "All the Land That's Next to Mine!" *Farm Quarterly*, 13 (Autumn, 1958), 63, 103; E. Merton Coulter, *James Monroe Smith, Georgia Planter, Before Death and After* (Athens, Ga., 1961), 36. Coulter's biography is sympathetic toward Smith.

25. Coulter, *James Monroe Smith*, 80.

26. Koch, "All the Land That's Next to Mine!" 104.

him, Morrison denied that Smith had deceived or mistreated him or his wife.[27]

Justice Department lawyers were unable to find a worker on Smith's farm who would admit mistreatment. Yet the U.S. Attorney's office received a stream of complaints from relatives of Smith's laborers, citing details of "Jim Smith slavery."[28] Investigators saw that the workers on this plantation were afraid to talk. U.S. Attorney E. A. Angier determined that conditions at Smithonia were worse than those described by Harriet Beecher Stowe in *Uncle Tom's Cabin*.[29] In 1909 an attorney filed charges on behalf of fifty blacks who had escaped from Smithonia and were "living in constant dread of being captured and taken back on some slight pretext."[30] Smith denied accusations of peonage, declaring he paid the highest wages of any farmer in his section. "No one has done more, if so much, as I have done for the general good of the negro," said Smith. "It has often been used against me that I was doing too much for the negro." He sadly concluded, "It is said the negro has no gratitude. I believe it." The millionaire farmer and former gubernatorial candidate was never convicted.[31]

Convictions for peonage were uncommon. Angier reported that of thirty cases presented to a federal grand jury in Athens in April 1905, he withdrew the final twenty-five indictments because the grand jury was "manifestly getting ready to return no bills in plain palpable cases of unquestioned, overwhelming guilt."[32] Blacks agreeing to testify were intimidated. In one case white farmers told witnesses they would "use all means to put in the chain gang every colored man, woman and child who has complained to the Federal Courts," threatening to return to peonage those who could not be jailed, and to kill those who could not be

27. *Ibid.*, 104–5; Luther R. Faner to Attorney General, June 21, 1905; James Stansberry to Dept. of Justice, Dec. 1, 1906; Assistant U.S. Attorney C. D. Camp to Attorney General, Nov. 28, 1903; Mentha Morrison to President Theodore Roosevelt, Oct. 22, 1903, Justice Dept. Records.

28. Stansberry to Dept. of Justice, Dec. 1, 1906; Camp to Attorney General, Nov. 28, 1903; E. A. Angier to Attorney General, Feb. 23, 1904, Justice Dept. Records.

29. Camp to Attorney General, Nov. 28, 1903; Angier to Attorney General, Feb. 23, 1904, *ibid.*

30. Atlanta *Constitution*, Aug. 22, 1909.

31. *Ibid.*, Aug. 29, 1909; Coulter, *James Monroe Smith*, 51.

32. Angier to Attorney General, May 16, 1905, Justice Dept. Records.

reduced to servitude.[33] About the same time Judge E. C. Kinnebrew wrote that potential witnesses were being arrested to prevent or discredit any testimony they might offer. While an average
number of indictments was fifteen or twenty, during the spring
term the grand jury indicted a hundred and fifty blacks, a number
"unprecedented in the annals of the county." The judge specu-
lated, "It may be the object of the projectors of this movement to
run all expected witnesses in peonage cases off where United
States officers can't find them, or if they are found to hold them
up before Federal juries who try peonage cases as being themselves criminals and unworthy of belief."[34]

The Atlanta *Constitution* probably reflected white Georgia's
attitude by labeling these prosecutions for peonage a "disaster"
which demoralized the agricultural market. Since the Civil War
the South had shown "humane and practical treatment" toward
Negroes, and although there probably were isolated cases of
tenant mistreatment, peonage "has never existed in a Southern
state."[35] Whites rarely challenged this myth. Judge Emory Speer
of the Southern District of Georgia, a former congressman, was
one of the few who did:

> What hope can the respectable Negro have—what incentive to
> better effort or better life—if he, his wife, his daughter, or his
> sons, may in a moment be snatched from his humble home and
> sold into peonage? Let us for a moment put ourselves in his place,
> and imagine our furious indignation or hopeless despair if our
> loved ones or ourselves could be subjected to such a condition of
> involuntary servitude. Nor if conditions like those described in
> the indictment shall continue, will the Negro remain the sole
> victim of peonage.[36]

Prosecutions reached a peak during the first ten years of the
twentieth century, and as early as 1906 President Theodore
Roosevelt believed the government had "pretty well broken up"
the practice. Fewer cases were tried during the next decade, but
the practice had not diminished, and prosecutions increased fol-

33. Angier to Attorney General, Apr. 18, 1904, *ibid.*
34. E. C. Kinnebrew to Angier, May 16, 1904, *ibid.*
35. Atlanta *Constitution*, Apr. 18, 1904.
36. *United States* v. *McClellan et al.*, 127 Fed 971.

lowing World War I.[37] In 1921 the Attorney General reported peonage existed "to a shocking extent" in Georgia. The NAACP investigated so many violations that the Atlanta branch revived the Underground Railroad to facilitate escape from rural areas.[38] One particularly brutal case of peonage focused national attention on Georgia.

John Williams, fifty-four, father of twelve and a "giant in stature," owned a 2,700-acre plantation near Monticello in Jasper County, between Macon and Atlanta in central Georgia. For several years he had obtained labor by paying fines for blacks convicted of minor offenses in nearby towns. Politically influential, Williams was a cousin of the Jasper County sheriff.[39] Justice Department agents visited Williams's farm on February 23, 1921, to investigate allegations of peonage. They did not file charges. Several weeks later a black hired hand, Clyde Manning, confessed that after the initial investigation he and Williams destroyed evidence by murdering eleven blacks.[40] Williams and Manning shot one victim, killed four others with an ax, and bound and weighted the other six men with stones before throwing them into the river. Asked why he cooperated, Manning replied that Williams would have killed him had he refused. "I know he meant what he said," Manning declared. "I know him like he knows a book."[41]

Williams's trial revealed other cruelties, including more murders, but the defense attorney pleaded with the jury not to hang a white man on the testimony of "a worthless negro."[42] The jury found Williams guilty but recommended mercy, and the judge sentenced him to life imprisonment—a compromise verdict, because although eight jurors favored the death penalty, the other four would have held out for a mistrial rather than accept a death sentence.[43]

37. Roosevelt to Owen Wister, Apr. 27, 1906, Owen Wister Papers, Manuscript Division, Library of Congress.

38. Dept. of Justice, *Annual Report of the Attorney General of the United States* (Washington, 1921), 198; see also reports for 1911 to 1920. Report of the Atlanta branch of the NAACP, June 20, 1921, Branch File, NAACP Papers.

39. New York *Tribune*, Mar. 27, 1921; Savannah *Press*, Mar. 28, 1921; *Literary Digest*, 69 (Apr. 16, 1921), 13–14; Daniel, *Shadow of Slavery*, 110.

40. New York *Times*, Mar. 27, 1921.

41. *Ibid.;* Daniel, *Shadow of Slavery*, 117–18.

42. New York *World*, Apr. 9, 1921.

43. Atlanta *Constitution*, Apr. 12, 1921. Later Manning also received a life sentence. For a detailed account of the *Williams* case, see Daniel, *Shadow of*

Following the *Williams* case Georgia Governor Hugh M. Dorsey published a pamphlet describing seventeen peonage cases and called upon white Georgians to stop the practice. But peonage would not disappear quickly. It is difficult to determine how common peonage was in Georgia and the rest of the South; that it was widespread is evident. One authority estimated in 1907 that investigations in Georgia, Alabama, and Mississippi would "prove that 33⅓ per cent of the planters operating from five to one hundred plows, are holding their negro employees to a condition of peonage, and arresting and returning those that leave before indebtedness is paid."[44] As late as 1939 the white Georgia Baptist Association adopted a resolution, perhaps overstated, that "Peonage or debt slavery has by no means disappeared from our land. There are more white people affected by this diabolical practice than there were slave holders: there are more Negroes held by these debt slavers than were actually owned as slaves before the war between the states. . . . The method is the only thing that has changed."[45]

Peonage in rural Georgia was difficult to measure because of its similarity to farm tenantry. Although some poor whites were peons, most victims were black. Thousands of black share-croppers, mistreated by their employers, were not much better off than slaves or debtors forced to do equal work for the same wages. The crop lien system often had the same effect on the free laborer as the court fine on the peon and the threat of violence on the slave.

Convicts were another source of forced labor. Misdemeanor offenders worked on county chain gangs, and private individuals and corporations leased felony convicts from the state. Convict leasing had begun in Georgia in 1868, when the military governor

---

Slavery, 110–31. Daniel's interesting book is the best study of peonage in the South.

44. Hugh M. Dorsey, *A Statement from Governor Hugh M. Dorsey as to the Negro in Georgia* (Atlanta, 1921); A. J. Hoyt to Attorney General, Feb. 4, 1907, quoted in Daniel, *Shadow of Slavery*, 22. Hoyt had spent years investigating peonage and whitecapping.

45. Quoted in *Cong. Record*, 77th Cong., 1st sess., Appendix, p. A2848 (June 13, 1941); William Henry Huff to Julian L. Harris, May 20, 1941, Julian L. Harris Papers, Special Collection, Robert W. Woodruff Library, Emory University.

leased a hundred convicts to the Georgia and Alabama Railroad for one year as an alternative to rebuilding the state penitentiary, destroyed in 1865 by Union troops.[46] The legislature experimented with various arrangements and in 1876 passed a comprehensive lease law which dominated legislation for the next thirty years. It provided that felony convicts be leased for a twenty-year period to one or more individuals or corporations. The lessee would meet management expenses, including food, clothing, and housing, and would have authority to control and punish prisoners. The state furnished a physician and a chaplain "to aid in reforming the moral character of the convicts."[47] Although some convicts worked on plantations, the lease system was better suited to larger operations, and most worked in brickmaking factories, lumber and saw mills, road and railroad construction, and iron and coal fields.[48]

From the beginning, convict lease holders were involved in politics, with two of the major twenty-year lessees, Senator Joseph E. Brown and Governor John B. Gordon, among Georgia's leading politicians. Wealth amassed from prison labor and authority to sublease convicts gave lessees great power. Some judges gained local favor by sentencing prisoners—usually blacks—to excessive terms. Rebecca Latimer Felton, wife of a former congressman, claimed that a judge in her district won the Democratic nomination and a seat in Congress as reward for sending blacks to prison.[49]

Of the more than 1,200 felony convicts in 1879, 90 percent were black. (In 1908, the year the legislature abolished leasing, 2,219 of the 2,566 convicts were black.) An investigation in 1882 showed blacks serving sentences twice as long as whites for burglary and five times as long for larceny; black convicts suffered higher death

46. Fletcher M. Green, "Some Aspects of the Convict Lease System," in *Democracy in the Old South: The Essays of Fletcher Melvin Green* (Vanderbilt, 1969), 274.
47. *Ibid.; Georgia Laws*, 1876, pp. 40–43; A. Elizabeth Taylor, "The Origin and Development of the Convict Lease System in Georgia," *Georgia Historical Quarterly*, 26 (June, 1942), 118–19.
48. Du Bois, ed., *Negro American Family*, 51.
49. Rebecca Latimer Felton, "The Convict System of Georgia," *Forum*, 2 (Jan., 1887), 486; Wingo, "Race Relations in Georgia," 248; Hugh C. Bailey, *Liberalism in the New South: Southern Social Reformers and the Progressive Movement* (Coral Gables, Fla., 1969), 64.

rates and received a smaller proportion of pardons than whites.[50] When abuses in the system became notorious, some Georgians began working to abolish it. As early as 1869 the principal keeper of the penitentiary, John Darnell, argued that the legislature erred in leasing convicts. The Georgia House of Representatives discussed but defeated a bill to abolish the system in 1877, and the Senate behaved similarly two years later.[51] The Senate Commission on the Penitentiary investigated and condemned convict leasing in 1878, reporting that in some camps men and women were chained together and occupied the same bunks. The commission blamed these arrangements for the twenty-five illegitimate children born in prison camps, but guards did their share to increase the prison population.[52] In the autumn of 1880 George Washington Cable investigated prison camps in Georgia and found life "cruel, brutalizing, deadly; chaining, flogging, shooting, drowning, killing by exhaustion and exposure were daily occurrences."[53] Tom Watson attacked the lease system in the campaign of 1880, and abolition became a plank in the Georgia Populist platform in the 1890s.[54] Governor W. Y. Atkinson made a similar plea in his annual message to the General Assembly in 1897, but his effort failed.

Abolitionists had cause for concern, as each investigation uncovered appalling conditions in convict camps. Evils of the old slave system existed, but the restraining influence on slaveowners —the economic value of slaves as property—was no longer a factor. State officials, assigned to inspect camps regularly and report abuses to the Prison Commission, received salaries from the lessees and were reluctant to accuse their "employers" of wrongdoing.[55] The three-man Prison Commission, created in 1897 to

50. Bailey, *Liberalism in the New South*, 159; Wingo, "Race Relations in Georgia," 254–55. The ratio of black women to white women in prison was much higher than that of black men to white men.
51. *Report of the Principal Keeper of the Georgia Penitentiary* (1869), 10, quoted in A. Elizabeth Taylor, "The Abolition of the Convict Lease System in Georgia," *Georgia Historical Quarterly*, 26 (Dec., 1942), 273.
52. Felton, "The Convict System of Georgia," 488.
53. George Washington Cable, "The Convict Lease System in the Southern States," *Century Magazine*, 27 (Feb., 1884), 582–95, quoted in Bailey, *Liberalism in the New South*, 157.
54. Taylor, "Abolition of the Convict Lease System," 273.
55. Alexander McKelway, "The Convict Lease System of Georgia," *Outlook*, 90 (Sept. 12, 1908), 71.

increase regulation of camps, adopted a laissez-faire attitude; their annual reports spoke glowingly of conditions.[56]

When a legislative committee, spurred by a series of articles in the Atlanta *Georgian* in the summer of 1908, made its own investigation, findings shocked Georgians to action. Officials of the Durham Coal and Coke Company worked convicts from sunrise till late at night seven days a week under terrible conditions. One convict reported working waist deep in water during the winter. Owners required convicts to mine daily quotas, whipping those who failed.[57] A former prison guard in another camp saw from twenty-five to forty men beaten at one time, including a sixteen-year-old white boy given forty lashes.[58] Living conditions were pitiful. In one camp sixty-one men slept in a room seventeen by nineteen by seven feet, subsisting on a diet of cornbread and spoiled pork. Bedding, clothes, and eating quarters were filthy, and some men contracted gangrene where iron shackles rubbed their legs. Medical attention was rare.[59]

Life was cheap in the camps. In May 1900 Deputy Warden Willis Ponder of the convict camp at Jakin in Early County placed a black convict, Fred Kent, in a room by a hot stove and covered him with fifteen blankets. After "sweating" him for nearly two hours, Ponder released Kent, by then suffering from exhaustion; the convict died that night. The camp physician recorded death due to lung congestion, and there was no investigation. When a black convict was whipped to death, the physician listed the cause as congestion from drinking too much water. A sixteen-year-old black youth serving a three-month sentence was shot while escaping; he lay dead for over a week before he was buried.[60] The Prison Commission suppressed information about these and other killings. In its report for 1908, the year of the

56. *Annual Report of the Prison Commission of Georgia* (1897–1908).

57. Atlanta *Georgian*, July 25, 1908; Taylor, "Abolition of the Convict Lease System," 281; "Report of the Convict Investigating Committee to the Extraordinary Session of the General Assembly," *Georgia Laws*, 1908, p. 1072 (hereafter cited as "Convict Investigating Committee").

58. Atlanta *Georgian*, July 17, 1908.

59. *Ibid.*, July 13, 1908; Du Bois, ed., *Some Notes on Negro Crime*, 4; "Convict Investigating Committee," 1072.

60. "Convict Investigating Committee," 1080–82; Savannah *Tribune*, Aug. 2, 1902; McKelway, "Convict System of Georgia," 69; Atlanta *Georgian*, July 25, 1908.

investigation, commissioners gave this sanguine description of
life in the camps:

> So far as food, clothing, bedding, medical attention and general
> maintenance goes, the convicts in the . . . [camps] are in a better
> condition than ninety-five per cent of them were before convic-
> tion, and enjoy more of these necessaries than many honest labor-
> ers in any community in the state. The discipline is strict, and in
> some cases necessarily severe, the labor is hard as required by
> law, but no harder than many honest laborers undergo daily in
> order to earn a livlihood [sic] for themselves, and their families.
> With rare exceptions their treatment is kind, considerate, and
> humane, and such exceptions, however deplorable, will some-
> times occur in all penal institutions.[61]

Exposure of camp conditions caused Georgians to abolish the
lease system in 1908, only to replace it with a state-sponsored
chain gang.[62] The legislature put felony convicts to work on
county roads and other public works, and while conditions varied
from county to county, the spectacle of prisoners in striped uniforms, chained together, herded from one place to another packed
in cages became common.[63] A former inmate of the Dougherty
County chain gang recently recalled conditions in his camp:
"Between 3:30 and 4:30 in the morning the guard would walk
into the bunkhouse where the inmates were sleeping, with his
strap hanging on his arm. He made each inmate sit at the foot of
his bunk. He'd start on the right going in. The building was one
hundred feet long. He'd go from one end to the other. By the
time he'd get back to the front door, he'd be steppin' in blood in
the aisle-way. He'd do this just about every morning, especially
Monday." The guard would whip all but about two or three of the
black prisoners, but would not whip any of the half-dozen white
convicts.[64]

John L. Spivak investigated road camps in Georgia in the early

61. *Annual Report of the Prison Commission of Georgia* (1907–8), 6.
62. The movement to abolish the convict lease system will be discussed in the
chapter on "Race and Reform."
63. For firsthand descriptions of life on Georgia's chain gangs in the 1920s
and 1930s, see John L. Spivak, *Georgia Nigger* (New York, 1932), and Robert E.
Burns, *I Am a Fugitive from a Georgia Chain Gang* (New York, 1932).
64. Interview between Henry Williams and Mr. Monroe Clark, Aug. 17, 1973,
Albany.

1930s and concluded from conversations with guards that they
were "abysmally cruel men who vented their own frustrations
on those less fortunate than themselves."[65] Other investigations
revealed instances of torture equaling or surpassing the cruelty
of convict leasing.[66] Recalling conditions during his administration
in the 1940s, former governor Ellis Arnall admitted that "the
Georgia penal system was bad; it was evil; it was inhuman." The
function of convicts, to make or save money for the county and
state, left no room for rehabilitation. Georgia whites, aware of the
chain gang and its horrors, would rather not hear how the state
built and repaired public roads so cheaply.[67]

While legislators grappled with some of the problems presented
by felony convicts, a much larger group of prisoners received little
attention. Men, women, and children convicted of misdemeanor
offenses such as vagrancy, disorderly conduct, and drunkenness
were tried by the city recorder, who was both judge and jury and
often imposed severe sentences. Nine out of ten persons arrested
for municipal offenses in Georgia were black.[68] One recorder
sentenced a woman to three years on the chain gang for disorderly
conduct. A ten-year-old black child, arrested for vagrancy in
Atlanta, received a thirty-day sentence. The recorder at Waycross
sent eleven-year-old Carrie Christian to the chain gang for stealing a ring.[69]

Municipal courts were commonly the best single source of
peon labor. Some recorders worked with local farmers who paid
fines levied against black misdemeanants in return for contract-
ing their labor. The first decade of this century was accompanied
by a shortage of black farm and domestic labor. Enforcement of
the state's vaguely worded vagrancy law was effective in secur-
ing workers, for anyone without proof of steady employment was

65. John L. Spivak, *A Man in His Time* (New York, 1967), 175.

66. *Ibid.*, 179; Atlanta *Constitution*, Jan. 30, 1914; *Journal of the Senate of the State of Georgia*, 1912, pp. 882–83 (hereafter cited as *Senate Journal*).

67. Ellis Arnall, in Vincent Godfrey Burns, *The Man Who Broke a Thousand Chains* (Washington, 1968), 7; Spivak, *A Man in His Time*, 179; Prison Indus-tries Reorganization Administration, *The Prison Labor Problem in Georgia* (Wash-ington, 1937), 25, 34.

68. Savannah *Tribune*, Jan. 27, 1906.

69. Alexander Akerman, address before the Georgia State Bar Association, quoted in *Voice of the Negro*, 3 (Sept., 1906), 619–20; Atlanta *Constitution*, Apr. 28, 1898; *Crisis*, 14 (Oct., 1917), 316.

fair game for court officials.[70] Threat of enforcement was often enough to force unemployed blacks to take undesirable, low-paying jobs as servants and common laborers. The public appeared to sanction misuse of the law, and the Atlanta *Constitution* went so far as to demand that able blacks be compelled to work six days a week; those refusing employment "should be promptly hauled to the recorder's court and there they should find a justice which has no mercy side-issue."[71]

Those convicted of vagrancy and other misdemeanors and who did not have their fines paid were put on local chain gangs and confined in jails. The most notorious was the stockade in Atlanta, a city with one of the highest arrest rates in the country. (In 1900, of the 14,045 cases tried, over 9,500 involved blacks. In 1906, the year of the race riot, the number of blacks arrested had jumped to 13,500.[72]) An investigation of the stockade in 1909 revealed unventilated living quarters overrun with cockroaches and rats, and a dining room next to an open toilet. Prisoners wore riveted shackles which bore into their flesh; only inmates with money could purchase devices from the guards to protect their legs. Punishment for unruly, uncooperative, or unpopular prisoners was frequent, with offenders strapped into a "bucking machine" (a device resembling a pillory invented by the prison superintendent) and whipped with a riveted strap. The stockade physician testified that a small thirteen-year-old black girl wearing only two thin undergarments was whipped in the bucking machine by Assistant Superintendent R. M. Clay while Superintendent D. M. Vining looked on. The girl became hysterical when released and said something unintelligible to the superintendent; he ordered her back into the chair, where Clay beat her again. Clay said he whipped her because she was "mean and fussing with other prisoners."[73]

On an earlier occasion City Recorder Nash Broyles, who made

---

70. *Georgia Laws*, 1903, pp. 109–11; Evans, "The Labor Movement in Georgia," 316–20.

71. Atlanta *Constitution*, Aug. 26, 1906.

72. Thomas H. Martin, *Atlanta and Its Builders, A Comprehensive History of the Gate City of the South*, II (Atlanta, 1902), 204; Charles Crowe, "Racial Massacre in Atlanta, September 22, 1906," *Journal of Negro History*, 54 (Apr., 1969), 170. Atlanta had the highest per capita arrest rate in the nation.

73. Atlanta *Georgian*, Dec. 30, 31, 1909; Jan. 1, 13, 14, 1910.

his reputation by stuffing the stockade with black men, women, and children, admitted he never sent white children there, despite the fact that so many of them had committed serious offenses. "To do so," commented Broyles, "would mean their complete ruin."[74]

Evidence of peonage, injustice in the courts, inhuman treatment of convicts, and exploitation of free black labor points to a new system of involuntary servitude in Georgia. Like its antebellum predecessor, the new slavery was based upon the need for a large supply of cheap labor and governed by racist assumptions. Poor whites were among the system's victims, but the black masses were hardest hit. The regimen of severity, recounted here, so narrowed the bounds of livelihood that for many blacks the life of freedom was not so different from the days of slavery. Black leaders, along with some concerned whites, fought peonage, convict leasing, and the chain gang with limited success. The system of forced labor was deeply rooted in Georgia, surviving both the Civil War and Reconstruction to remain an essential part of economic life well into the twentieth century.

74. Martin, *Atlanta and Its Builders,* II, 205.

Racial Politics

THE PARTY of Lincoln was the political voice of black Georgia. Republicans held power briefly after the Civil War, but Democrats took over again in 1872 and thereafter controlled state and local politics. We have seen that in the 1890s white Populists led by Tom Watson tried to enlist black support against conservative Democrats. Although many blacks voted Populist, several of their spokesmen reacted differently. The leading black Republican, William A. Pledger, rejected Watson and his radical agrarians in favor of the "wealth and intelligence" of paternalistic Democrats, a view shared by other middle-class blacks who regarded poor whites as their worst enemies.[1] Nonetheless, the Populist challenge was a last opportunity for black Republicans, for only by joining with a genuine grass-roots movement could they hope to influence government. But attempts at fusion were half-hearted and came too late, and the Populist party declined. The beginning of the twentieth century saw Georgia politics settling back into their familiar pattern.

For Georgia Republicans, the normal routine involved lobbying for federal patronage and scrambling for delegate seats to the national convention. The state party had not fielded a full slate of candidates since 1882; its leaders appeared content to fight among themselves. Most whites viewed the Georgia Republican party with contempt, labeling it a "Negro party" led by corrupt whites and a few black spoils-seekers.[2] Such charges were not

1. Atlanta *Constitution*, Oct. 3, 1896, quoting Pledger. A self-made man who rose to prominence in the Georgia Republican party before he was thirty, Pledger maintained his influence in party affairs throughout the 1880s and 1890s.
2. Bacote, "The Negro in Georgia Politics," 516.

without basis. Except for an interval of Negro control in the early 1880s under Pledger, whites had held the top positions in a party 90 percent black, largely because the national organization opposed black control of southern Republicanism.[3] White leaders left much to be desired, and men like Pledger had an eye on the main chance. Still, blacks exerted considerable influence in the state party's higher councils, and able men were active on all levels. Particularly impressive were Republican leaders appointed to important positions.

Georgia led the South in the number of blacks holding federal jobs, thanks to the patronage policies of President William McKinley.[4] The best offices went to three men long active in party affairs: John H. Deveaux served as collector of customs in Savannah; Henry L. Rucker became collector of internal revenue in Atlanta; and Judson Lyons of Augusta moved to Washington to become register of the United States Treasury, the highest appointive federal office held by a black. All were capable administrators subsequently reappointed by McKinley's successor, Theodore Roosevelt. A leader of Savannah's Negro aristocracy, Deveaux founded the Savannah *Tribune* and had held several government posts prior to becoming collector. His appointment to the Savannah post evoked strong reaction from whites, particularly members of the powerful cotton exchange. Through hard work and honest administration of the customs house Deveaux neutralized many critics, and his reappointment encountered little resistance.[5]

Atlanta businessman Henry Rucker had smoother sailing in his confirmation, winning endorsements from leading Atlanta Democrats, including the mayor, most city and county officers, and wealthy businessmen, all of whom seemed resigned to accepting a black in that position. Attorney Judson Lyons became register of the Treasury after his previous appointment as postmaster of Augusta met such white hostility that it had to be withdrawn. A graduate of Howard Law School, Lyons had an outspoken com-

3. Clarence A. Bacote, "Negro Officeholders in Georgia under President McKinley," *Journal of Negro History*, 44 (July, 1959), 233.

4. *Ibid.*, 222–29.

5. Matthews, "Studies in Race Relations," 11; John H. Deveaux to Washington, Apr. 29, 1906, Washington Papers.

mitment to civil rights which set him apart from many black officeholders.

Rucker, Lyons, and Deveaux were Georgia's most important black Republicans during the first decade of the century. Rucker, a son-in-law of Reconstruction congressman Jefferson Long, attended his first Republican convention as a delegate in 1880. Deveaux had long been the Republican power on the Atlantic coast, and Lyons had been the state's national committeeman since 1896.[6] Behind them was the awesome figure of Booker T. Washington. All three owed reappointment to their offices to him, and the Tuskegean demanded loyalty in return. Once, when Henry Rucker balked at a Washington request, Tuskegee secretary Emmett J. Scott testily replied: "Your present tenure is due altogether to efforts which emanated from Tuskegee. . . . I am very sorry that . . . you could not see your way clear to serve him in view of the unselfish devotion which has characterized all of his efforts in your behalf."[7] Rucker soon got back into line. Deveaux also stayed on Washington's good side, and was especially solicitous when his commission came up for renewal in 1906.[8] Lyons, on the other hand, was something of a rebel. While reappointed register in 1901 with Tuskegee approval, Lyons proved his own man in supporting the radical, anti-Bookerite programs of Monroe Trotter and W. E. B. Du Bois. Lyons did not win reappointment when his second term expired in 1906 largely because, in the words of the Washington *Bee*, "he has not danced while Mr. Washington played the fiddle."[9] Washington's blessing was the key to success for black Republicans during the Roosevelt years, and none of the infighting which was the trademark of Georgia Republicanism escaped Tuskegee's notice.

A typical intra-party clash occurred in Savannah before the presidential campaign of 1900. There Deveaux's control of party

6. Olive Hall Shadgett, *The Republican Party in Georgia from Reconstruction through 1900* (Athens, Ga., 1964), 170–73.

7. Scott to Henry L. Rucker, June 3, 1906, Washington Papers.

8. Deveaux to Washington, Apr. 29, 1906; Scott to Deveaux, May 1, 1906, Washington Papers. Rucker had been asked to invite his chief antagonist, Ben Davis, along on an excursion to Tuskegee which Washington was planning.

9. August Meier, *Negro Thought in America, 1880–1915, Racial Ideologies in the Age of Booker T. Washington* (Ann Arbor, 1963), 237; Washington *Bee*, Dec. 16, 1905. See also Melvin J. Chisum to Washington, Feb. 16, 1906, Washington Papers.

machinery was challenged by black leaders E. K. Love, pastor of the oldest Baptist church in Georgia, and R. R. Wright, principal of the state industrial school.[10] The dispute centered around control of the district nominating convention, the first step in choosing national delegates. After a series of meetings marked by fights and police intervention, the Deveaux faction prevailed. Part of the problem was that the Deveaux people were identified with Savannah's light-skinned elite, while Love and Wright were leaders of a "black" faction.[11] A similar division occurred in Augusta, where Judson Lyons and editor William J. White were opposed by a rising group of dark-skinned ex-slaves led by Reverend Charles T. Walker.[12] Skin color, however, was not as important as political allegiance and ideology in separating black Republicans.

The major factional dispute began in 1904, when Ben Davis employed the editorial columns of his new weekly to attack "boss rule" by the Deveaux-Rucker-Lyons triumvirate. Along with his ally, attorney "Linc" Johnson, Davis attempted to discredit the big three. After the state Republican convention Davis blasted Deveaux, asserting that the collector was "more resourceful than Lyons but is not as big a 'Nigger.' . . ." Lyons, in Davis's opinion, was "a stuffed shirt."[13] Henry Rucker was the prime target of the Davis-Johnson clique, which tried to replace him as collector. Davis criticized Rucker for referring to Democrats as "mobbers, lynchers, and repressionists," then turned and accused him of hiring mostly Democrats to work in his office.[14] Both sides appealed to Tuskegee for help. Washington told Johnson that he would remain above the fray, but secretly he interceded with President Roosevelt for Rucker.[15] The collector kept his job, but Davis and Johnson had only begun to operate.

10. Love died that same year, but Wright remained politically active in Georgia for many years.
11. Savannah *Morning News*, Jan. 19, 25, 28, 30, 1900; Feb. 1, Mar. 8, Apr. 6, 1900.
12. Meier, *Negro Thought in America*, 156.
13. Atlanta *Independent*, Apr. 2, 9, May 7, 14, 1904.
14. *Ibid.*, Dec. 3, 1904; Jan. 14, 1905.
15. For Washington's role in the Davis-Rucker controversy, see Washington to Rucker, Nov. 21, 1904; Nov. 9, 1905; Washington to Ben Davis, Oct. 25, 1905; Rucker to Scott, May 31, Nov. 8, 1905; Scott to Rucker, June 6, Aug. 2, 1905; Washington to Rucker, May 16, 1905; Washington to Davis, Aug. 29, 1905, Washington Papers.

One by one the big three fell from power. Lyons's failure to be reappointed register preceded his replacement as national committeeman in 1908, a feat engineered by Johnson at the request of William Howard Taft's campaign manager. (Lyons's successor as committeeman was Henry Blum, a white man who tried unsuccessfully to purge Georgia Republicanism of any black influence.) Johnson's reward for getting rid of Lyons was the office of Recorder of Deeds.[16] John H. Deveaux died in the summer of 1909, and Henry Rucker lost his job to a white man the following year, in keeping with President Taft's policy of appointing no southern blacks to office.[17] Linc Johnson and Ben Davis stepped into the leadership void they helped create. Both men would achieve positions of some influence in the party, despite—or perhaps because of—their unscrupulous politics.

Paralleling the decline of the Republican party and federal patronage for blacks was the movement to disfranchise the Negro in Georgia. The first disfranchisement law was the cumulative poll tax, passed by the state legislature in 1887. Under the terms of this statute a person neglecting to pay his poll tax over a period of years would have to pay up all back taxes in order to vote in any election. One contemporary student of southern race relations believed this law to be "the most effective bar to Negro suffrage ever devised."[18] After 1900 fewer than 10 percent of eligible Georgia blacks appear to have voted.[19] Still, since a number of black men continued to exercise their franchise in the larger cities, urban politicians responded with the white primary, enacted in Atlanta in 1892 and later in the other major cities.[20]

The white primary was simply a decision by local Democratic

16. Charles Anderson to Washington, Sept. 29, Oct. 2, 12, 1908; Jan. 8, 1909; Washington to William Howard Taft, Feb. 19, 1910, *ibid.*; Meier, *Negro Thought in America*, 252; Augustus A. Adair, "A Political History of the Negro in Atlanta, 1908–1953" (Master's thesis, Atlanta University, 1955), 18. Taft removed J. C. Dancee, a Washington man, as Recorder of Deeds to make way for Johnson.
17. Savannah *Tribune*, Apr. 16, 23, July 2, 1910.
18. J. Morgan Kousser, *The Shaping of Southern Politics, Suffrage Restriction and the Establishment of the One-Party South 1880–1910* (New Haven, 1974), 65, quoting Alfred Holt Stone, *Studies in the American Race Problem* (New York, 1908), 355. Kousser's excellent book examines disfranchisement laws and practices throughout the South.
19. Kousser, *Shaping of Southern Politics*, 211.
20. Augusta adopted the white primary in 1900, Macon in 1901, and Savannah in 1904. See Matthews, "Studies in Race Relations," 86.

leaders to limit the franchise to white males in the Democratic primary. Since in Georgia winning the Democratic nomination meant certain election, eliminating black voters from the party's primary disfranchised blacks without passing a law, which might run afoul of the Fifteenth Amendment. State Democratic leaders adopted the primary system of nominating candidates in 1898, and two years later they limited participation to white voters in all state Democratic primaries.

So important was preservation of white supremacy at the polls that whites rarely challenged primary outcomes, even if the winner was corrupt or incompetent. When James Woodward, a public drunk, won a bare plurality over four other candidates in the 1904 Atlanta mayoral race, none would challenge him in the general election, where blacks could vote. James L. Key, a defeated candidate and a progressive who should have known better, declared that "Our white primary as an institution is one of the most satisfying we have and any effort to destroy its stability in the community is a bad thing." But four years later, after winning renomination, Mayor Woodward became embarrassingly inebriated while visiting Jacksonville, Florida; this time reformers challenged and defeated him in the general election, soliciting and receiving black votes.[21]

Democratic party officers justified the white primary as a progressive reform to "purify" the ballot, for it would stop white candidates from buying black votes in general elections, a practice widespread in the urban South. Often on the night before an election bribable Negro men were rounded up and herded into makeshift cattle pens near the polling booths. Political henchmen would build fires, hire brass bands, and furnish an abundant supply of liquor for the blacks. The next morning wardheelers would rouse them and march them to the polls, there to vote early—and sometimes often—for the white statesman who had provided the election-eve entertainment and slipped them a dollar or two for performing their civic duty.[22] The white primary, then,

21. Clarence A. Bacote, "The Negro in Atlanta Politics," *Phylon,* 16 (Fourth Quarter, 1955), 340; Atlanta *Journal,* Oct. 6, 1904.

22. Interview with Mr. Robert W. Gadsden, July 20, 1974, Savannah; Richard H. L. German, "The Queen City of the Savannah: Augusta, Georgia, During the Urban Progressive Era, 1890–1917" (Ph.D. dissertation, University of Florida, 1971), 46.

would eliminate such gross improprieties by limiting the franchise to Caucasian males, by definition honest and upright.

A look at Augusta's first white primary is instructive, for, according to the conservative Augusta *Chronicle*, "Vote buying was practiced to a greater extent . . . than possibly ever before. . . . Many white men who would not sell their votes under the old regime along with the negroes, now barter them in the most brazen manner." White voters cheered when a candidate's men arrived early at the polls flashing rolls of bills; by mid-morning votes were selling for as much as fifteen dollars.[23] Black Augustans got to the heart of the problem when they wrote, "If bribery and vote selling have too often made popular elections in Georgia a farce, then proscribe bribery and vote selling; and not colors." They pointed out that many blacks refused to sell their votes, and that while the black man did not aspire to be mayor of Augusta, "he did want a voice in the election of one."[24] However, once established, the white primary became a fixture on the southern scene. It did not stop vote-buying, nor did it lead to better government.

The white primary did eliminate the last vestiges of black power at the polls, so it came as a surprise to many Georgians when several politicians began a campaign to disfranchise blacks by state law. The earliest attempts met with resounding defeat. Georgia lawmakers debated an 1899 disfranchisement bill introduced by Thomas Hardwick, a Tom Watson protégé, defeating it 137 to 3. A coalition of white ministers, labor leaders, and machine politicians joined blacks to oppose the bill. Booker T. Washington actively lobbied against the proposal and twenty-four blacks, including W. E. B. Du Bois and John Hope, petitioned the legislature.[25] Hardwick's bill failed for two major reasons. First, most whites felt the law unnecessary. The cumulative poll tax had disfranchised most blacks, while the white primary shut the door on remaining Negro voters. Second (and somewhat paradoxically), under the existing law conservative Democrats could

23. German, "Queen City of the Savannah," 146, 150; Augusta *Chronicle*, Nov. 21, 1900.
24. German, "Queen City of the Savannah," 136.
25. "Disfranchise Defeated in Georgia," *Independent*, 51 (Dec. 7, 1899), 3306; Atlanta *Constitution*, Nov. 10, 18, 1899; Washington to T. Thomas Fortune, Nov. 7, 10, 1899, Washington Papers; Lynwood M. Holland, *The Direct Primary in Georgia* (Urbana, 1949), 54; Savannah *Tribune*, Nov. 23, 1901.

hold the black vote in reserve for use in general elections against Populists or any other group challenging their power.[26] In case a reform group made a serious challenge within the party, the Democratic leadership could, in the words of Tom Watson, "drop the white primary, declare for a general election, pay up the Negro's back taxes, register him as a voter, and use him as a prop to their power."[27] An unlikely prospect. But with the memory of the Populist revolt still haunting them, the Democrats were not yet ready to eliminate their Negro option.

At the turn of the century few people believed blacks would ever again be politically important. In rural Terrell County, for example, seventy black voters, all farmers, were on the books in 1900 in the fourth district. That number fell to twenty-two in 1902, and none remained by 1904.[28] In that year John Hope said Georgia blacks had such little influence that most, himself included, did not know the name of their ward alderman. "Any discussion as to the fitness and honesty of municipal and state candidates hardly touches me," Hope sadly confessed, "as I know I cannot lift a finger to promote the interests of any one of them. I have no voice."[29] But Tom Watson remained unsatisfied with the status quo, believing that legal elimination of the black vote would permit white voters to divide on issues affecting their self-interest, and in any contested election his Populist followers would hold the balance of power.[30]

Watson made his move in the gubernatorial campaign of 1906. Along with Tom Hardwick, he threw his support behind reform candidate Hoke Smith, the former Secretary of the Interior, who was running against conservative Democrat Clark Howell, editor of the Atlanta *Constitution*. Watson's price was Smith's acceptance of an election law to disfranchise blacks.[31] At the cam-

26. Bacote, "Negro in Georgia Politics," 426.

27. Tom Watson, "Temperate Comment Upon a Peculiar Situation," *Tom Watson's Magazine*, 3 (1906), 265.

28. Terrell County Court of Ordinary, "Voter Registration," microfilm 145–40, Georgia Department of Archives and History.

29. John Hope, "Negro Suffrage in the States Whose Constitutions Have Not Been Specifically Revised," in Archibald H. Grimké *et al.*, *The Negro and Elective Franchise*, American Negro Academy *Occasional Papers* No. 11 (Washington, 1905), 55–56, 59; Wingo, "Race Relations in Georgia," 104.

30. Watson, "Temperate Comment," 265; Woodward, *Tom Watson*, 372.

31. Hardwick worked behind the scenes to persuade his friend Watson to endorse and support Smith, despite the latter's history of conservatism and anti-

paign's outset Smith's theme was domination of state government by corporations, particularly the railroads. Race became the major issue when Howell attempted to draw attention away from his close railroad connections by attacking Smith's disfranchisement plan.

At a debate in Rome, in northwest Georgia, Howell pressed the attack he had already begun in *Constitution* editorials, claiming the disfranchisement amendment was unnecessary because Negroes were already "white-primaried." A Smith provision permitting a man to qualify to vote by interpreting a section of the state constitution would, in Howell's opinion, inspire more blacks to go to school, ultimately increasing their numbers at the polls at the expense of illiterate whites. "Already," he warned, "throughout the state countless thousands of negro children are getting bowlegged with the burden of carrying their books to school."[32] Smith retorted that his educational qualification would apply so harshly to blacks that "if they brought every teacher from New England for ten years, it would not give ten percent of the niggers in Georgia the privilege of voting." Election managers, Smith later explained, could require black applicants to interpret a constitutional sentence containing a Latin phrase, while a single English sentence would suffice for whites.[33]

A favorite Smith tactic was to haunt his audiences with the specter of "Negro rule," singling out the coastal county of McIntosh as proof of black potential. McIntosh was something of an anachronism in Georgia politics. Sixty-three counties had black majorities and four were blacker than McIntosh, yet that county alone continued to send a black legislator to Atlanta. Several factors appear to account for this vestige of black power. Although McIntosh was one of Georgia's poorest counties, black landowners outnumbered whites more than two to one. Land own-

Populism. Once the campaign heated up, Watson's support of Hoke Smith became an issue itself. For more on this election, see Dewey W. Grantham, Jr., *Hoke Smith and the Politics of the New South* (Baton Rouge, 1958), 131–55, and Woodward, *Tom Watson*, 370–78.

32. Atlanta *Journal*, Jan. 10, 1906.

33. Atlanta *Constitution*, June 24, 1906; Josie Spencer Walls, "The Negro in Meriwether County, Georgia as Reflected in the Meriwether *Vindicator*, 1873–1910" (Master's thesis, Atlanta University, 1971), 28, quoting Meriwether *Vindicator*, Mar. 16, June 1, 1906.

ership gave these men a margin of political and economic independence denied the sharecropper or agricultural worker in other black counties. McIntosh blacks also kept alive the political legacy of Reconstruction. While for years the governor had appointed the mayor and aldermen of Darien, the county seat, to prevent a black takeover, as late as 1906 blacks could boast of three elected justices of the peace, all the county's deputy sheriffs, and the entire Darien police force. These key officials could protect blacks in the exercise of their franchise. Indeed, when candidate Smith was campaigning in Darien, he looked up to see a black policeman conspicuously located in front of the courthouse, with a big pistol strapped to his side. Smith liked to remind his audiences that here neither the poll tax nor the white primary was effective, for tax-paying blacks could hold their own primary and outvote the whites in the general election. His disfranchisement plan, he persuasively argued, would finally redeem McIntosh.[34]

Although each candidate claimed to be an ardent white supremacist, both had to overcome reputations as racial moderates. Smith criticized his opponent for voting aid to black schools while in the legislature, and Howell revealed Smith's contribution to all-black Morris Brown College.[35] Howell noted that Smith asked Bishop Turner to recommend him for the Secretary of the Interior post, and returned the favor by giving jobs to some of Turner's relatives. But Smith had a way of neutralizing potentially damaging information. Challenged to defend his federal appointment of a black man as superintendent of Freedman's Hospital, Smith shot back: "That was a nigger hospital. There was nobody but niggers there. There was never anybody but niggers in charge of it as far as I know. A nigger ought to be in charge of it."[36] Here, as in the campaign generally, Hoke Smith simply "out-niggered" his opponent.

A typical Smith speech would blame the Negro for the state's

34. Atlanta *Constitution*, June 24, 1906; Bacote, "Negro in Georgia Politics," 105, 114, 387, 411; McIntosh County *Tax Digest*, 1871, 1878, 1880, 1885, 1890, 1892, 1900, 1910, 1919; Census, *Negro Population*, 127, 131.

35. Clipping from Atlanta *Journal*, Jan. 10, 1906, in Smith scrapbook, Hoke Smith Collection, Special Collection, University of Georgia Library.

36. Atlanta *Constitution*, June 24, 1906.

ills, promising that removal of blacks from politics would not only eliminate Negro officeholders, but would also curb the black man's desire for an "intermingling" of the races, protect white womanhood, and improve race relations.[37] If whites did not achieve these ends legally, Smith predicted, violence might be necessary. Referring to a North Carolina riot which left at least twenty-five blacks dead, he said that "we can handle them as they did in Wilmington," where the woods were "black with their hanging carcasses." Smith challenged cheering audiences with "Shall it be ballots now or bullets later?"[38]

This rhetoric infuriated blacks. Bishop Turner, who had regarded Hoke Smith as a friend of the race, was dismayed by the apparent transformation. The black-owned Savannah *Tribune* expressed displeasure over the drift of events, lamenting: "God help the civilization and future of the Democratic white man if Hoke Smith represents his ideas."[39] But the militant *Voice of the Negro* believed Smith no different from most Georgia whites, including his opponent:

> The race has nothing to gain in the election of either one of these gentlemen. They both are set in their religious convictions to keep the race down and both of them appeal to the ignorant whites with the all-inclusive argument that black men have no rights which white men are bound to respect. In this situation in which we are the target for their poisoned arrows and are their only stock argument for the imperative stomp harangue, we advise our race, "Hands Off!"[40]

Hoke Smith won the primary in a landslide, receiving more votes than the combined total of Howell and three minor candidates, including planter James Monroe Smith and Richard Russell, Sr. Supporters hailed the outcome as a victory for reform. The election of 1906 was significant for another reason: the fact and the manner of Smith's victory contributed to racial polarization in the state. Shortly after the election Atlanta mobs attacked

37. Atlanta *Journal,* Aug. 20, 1905.
38. Atlanta *Constitution,* Nov. 9, 1906. Charles Crowe, "Racial Violence and Social Reform—Origins of the Atlanta Riot of 1906," *Journal of Negro History,* 53 (July, 1968), 243, quoting Smith.
39. Savannah *Tribune,* Aug. 25, 1905; clipping from Atlanta *Constitution,* Sept. 2, 1905, in Smith scrapbook, Smith Collection.
40. *Voice of the Negro,* 3 (Mar., 1906), 216–17; 2 (Nov., 1905), 748.

and killed blacks in a four-day riot, climaxing the year and a half during which Smith had stirred up hatred.[41] A man of culture and family, he had made acceptable the demagoguery of James K. Vardaman and Ben Tillman, and together with Tom Watson set the tone for the next half-century of Georgia campaigning. Smith was not the first office-seeker to appeal to voter emotions, but after the 1906 contest race became the essential issue for Georgia politicians.

When the General Assembly met in 1907 nearly everyone expected some disfranchisement measure. Considerable debate ensued, with representatives from north Georgia districts opposing any plan which might deny the vote to illiterate whites.[42] The final bill, written as a constitutional amendment and subject to voter ratification, required registrants to meet any one of five qualifications. The first category included all war veterans, whose descendants received the vote under the "grandfather clause." The only black legislator, William H. Rogers of McIntosh County, attempted to include under this clause "all persons in involuntary servitude prior to January 1, 1863, and their children." His was the only aye vote.[43]

The next section gave the vote to men "of good character," with the registrar as sole judge. This clause, intended to enfranchise whites failing to meet other qualifications, gave registrars the opportunity to deny the vote to political opponents.[44] The registrar was to evaluate the constitutional test where one qualified by reading and writing, or by interpreting any paragraph of the United States Constitution. Another qualification allowed the vote to any man owning forty acres of land or property assessed at five hundred dollars. Finally, all voters had to pay a poll tax at least six months before an election.[45]

Blacks lobbied to defeat the amendment. One petition, bearing the signatures of Henry L. Rucker and Judson Lyons, businessmen Alonzo F. Herndon and Moses Amos, Professor George A.

41. Du Bois, "Looking Seventy-five Years Backward," 244.
42. Dewey W. Grantham, "Georgia Politics and the Disfranchisement of the Negro," *Georgia Historical Quarterly*, 32 (Mar., 1948), 15.
43. Savannah *Tribune*, Aug. 17, 1907.
44. "Inviting Corruption," *Outlook*, 87 (1907), 57–58.
45. *Georgia Laws*, 1907, pp. 47–50.

Towns and Reverend H. H. Proctor, asked the legislators not to
"disregard your solemn vows and trample your honor in the dust
by passing this bill."[46] The measure passed the Senate 37-6 and
the House 159-16, with only Representative Rogers opposing the
bill because it would disfranchise blacks. Eleven of the fifteen
white House members voting against the bill represented white
counties. They feared that the new law would also disfranchise
whites.[47]

Hoping to defeat the amendment in the general referendum,
blacks helped organize the Georgia Suffrage League to oppose
disfranchisement and encourage black registration. The Atlanta
Independent and other weeklies urged people to qualify and
vote, but registration was disappointing.[46] Fewer than 1,800
blacks—less than 10 percent of those eligible—registered in
urban Fulton County, while figures were lower in rural areas
where night riders sometimes terrorized blacks.[49] On election
day the amendment carried by almost a two-to-one majority, although the 42,000 votes against it indicated that many whites
were unconcerned about Negro rule.[50] Ben Davis charged that
blacks had disfranchised themselves, as there were 20,000 more
eligible black voters than the total vote cast for the amendment.
"Our absence from the polls argues conclusively our unfitness for
the ballot," he concluded.[51] In light of the intimidation that kept
many blacks from the polls, Davis's judgment was harsh. Moreover, most blacks had not voted in a state election since 1896
and thus owed at least twelve years of back poll tax, more than
they could pay.[52]

Disfranchisement did not eliminate the black vote altogether.
Figures vary, but during the decade after disfranchisement from
ten to fifteen thousand blacks were registered, mostly in urban

46. Atlanta *Constitution*, July 28, 1907.
47. Grantham, *Hoke Smith*, 159–60; Kousser, *Shaping of Southern Politics*, 221.
48. Atlanta *Independent*, Mar. 10, 1906; June 15, 22, 1907.
49. Atlanta *Journal*, Oct. 1, Nov. 3, 1908; Bacote, "Negro in Georgia Politics,"
499.
50. Atlanta *Constitution*, Oct. 8, 1908. The totals were 79,963 for and 42,260
against. Both Fulton (Atlanta) and Bibb (Macon) counties voted against the
amendment. Only one-fourth of the white electorate voted. See Kousser, *Shaping
of Southern Politics*, 222.
51. Atlanta *Independent*, Oct. 17, 1908.
52. Bacote, "Negro in Georgia Politics," 503.

areas. Of these, only a few hundred were politically active.[53] In rural counties blacks disappeared from the voting rolls. Sumter County in southwest Georgia had a population of about 27,000, with nearly three-fourths of its citizens black. After the disfranchisement amendment passed, the vast majority of white men who registered did so under the grandfather clause. In fifteen districts election officials enrolled a total of four blacks: three farmers and a preacher. All were in the Americus district and were registered under the "good character" clause. Two years later even those token blacks were dropped from the lists, and all registration sheets bore the heading: "List of White Registered Voters for the ——— District." Throughout the state black registration dropped from 28.3 percent in 1904 to 4.3 percent in 1910.[54]

Fewer whites registered under the law. In his 1911 message to the legislature Governor Joseph M. Brown estimated that the 1908 law discouraged 85,000 white men from registering, a figure no doubt exaggerated for political effect.[55] Tom Watson, now at odds with Hoke Smith, supported Brown in the 1908 election, accusing his former ally of intending to disfranchise poor whites all along. After charging Smith with soliciting the Negro vote, Watson warned an Atlanta audience that "unless something is done for the white men of Georgia the heel of the Negro will be upon our necks." His new solution: the legislature should nullify the Fifteenth Amendment, repeal the disfranchisement law, and make "a white face and set of tax receipts" the only qualification for voting.[56] Confident that the new law solved what they had perceived as the problem of black voting, most whites ignored Watson's plea. Actually, intimidation, the poll tax, and the white primary were as effective in reducing the black vote as was the law. Nor had the disfranchisement statute purified elections as its advocates had predicted, for ballot-box stuffing, coercion, and

53. Atlanta *Journal,* June 23, 1910; Jan. 2, 1916; *Crisis,* 4 (Dec., 1912), 59; Joseph M. Brown, *Annual Message,* June 28, 1911, in *Journal of the House of Representatives of the State of Georgia,* 1911, p. 18 (hereafter cited as *House Journal*).

54. Sumter County, Court of Ordinary, "Registered Voters, 1909, 1911–1913," microfilm 135–48, Georgia Department of Archives and History; Kousser, *Shaping of Southern Politics,* 223.

55. Brown, *Annual Message,* 1911, p. 18.

56. Atlanta *Constitution,* Sept. 3, 1910.

vote-buying remained part of the Georgia political scene long
after the disappearance of blacks from the polls.[57]

The campaign for disfranchisement underscored the weakness
of the Georgia Republican party. With no grass-roots organization, the party could not generate a mass movement against ratification. Most blacks had by then become disenchanted with the
party, whose central committee had long since abandoned interest in Georgia affairs, "except as Uncle Sam's crib may be involved."[58] It was the aura of glamour and success surrounding
the national party that kept Republicanism from dying out in the
state. Too, Georgia Republican leaders had influence among
presidential aspirants. At the national convention the ballots of
Georgia delegates counted the same as others, and these votes
were sought—and often bought—by supporters of every serious
contender.[59] But even here change was occurring, for it was in
the early twentieth century that the national Republican party
reexamined its position toward the Old Confederacy and groped
toward a new southern strategy.

Theodore Roosevelt won the allegiance of black Americans
shortly after becoming President when he invited Booker T.
Washington to dine in the White House. His strong defense of
black political appointees in the South increased his following,
and blacks gave the President enthusiastic support in the 1904
election. From the beginning of his second term Roosevelt gave
indications of selling out to the white South. While the President
charmed whites on his southern tour in 1906, his patronizing,
conservative references to the race problem upset many blacks.[60]
His discharge of a battalion of black soldiers after several were
unjustly accused of shooting up Brownsville, Texas, embittered
many more.[61] But Roosevelt's racial views were consistent. Writ-

57. It is worth noting that Georgia did not enact the Australian ballot until
1922, fourteen years after Negro disfranchisement.

58. William J. White to Henry P. Farrow, Feb. 24, 1906, Henry P. Farrow
Papers, Special Collection, University of Georgia Library; Bacote, "Negro in
Georgia Politics," 386.

59. *Crisis*, 19 (Apr., 1920), 297.

60. Atlanta *Independent*, Jan. 21, 1905; Bacote, "Negro in Georgia Politics,"
368–70.

61. See Washington to William Howard Taft, Nov. 19, 1906, Washington
Papers. Washington told Taft: "I have never in all my experience with the race

ing to a southern white friend, author Owen Wister, he admitted the Booker T. Washington dinner may have been unwise, although he did not "know a white man of the South who is as good as Booker Washington today."[62] Roosevelt agreed with Wister that as a race Negroes were "altogether inferior to the whites," but he would not accept the racist view that all blacks should be disfranchised, that none was qualified for leadership, or that black education was harmful.[63] He believed blacks should receive decent treatment and have opportunities to develop their talents. The President could not remain philosophical, for his actions had angered the white South as had those of no other President since Lincoln. Southern criticism of black appointments disturbed him, for he was only following precedent. Defending his policy to Clark Howell, Roosevelt wrote: "I certainly cannot treat mere color as a permanent bar to holding office, any more than I could treat creed or birthplace." He asked the *Constitution* editor whether in the long run it was not better to "act on the motto 'all men up' rather than that of 'some men down'?" Yet Roosevelt wanted to be judged "not by what I say but by what during the last seventeen months I have actually done." The President cited instances where he replaced black officeholders with whites, and confessed to being "surprised and somewhat pained, at what seemed the incomprehensible outcry in the South about my actions."[64] The President's plea did not placate Howell, whose newspaper continued to speak of "the negrophile Mr. Roosevelt."[65]

Two years later Howell and other southern whites had kinder thoughts about the President's views. In drafting his annual message for 1907, Roosevelt sought advice on the section concerning the race question; Howell responded, "it is exactly on the right line."[66] W. E. B. Du Bois, then teaching at Atlanta University,

---

experienced a time when the entire people have the feeling that they have now in regard to the administration." For the story of what happened at Brownsville, see John D. Weaver, *The Brownsville Raid* (New York, 1970).

62. Roosevelt to Wister, Apr. 27, 1906, Wister Papers.
63. *Ibid.*
64. Roosevelt to Clark Howell, Feb. 24, 1903, copy in Julian L. Harris Papers.
65. Atlanta *Constitution,* Nov. 7, 1904.
66. Howell to Roosevelt, Oct. 31, 1906, Theodore Roosevelt Papers, Manuscript Division, Library of Congress.

disagreed: "If the truth must be told, Theodore Roosevelt does not like black folk. He has no faith in them. I do not think he really ever knew a colored man intimately as a friend. . . . He is an American. The pity of it is, we expected more."[67] Roosevelt's Negro policy varied with the political climate. He courted the black voter when he needed him in 1904, then disregarded him during his second term. Later he flattered southern black audiences prior to the Republican nominating convention in 1912. Ultimately he endorsed a lily-white Progressive party in the South during the 1912 campaign.

The man whom Roosevelt designated his presidential successor, William Howard Taft, accelerated the Republican party's move away from Georgia blacks. By the turn of the century the conservative Republican ideology was attracting some southern whites who had voted for Democratic presidential candidates before the rise of William Jennings Bryan. These new "National Republicans but State and Local Democrats" were anti-Negro and wanted to rid the party of black members. Taft encouraged this white faction and, ignoring the largely black regular Republican organization, named the lily-white Taft Club to head his Georgia campaign in 1908.[68] Black Republicans like Ben Davis stuck with Taft, defending him from attacks by Du Bois and other disillusioned blacks. A spokesman for the anti-Taft forces, Du Bois made a northern tour urging blacks to vote for Bryan. Anticipating the political realignment of the New Deal era, Du Bois urged listeners to "emancipate the Democratic party from its enslavement to the reactionary South."[69] Davis responded by instructing Atlanta University to fire the outspoken professor, for "a Negro teacher who votes for the party of disfranchisement can't teach Negro boys and girls." Taft received the great majority of black votes, but a number of blacks voted for Bryan.[70]

As President, Taft appointed no southern black to office. Conceding that the decision to enfranchise southern blacks had "proved to be a failure," he gave clandestine support to the lily-

67. *Horizon*, 1 (Jan., 1907), 8–9.
68. Farrow to Walter H. Johnson, July 5, 26, 1904, Farrow Papers; Atlanta *Independent*, Nov. 7, 1908.
69. *Horizon*, 4 (July, 1908), 10; (Aug., 1908), 3.
70. Atlanta *Independent*, Oct. 24, 1908; August Meier, "The Negro and the Democratic Party, 1875–1915," *Phylon*, 17 (Second Quarter, 1956), 187.

white movement in the South.[71] Taft remained insensitive toward problems facing blacks. "I have heard it said that your lot in the South is a hard one," the President told a group of Atlanta blacks assembled in the Central Avenue M.E. Church. "I do not believe it; you are now in the South and you look reasonably happy." When he remarked that education would solve the South's problems, a man in the audience shouted, "We don't get it!" Taft replied, "You must realize that it takes time and money to perfect systems of education."[72] After touring Georgia State Industrial College in Savannah and drinking a glass of the dairy department's buttermilk, Taft commended students on Negro progress, then added: "You have had your association with a moral race and your condition today would not be what it is but for that association. . . . And I want you to listen," the President concluded dramatically, "the best friend the Southern Negro has is the Southern white man."[73]

The campaign of 1912 divided Georgia voters. At the national convention most black Republicans delivered their votes to Taft, despite efforts of Roosevelt backers to woo them. (One report stated that the going rate offered by Roosevelt men was $1,500 per vote; TR supporters charged that Taft had already bought the Georgia delegation before the convention.[74]) After Roosevelt bolted and called for a new party, black Republicans like Henry L. Rucker and Judson Lyons were eager to follow. The Georgia White League called a state meeting to choose delegates to the national Progressive party convention. Blacks too held a meeting, selected a contesting delegation and threatened to send it to the national gathering at Chicago. No agreement was possible, and at the convention Georgia went unrepresented.[75]

Three months before the election Roosevelt wrote to Julian Harris, editor of *Uncle Remus's Home Magazine* and TR's prin-

71. Atlanta *Independent,* Mar. 13, 1909; David W. Southern, *The Malignant Heritage: Yankee Progressives and the Negro Question 1901–1914* (Chicago, 1968), 71.

72. Savannah *Tribune,* Apr. 1, 1911.

73. Atlanta *Independent,* May 18, 1912.

74. *Ibid.,* Apr. 20, June 29, 1912.

75. George E. Mowry, "The South and the Progressive Lily White Party of 1912," *Journal of Southern History,* 6 (May, 1940), 240, 243; Atlanta *Independent,* July 27, 1912.

cipal Georgia supporter, detailing his views on the Negro and the Progressive party. Taking a middle position between those who demanded that southern blacks be brought into the new party's councils and those calling for a white man's party, Roosevelt advocated black representation in northern delegations only. He contended that the Progressive party had the true interests of black people at heart, for Democrats ignored the Negro and Republicans were hypocritical.[76] Cynics accused the former President of maneuvering to get southern white votes without losing support from northern blacks.

Meanwhile Georgia Democrats were holding a presidential primary. The two leading candidates were Senator Oscar Underwood, an Alabama conservative, and Governor Woodrow Wilson of New Jersey. Wilson was born in the South, had married a southern woman, and had spent a year in Atlanta as a struggling young lawyer. These credentials were unacceptable to Tom Watson, who disliked Wilson personally. Watson campaigned for Underwood, portraying Wilson as "ravenously fond of the negro." These attacks were largely responsible for the governor's defeat, for although he won every urban area except Columbus, he lost the farm vote. In the general election Wilson would gain strong rural support.[77]

The 1912 election campaign in Georgia was bitter and racist. Wilson supporters emphasized his southern origins and segregationist views. Roosevelt's followers claimed that theirs was the white man's party best representing southern interests. The state's blacks split three ways. Conservative editors and politicos remained with Taft, characterizing Roosevelt as "so changing in his principles that it would not pay to follow in his wake."[78] Roosevelt appeased some blacks with his explanation of their exclusion from the party in the South. Others followed Du Bois

76. Roosevelt to Harris, Aug. 1, 1912, in Arthur S. Link, ed., "Correspondence Relating to the Progressive Party's 'Lily White' Policy in 1912," *Journal of Southern History,* 10 (Nov., 1944), 480–90.

77. Arthur S. Link, "The Negro as a Factor in the Campaign of 1912," *Journal of Negro History,* 31 (Jan., 1947), 83; Link, "The Democratic Pre-Convention Campaign of 1912 in Georgia," *Georgia Historical Quarterly,* 29 (June, 1945), 143–58.

78. Savannah *Tribune,* July 20, 1912.

into the Democratic column, assured by Wilson's eleventh-hour statement that he would work for the welfare of black people.

After Wilson carried the state with 80 percent of the vote, the Progressive party chairman blamed the "negro issue" for Roosevelt's poor showing.[79] Three days before the election, circulars showing TR dining with Booker T. Washington and throwing his arms around black delegates at the Chicago convention went into every county. In forty key counties every voter received one. On election day some Wilson supporters stood around voting tables shouting "Nigger!" at everyone supporting the Progressive ticket, climaxing a newspaper campaign which had rehearsed Roosevelt's old sins against the South and championed Wilson as the white man's candidate.[80]

Georgia politics after 1912 returned to normal—white Progressives came home to the Democratic party, while disillusioned blacks went back to what remained of the party of Abraham Lincoln. The campaign proved again that in Georgia the Democrats were not easy to challenge. The party accurately reflected the state's prejudices against blacks; it was standpat and thereby safe. The party symbolized the year 1850, not the year 1912 or indeed any year since 1860. But that was the way white Georgians wanted it. In many ways—in the growth of Atlanta from a town to a metropolis, in the increasing prosperity of agriculture, in the beginnings of industry—Georgia was looking to the future. In social and political behavior, it preferred to look to the distant past.

79. Atlanta *Constitution,* Nov. 6, 1912.
80. Roger A. Dewar to Harris, Nov. 13, 1912, Harris Papers.

Race and Reform

SENATOR ROBERT M. LA FOLLETTE'S observation that the progressive movement had bypassed the South was not entirely accurate.[1] The South did have reformers, mostly urban business and professional men who entered politics hoping to change their communities and states.[2] Regulation of railroads and utilities, election reform, increased support of public education, abolition of convict and child labor, and Prohibition concerned southern reformers. But in Georgia, at least, the two decades preceding World War I were marked more by continuity than change. Georgia progressives were, at heart, conservative Democrats who distrusted direct democracy; they were interested more in improving their own comfortable existence than in uplifting the masses, black or white. Progressive reform in Georgia was conservative, elitist, and above all racist.

For blacks in Georgia cities the progressive era meant further proscription. Segregation by local ordinance in residential areas and public places, exclusion from parks and libraries, and continued denial of basic city services was the rule for every government, honest or corrupt, reformist or reactionary. Augusta is a good example of a municipal government dedicated to progressivism for rich whites only. There, where conservative businessmen held sway, paved roads, sewers, and garbage collection were unheard of in most black areas, and disease was rampant in the densely packed "Terri."[3] Poor whites, most of whom lived near

1. Robert M. La Follette, quoted in Arthur S. Link, "The Progressive Movement in the South, 1870–1914," *North Carolina Historical Review*, 23 (1946), 173.
2. C. Vann Woodward, *Origins of the New South 1877–1913* (Baton Rouge, 1951), 371; Tindall, *Emergence of the New South*, 32.
3. German, "Queen City of the Savannah," 383–86.

the mills, did not fare much better. Historian Richard H. L. German has written that the rise of progressivism in Augusta was accompanied by racism and class antagonism, concluding that

> the "Good Government" reform struggle in Augusta was not fought to achieve liberal, democratic, egalitarian and progressive ideals at all; but to sustain illiberal, anti-democratic and oligarchic privileges. The goals of the reformers were clear and simple: to prevent government by all the people by restricting the franchise to as few as possible, [and] to protect the special interests of the urban elites through favorable government policies for the business community. . . .[4]

Blacks in Augusta and other Georgia cities viewed those marching under the banner of reform with cynicism and dismay, for they knew from experience that most "progressive" urban reforms either excluded blacks or were directed against them.

This pattern also held true on the state level. The Atlanta *Independent* expressed the disillusionment of black Georgia when it observed, "Reform legislation used to mean remedial and helpful legislation for all the people, and special privileges to none, but under the present regime at the state capitol it means special favors for white people and the downright outlawry of the black man's rights."[5] During the progressive era almost every major legislative proposal brought before the General Assembly was either anti-black, devoted to white interests, or defeated by racist arguments. The first administration of Hoke Smith marked the high point of reform in Georgia, with disfranchisement its proudest achievement. Other major pieces of Smith's legislative program indicate that, far from being forgotten, the Negro was at the center of progressive consciousness.

The most sweeping reform legislation of the period was Prohibition, and here, too, racial fears were a catalyst for change. Under Georgia's local option law 125 of the 145 counties had adopted Prohibition. Large urban centers remained wet, and a 1904 law made it more difficult to end liquor sales in remaining wet counties. Liquor had not been a large factor in the 1906

4. *Ibid.*, 375, 389.
5. Atlanta *Independent*, Aug. 10, 1907.

campaign, for both major candidates opposed statewide Prohibition.[6]

The Atlanta race riot revived the issue and led to passage of legislation. Unwilling to accept blame for the tragedy, white leaders found a scapegoat in "demon rum" and called for measures forbidding liquor sales to blacks.[7] The riot rejuvenated the Prohibitionists, who now added the white man's burden to their arsenal. "It was the deliberate determination of the stronger race to forego its own personal liberty on this for the protection of the weaker race from the crimes that are caused by drunkenness," wrote a leading white progressive, Alexander J. McKelway.[8] The Reverend Lovick P. Winter agreed the riot had rekindled the movement, and he accused blacks of voting wet whenever a local-option bill was on the ballot.[9] Black minister H. H. Proctor retorted that in the last Prohibition election in Atlanta the only precinct to vote dry had a majority of black voters.[10] The stereotype of the drunken black man persisted among white progressives; they contended that just as the federal government had protected "that other weaker race," the Indian, from liquor traffic, so should Georgia protect its Negroes.[11] Booker T. Washington defended Prohibition in a manner similar to that of McKelway and other progressives. Always one to look on the brighter side, he noted that not only had the race riot emptied Atlanta's saloons, but it also had stimulated Birmingham to close its barroom doors.[12] Factors other than race were important in developing Prohibition sentiment, but the progressive's attitude of *noblesse oblige* and the reactionary's identification of liquor, blacks, and rape hastened dry legislation.[13]

When Governor Smith signed the bill, drys exuberantly pa-

6. Grantham, *Hoke Smith*, 162–63; *Georgia Laws*, 1904, p. 63.

7. Atlanta *Journal*, Sept, 26, 1906.

8. Alexander J. McKelway, "State Prohibition in Georgia and in the South," *Outlook*, 86 (1907), 947.

9. Lovick P. Winter, "Prohibition in Georgia," *Independent*, 63 (Aug. 15, 1907), 443–44.

10. H. H. Proctor, quoted in *Independent*, 62 (Jan. 3, 1907), 52. See also John Hammond Moore, "The Negro and Prohibition in Atlanta, 1885–1887," *South Atlantic Quarterly*, 69 (Winter, 1970), 38–57.

11. McKelway, "State Prohibition in Georgia," 949.

12. Booker T. Washington, in *Southern Workman*, 37 (Jan., 1908), 7–8.

13. National Prohibitionists employed a similar tactic during World War I, when they linked beer drinking with the German army.

raded through the streets, making calls on the governor and speeches before Henry Grady's monument. Their joy was short lived, for the law only prohibited manufacture and sale of intoxicants without curtailing consumption or import.[14] Locker clubs, where members kept bottles in private compartments, sprang up; many clubs soon discarded this sham and again sold liquor by the drink. "Near beer" saloons served alcoholic beverages to the less affluent.[15] Booze flowed in from other states. The Southern Express Company rented a vacant store in Atlanta as a depot and brought extra wagons to the city. One spring day in 1908 the company delivered 265 cases of whiskey and six barrels of beer to a single residential area. Service was so fast that an Atlantan who ordered a quart of whiskey from Chattanooga, 140 miles away, claimed his order came in thirty minutes. Widespread violation of the spirit and letter of the Prohibition law must have appalled Alexander McKelway, who had boasted after the law's passage: "We have a white population that is tremendously on the side of the law and bent on enforcing it. Its violations will be mainly by the negroes."[16] Less than a year later police uncovered a large bootlegging ring operating in the halls of the state capitol![17]

Both races broke the law. The General Assembly passed more legislation to tighten enforcement, and the state officially went "bone dry" in 1917.[18] In proposing this drastic law, which called for a thousand-dollar fine and/or a year in prison for possession of intoxicating beverages, Governor Nathaniel Harris spoke in apocalyptic terms:

> The need for this legislation grows out of our social environment. Two antagonistic races are living in the South side by side, utterly separate and diverse, with the strongest race prejudice that was ever developed in the history of the world. . . . Liquor arouses the dominant feeling of race hatred, deadens all sense of responsibility —either to law or to humanity—and, if its use were not controlled, would inevitably bring anarchy and race war in our midst

14. *Georgia Laws*, 1907, pp. 81–83.
15. S. Mays Ball, "Prohibition in Georgia: Its Failure to Prevent Drinking in Atlanta and Other Cities," *Putnam's Magazine*, 5 (Mar., 1909), 695–96.
16. McKelway, "State Prohibition in Georgia," 948.
17. Ball, "Prohibition in Georgia," 696–97.
18. *Georgia Laws*, 1917, pp. 1–19.

at an early date. Prohibition is self-protection, it is the last hope of the two races—to preserve harmony and maintain peace in their midst.[19]

In many ways Prohibition in Georgia was a rehearsal for the national experiment, but injection of the race issue was a southern contribution to Prohibition rhetoric and a major reason why Georgia and sister states in the South went dry nearly a decade before passage of the Eighteenth Amendment.

Like Prohibition, the convict lease system was not an issue in the 1906 campaign. Although few Georgians defended it, convict leasing had brought in considerable state revenue, and most people feared higher taxes without it. Lessees of convicts were powerful politically and fought efforts to end their profitable arrangement with the state.[20]

In the summer of 1908 the Atlanta *Georgian* began a campaign to abolish convict leasing, rallying public opinion to demand that the legislature end the practice. The *Georgian* attacked leasing on many levels. Exposing the cruelty of the system, an early editorial noted that these evils had "advertised us to the outside world as a barbarous people."[21] Meeting the revenue issue head on, the paper recommended higher taxes to compensate for lost income and pay for a real prison system. The newspaper revealed dealings between high prison officials and lessees, while focusing on gruesome reports of mistreatment of white prisoners.[22] Though 90 percent of state convicts were black, the editors no doubt believed white Georgians would act if atrocity stories dealt with their race. In all the public outcry rarely was the racial composition of the convict community mentioned, except to protest lack of segregated facilities in camps. It was almost as though whites could show sympathy for "convicts" where they could not for "Negroes." At any rate, mass meetings took place in Atlanta, Rome, and other cities in the summer of 1908, newspapers throughout the state lent support, and organized labor opposed

19. Nathaniel Harris, "Annual Message," in *House Journal*, 1916, pp. 124–25.
20. Alton D. Jones, "Progressivism in Georgia, 1898–1918" (Ph.D. dissertation, Emory University, 1963), 12.
21. Atlanta *Georgian*, June 26, 1908.
22. *Ibid.*, June 26, July 11, 15, 1908. Details of convict abuse are found in the chapter on "The New Slavery," above.

competition of convict with free labor.[23] Faced with such pressure the General Assembly responded. After long and bitter debate carried over into a special session, legislators passed a law to employ convicts on public roads and county lands, and prohibited individuals or corporations from leasing prisoners. Another section required segregation of black and white convicts when possible.[24] The chain gang replaced the private convict camps, and reformers heralded this change as humanitarian. The legislature had in fact traded the convict from one harsh taskmaster to another.[25]

Other legislatures passed laws proscribing black freedom. Back in the 1890s the General Assembly segregated blacks on streetcars and sleeping cars.[26] During a severe labor shortage just after the turn of the century the Calvin Vagrancy Law was enacted to insure a cheap labor supply and to control the growing urban black population.[27] After Governor Terrell denied the Lincoln Guards, a delegation of black troops, permission to attend Theodore Roosevelt's inauguration in 1905, the legislature disbanded all "colored troops of this state."[28] In another example of vindictiveness lawmakers abolished Negro branches of the Elks and Knights of Pythias.[29] After years of taxing gifts for schools and colleges, the 1917 Assembly granted exemptions for educational endowments, except to whites contributing to black schools and blacks contributing to white schools.[30]

Not all anti-black proposals became law. One unsuccessful bill would have empowered the jury to recommend castration in rape cases. The Columbus *Enquirer-Sun* noted that this bill was "peculiarly adopted to southern conditions."[31] The 1902 legislature

23. Thomas D. Clark, *The Rural Press and the New South* (Baton Rouge, 1948), 101; Taylor, "Abolition of the Convict Lease System," 279.

24. *Georgia Laws*, 1908, pp. 1123–24.

25. See pp. 86–87.

26. *Georgia Laws*, 1891, p. 114; 1899, p. 84.

27. Columbus *Enquirer-Sun*, Oct. 30, 1903; *Georgia Laws*, 1905, pp. 109–10; *Voice of the Negro*, 2 (Sept., 1905), 604.

28. Atlanta *Journal*, Jan. 29, Aug. 27, 1905; *Georgia Laws*, 1905, p. 166. For years the Negro contingent of the National Guard had held but a ceremonial function.

29. Atlanta *Constitution*, Aug. 15, 18, 1909; Atlanta *Independent*, Aug. 21, 1909. For more on the lodge controversy, see pp. 56–57.

30. *Georgia Laws*, 1917, pp. 39–41.

31. Columbus *Enquirer-Sun*, Oct. 27, 1900.

considered a bill establishing a rural police force of about 12,000 men, to be paid on the basis of arrests. This proposal was aimed at blacks, who would have had to carry identifying passes at all times. It was tabled.[32] Efforts to divide the school fund between the races in proportion to taxes paid and to bar whites from teaching black children were unsuccessful. (The Senate passed the latter bill 33-0, but the House killed it.[33]) After the Georgia Railroad strike of 1912, a measure to bar black firemen from locomotives on the Georgia Railroad passed the House but failed in the Senate. The proposal included a stiff educational requirement and had backing from the Georgia Federation of Labor. Harassment bills, like the one requiring circuses to give separate performances for white and Negro audiences, frequently appeared on the legislative docket.[34]

Failure of the General Assembly to provide sufficient funds for the education of black children, to enact any social legislation, or to pass laws against lynching and mob violence was even more detrimental to blacks than legislative efforts to bolster the caste system and codify white supremacy. Measures benefiting the black community never received serious consideration. Progressive legislators genuinely interested in humanitarian reform directed their energies toward the white working class, pushing for compulsory school attendance and elimination of child labor in factories. Ironically, racist arguments and attitudes would impede reforms designed primarily to benefit the white people of Georgia.

Although Georgia had no compulsory attendance law, public sentiment for required attendance increased between 1900 and 1910. In 1907 the president of the Georgia Federation of Women's Clubs and a leading supporter of compulsory education, Mary Ann Lipscomb, wrote that the "only barrier that seems to be in our way is that of the negro problem."[35] Advo-

32. Savannah *Tribune*, Nov. 15, 1902.

33. Silas X. Floyd, "The Georgia School Fund," *Independent*, 54 (Jan. 16, 1902), 160–61; *House Journal*, 1911, p. 906; *Senate Journal*, 1915, p. 272.

34. Atlanta *Constitution*, Aug. 8, 1912; *Crisis*, 4 (Oct., 1912), 273; Atlanta *Journal*, July 20, 1907.

35. Mrs. Mary Ann Lipscomb to Mrs. Rebecca L. Felton, Apr. 25, 1907, Rebecca Latimer Felton Collection, Special Collection, University of Georgia Library; quoted in Wingo, "Race Relations in Georgia," 206.

cates exploited the race issue. Rebecca Latimer Felton argued that more black than white children were attending school on a voluntary basis, and the Atlanta *Journal* cited the rapidly falling black illiteracy rate as proof that a compulsory statute was necessary to get white children into school.[36] In response to a northerner's suggestion that poor, illiterate southern whites might improve their stock by intermarrying with blacks, the chairman of the Committee on Compulsory Education, Mrs. Edgar A. Ross, retorted: "The heritage of the 'poor white' of our Southland is as pure as that of the rich white. Let compulsory education shake off their shackles of ignorance and poverty and they will rise, in state house and Congress, to refute such vile slanders."[37]

Legislators were influenced by arguments against a law which would have to require black children as well as white to attend school. White residents of black belt counties where few blacks attended school did not want to allocate funds for thousands of black pupils. Education was no asset for field hands who, they believed, became more criminal and less trustworthy with schooling. Governor Allen D. Candler in his 1899 annual message falsely declared that 90 percent of crimes attributed to blacks were committed by individuals having opportunity to attend free schools, and blamed the rising crime rate on education.[38] Others believed that educated black citizens, especially those qualified to vote, threatened white supremacy. Opposing these views, the chairman of the education committee of the Atlanta Chamber of Commerce, William J. Lowenstein, asked: "Is it wise or expedient to permit thousands of white boys and girls to grow up in ignorance, lest in forcing them into schools the aspirations of the negro child should be awakened? Shall the white man remain ignorant in order to encourage or compel the negro to remain ignorant? . . . The negro child needs no compulsory law to put him into school. He is already there whenever possible."[39]

When the General Assembly finally passed a compulsory education bill in 1916, only Mississippi remained without a law. The

36. Atlanta *Journal,* July 7, 1913; Jones, "Progressivism in Georgia," 257.
37. Clipping from Atlanta *Constitution,* Feb. 16, 1908, Baker Papers.
38. Allen D. Candler, "Annual Message," 1899, in *House Journal,* 1899, pp. 20–25; Jones, "Progressivism in Georgia," 231.
39. Atlanta *Constitution,* Aug. 7, 1916; *Uncle Remus's Home Magazine,* 4 (Aug., 1910), 13.

Georgia statute was full of loopholes. Children between eight and fourteen were to attend at least four months a year until they completed the fourth grade, but local authorities could easily exempt blacks from the law. Children from poor families or those living more than three miles from the nearest schoolhouse were not covered. A local school board could "for other good reason" excuse children from attendance, "such boards being authorized to take into consideration the season for agricultural labor and the need for such labor." These provisions could apply to poor white children as well, and many officials did not enforce compulsory attendance in economically depressed areas.[40] Some white Georgians had opposed forced attendance as interference with parental authority, others because they did not want additional taxes. But the assumption that educated black men and women would challenge white supremacy and no longer tolerate the caste system was a powerful argument against compulsory education, and whites expressing these fears did so with reason.

Related to the compulsory education movement was the drive to regulate child labor. Again race was an issue, though this time a subordinate one. In Georgia child labor was synonymous with textile mills, where for years children had worked, often beside their parents, under wretched conditions. Opposition to legislation came from mill owners, who were influential in the Georgia Senate. Thirty mill presidents, many of them from the North, appeared before legislative committees in 1900 and helped defeat child labor measures.[41] The Coca-Cola king, Asa Griggs Candler, expressed the sentiments of opponents when he told a convention of reformers that "The most beautiful sight that we see is the child at labor; as early as he may get at labor the more beautiful, the more useful does his life get to be." By 1911 Georgia was the only state permitting children under twelve to labor in factories or to work a sixty-six hour week.[42]

Reformers frequently drew racial comparisons to gain sympathy for their cause. Since prejudice prevented blacks from working in cotton mills, reformers claimed that while Negro children were in

40. *Georgia Laws*, 1916, pp. 101–2; Atlanta *Constitution*, Apr. 11, 1917.
41. Elizabeth H. Davidson, *Child Labor Legislation in the Southern Textile States* (Chapel Hill, 1939), 8.
42. Woodward, *Origins of the New South*, 418, quoting Candler; Alexander J. McKelway, "Child Labor Campaign in the South," *Survey*, 17 (Oct., 1911), 1025.

school white boys and girls were working in the mills, turning into physical and intellectual cripples.[43] Alexander McKelway led the crusade for child labor legislation in the South, repeating the theme that child labor jeopardized the purest racial strain in the entire country, the southern Anglo-Saxon.[44] Child labor reformers supported compulsory education, hoping passage of the law would get children out of the mills and into classrooms. They met with little success in either area. In 1914 the General Assembly passed a law regulating child employment, but it was so poorly written and enforced that as late as 1920 Georgia led the nation in the number of working children between the ages of ten and fifteen.[45] The mill owners were calling the tune in Georgia, and not even exaggerated appeals to white supremacy could rally support for effective legislation.

Detractors who claimed that Georgia was living in the Dark Ages had only to note that the age of consent there was ten, the lowest in the nation, to make their point. Efforts to raise the age to eighteen met with consistent failure, although inaction was not due to disrespect for white southern womanhood. The reason, members of the General Assembly informed a delegation from the Women's Christian Temperance Union, was that legislators objected to legal protection for young black girls! At this, the white North Georgia Conference of Southern Methodist Women unanimously adopted a resolution calling for "the protection of childhood and womanhood of Georgia without regard to race."[46] Other women's groups took similar stands, forcing the General Assembly in 1918 to raise the age from ten to fourteen. Yet this law provided that no man could be convicted on unsupported testimony of the victim, and the jury could reduce the crime from felony to misdemeanor in any case.[47]

The race question figured strongly in the crusade for women's

43. Georgia Federation of Labor, *Some Interesting Information Concerning Child Labor in Georgia* (Atlanta, n.d.), cover; *Outlook*, 107 (1914), 888; Atlanta *Constitution*, July 13, 1908.

44. Herbert J. Doherty, "Alexander J. McKelway, Preacher to Progressive," *Journal of Southern History*, 24 (May, 1958), 188.

45. National Child Labor Committee, *Child Labor Facts* (New York, 1928), 17; Jones, "Progressivism in Georgia," 79.

46. Lucy D. Hammond, *Southern Women and Race Adjustment*, John Slater Fund *Occasional Papers* No. 19 (Charlottesville, Va., 1917); "Committee on Social Service, Report No. 2" (Feb. 16, 1972), copy in NAACP Papers.

47. *Georgia Laws*, 1918, pp. 259–60.

rights, which then centered around the right to vote. The state campaign for women's suffrage was an uphill struggle with no widespread support, even among women. Many southern white men either placed their women on pedestals or believed them incapable of responsible political participation, or both. "Uncle Sam now stands before the world as the marvelous young giant of the West," claimed one male chauvinist. "He is the modern Samson, and this speech is my appeal to you not to give Delilah the shears with which to trim his locks and bring about the destruction of the temple."[48] The most convincing argument against female suffrage in the South was racial. Opponents feared that the proposed amendment would enfranchise black women, who would register and vote in large numbers. Even more distressing was concern that the Nineteenth Amendment would succeed where the Fifteenth had failed and bring black men back to the polls. "It means the final ratification of the Fifteenth Amendment to the Constitution of the United States, nothing less," warned State Representative Jackson Jones. "Of that amendment Frederick Douglass was the father and Susan B. Anthony, who received the negro in her home, the mother."[49] Senator Hoke Smith, leading the southern filibuster against the bill in Washington, predicted that passage would make it impossible to eliminate the Negro vote.[50] Anti-suffragist Mildred Rutherford feared revival of the two-party system in Georgia. "I remember well what Republican rule meant for the South," she told the legislature, "and I plead with you not to do anything to encourage the refastening of that rule about our necks. . . ."[51]

The suffragettes fought fire with fire. The Georgia Senate in July 1913 twice denied the Georgia Women's Suffrage Association use of its hall. The ladies quickly got permission to meet in the House chamber after giving every representative a handbill which read: "Negro men were allowed the use of the Capitol, but

48. Eugene Anderson, *Unchaining the Demons of the Lower World* (n.p., n.d.). This pamphlet was distributed by the Georgia Association Opposed to Women Suffrage, a women's group.
49. Atlanta *Constitution*, July 25, 1919; Kenneth R. Johnson, "White Racial Attitudes as a Factor in the Arguments against the Nineteenth Amendment," *Phylon*, 31 (Spring, 1970), 32.
50. Atlanta *Constitution*, May 27, 1919.
51. *Ibid.*, July 8, 1919.

Georgia women were debarred."[52] The president of the Association, Mary Latimer McLendon, led the counterattack: "The negro men, our former slaves, have been given the right to vote and why should not we Southern women have the same right?" Her sister, the crusading Rebecca Latimer Felton, echoed, "I do not want to see a negro man walk to the polls and vote on who shall handle my tax money while I myself can not vote at all. . . . Why this choice of negro men over your own wives and mothers?"[53]

Georgia women had to await congressional action before getting the vote. The Susan B. Anthony amendment passed in 1919, with Hoke Smith and all but one of Georgia's congressmen voting against it. Angry debate ensued when the Georgia General Assembly took up ratification of the amendment, but the outcome was never in doubt. The House voted it down 118–29, the Senate 39–10, giving Georgia the distinction of becoming the first state to reject the Nineteenth Amendment.[54] When it eventually became the law of the land Governor-elect Thomas M. Hardwick promised enforcement by encouraging "enfranchisement of all white women in accordance with the Anthony amendment and the disfranchisement of all black women on the same plan that the negro men are now disfranchised in Georgia."[55] Georgia blacks had always supported female suffrage, and black women tried to register when the books first opened. Only a few were successful, and in the short run the Nineteenth Amendment was of no benefit to Georgia blacks.[56]

If the spirit of progressivism did not ignore Georgia, neither did it have much effect. Several factors were responsible for failure of reform efforts during the first two decades. Cities were usually controlled by conservative Democrats whose "reforms" often

52. Columbus *Enquirer-Sun*, July 10, 1913; Jones, "Progressivism in Georgia," 216.
53. A. Elizabeth Taylor, "The Last Phase of the Woman Suffrage Movement in Georgia," *Georgia Historical Quarterly*, 43 (Mar., 1959), 17–18; Atlanta *Constitution*, July 3, 1919. Although only a few black men voted, the suffragettes were technically correct in their charge.
54. Atlanta *Constitution*, May 22, July 25, 1919.
55. Thomas M. Hardwick, quoted in Paul Lewinson, *Race, Class, and Party* (New York, 1932), 109.
56. Atlanta *Independent*, May 28, 1914; June 7, 1919; Savannah *Tribune*, June 28, 1919; Oct. 2, 9, 1920.

benefited only upper-class whites. Georgia was too poor to provide good schools and adequate public services, and was dependent upon northeastern bankers who controlled much of the state's
industry. Thus efforts on behalf of enforceable child labor legislation or other social reforms lacked any real chance for success.

Overshadowing all these problems was the race question. Responsible leaders could have blunted the effects of racism, but
politicians like Hoke Smith and Tom Watson fanned the flames
of anti-Negro sentiment to further their own careers. Lawmakers
applied the test of racial orthodoxy to every reform measure.
Racist attitudes brought about disfranchisement, influenced passage of Prohibition laws, prevented favorable state action on
women's suffrage, made a mockery of Georgia's age-of-consent
statute, and delayed compulsory school attendance for decades.
The General Assembly debated a number of bills curtailing black
freedom, enacting some proscriptive measures into law. The years
passed, and for the black people of Georgia the progressive era
came to have no more meaning than the decades which had
preceded it.

Race Violence

"Sit not longer blind, Lord God, deaf to our prayer
and dumb to our suffering.
Surely Thou, too, art not white, O Lord, a pale,
bloodless, heartless thing!"

"Whenever an aristocracy allows the mob to rule
the fault is not with the mob . . ."[1]

ALTHOUGH THERE was no Saturday afternoon concert at the Piedmont Driving Club, the terrace presented a lively scene, with tables surrounded by women dressed in airy summer fashions and men attired in light flannel suits. Back from a delightful summer trip to Massachusetts coastal resorts, Mrs. Henry Porter drove out to the club with Mrs. Louis Beck; and Mrs. Fleming Van Rensselaer enjoyed the half-holiday at a table with her friends Mrs. Richard A. Harris and Mr. and Mrs. James G. Miller. It was an Indian summer day in late September, and leaves drifting across the terrace from trees overhead foreshadowed a time when blazing log fires would beckon club members indoors. But for now these pillars of Atlanta society were content to sip their drinks in the warm sunlight, gently cooled by late afternoon breezes.

Not far away, on Decatur Street in downtown Atlanta, the usual Saturday afternoon crowd was gathering. Gambling dens, saloons, pawnshops, and cheap eateries lined both sides of the street, with

1. W. E. B. Du Bois, "A Litany at Atlanta," in *Darkwater* (New York, 1920), 27; Du Bois to W. D. Hooper, Oct. 11, 1909, in Aptheker, ed., *Correspondence of W. E. B. Du Bois,* I, 153.

second-floor lodgings just ill-disguised rooms of prostitution. Located in black Atlanta, the area drew pleasure-seekers of both races who drank and gambled together and shared the same women. As in most cities, vice was integrated in Atlanta. The "best" citizens of both races deplored the Decatur Street strip; ministers railed against it and civic leaders spoke of shutting it down. This kind of talk had been going on for years, and on Saturday, September 22, 1906, Decatur Street was swinging, as usual.[2]

Beneath the facade of abandon which characterized Saturday night on the town, Decatur Street—and the rest of Atlanta—was seething with racial tension. The city had been the focal point of Hoke Smith's race-baiting gubernatorial campaign which had ended just a month before. With no more election news, three evening newspapers boosted circulation by stirring racial passions. The Atlanta Evening News, Georgian, and Journal began featuring stories of alleged rape, citing details of "black fiends" assaulting defenseless virgins. The excitement rose at five o'clock on the afternoon of the 22nd, when the Evening News came out with the first of five extras announcing new attacks on white women. The Journal soon followed suit. Although false, banner headlines of "Two Assaults," "Third Assault," and "Fourth Assault" panicked Atlantans, sending hundreds who had been loitering on Decatur Street into action.[3]

The crowd turned into a mob shortly after nine o'clock when groups of white men began tormenting and beating up blacks. Mayor James Woodward was on the scene and ordered whites to disperse, but he was a weak man known for carousing, and the mob paid him no mind. As the mayor finished speaking at least 5,000 persons swarmed into the streets. The throng was young, in their teens and twenties; most were lower-class whites, yet more than a few were professional men, store owners, and college students. Between nine-thirty and eleven o'clock thousands of whites bought arms—one hardware store sold $16,000 worth. The sheriff of Fulton County banned sales but arrested only one owner (who had been selling weapons to blacks). By ten o'clock more

2. Atlanta Journal, Sept. 23, 1906.
3. Baker, Following the Color Line, 9.

than 10,000 whites, many armed, roamed downtown streets in search of blacks.[4]

Generally sympathetic to the rioters, the Atlanta police did little to quell the disturbance. A few policemen rescued blacks, yet it became apparent that officers would not use guns or night-sticks against whites. Mob leaders correctly interpreted police non-involvement as a blank check, and beatings of blacks gave way to murders. Equipped with revolvers, rifles, canes, and heavy stones, one segment of the mob attacked A. F. Herndon's barber shop on Peachtree Street. The two black barbers working at their chairs offered no resistance, and as one barber held up his hands a rioter hit him in the face with a brick. The mob shot both men, beat them to death, and dragged their mutilated bodies to the Henry Grady monument, where souvenir hunters went to work. In the furor at the barber shop a lame bootblack managed to escape. Young Walter White, helping his father deliver mail, saw the cripple pathetically trying to outrun the mob, only to be caught and beaten to death.[5] Farther on at the entrance to the Piedmont, Atlanta's finest hotel, hundreds watched a gang stab two blacks and moments later torture a man to death.[6]

Bands of rioters routed blacks cowering in alleyways or hiding in shops. After theaters let out and bars closed, throngs of well-dressed whites cheered these activities from the sidelines, often joining in. Police either stood by or participated. Driving all blacks from the streets, rioters turned to streetcar stops to await unsuspecting victims riding into the middle of the melee. Greeting every trolley with shouts of anticipation, the mob dragged black men and women from cars. The riot had been underway for two hours before the transit company stopped sending cars into the area, but by then twelve cars had been attacked.[7]

4. Crowe, "Racial Massacre in Atlanta," 155–57; New York *Times*, Sept. 23, 25, 1906; Atlanta *Georgian*, Sept. 24, 1906. Crowe's account of the riot is the best available. See also Baker, *Following the Color Line*, 3–25, and Glenn W. Rainey, "The Race Riot of 1906 in Atlanta" (Master's thesis, Emory University, 1929).

5. New York *Times*, Sept. 24, 1906; Baker, *Following the Color Line*, 10; Crowe, "Racial Massacre in Atlanta," 160–61; Benjamin Brawley, *A Short History of the American Negro* (New York, 1941), 170–71; Walter White, *A Man Called White* (New York, 1948), 9.

6. Crowe, "Racial Massacre in Atlanta," 159.

7. *Ibid.*, 161–62; Atlanta *Georgian*, Sept. 24, 1906.

Rioters demolished Negro barber shops and restaurants, smashed windows and looted stores owned by whites. Governor Joseph M. Terrell refused to declare martial law and delayed calling out state militia until shortly before midnight. By the time large numbers of troops had reported, the worst was over, because after blacks fled the central city the mob's ardor temporarily cooled. There was talk of invading outlying black residential sections and a few small gangs made tentative probes. Yet most knew that black Atlanta was now armed and waiting, and they had no stomach for a fight with unfavorable odds.[8]

Rumors of an impending racial clash had circulated through the city for days, and blacks had been quietly arming themselves. (Mortician David T. Howard had a load of guns shipped down from Chicago in a casket.[9]) Still, the hostilities of September 22 took the Negro community by surprise. Blacks trapped downtown thought only of escape, and those who struck back did so in self-defense. As the evening wore on and word of the riot spread into residential areas, groups there began organizing for both defensive and retaliatory action. Guerrilla bands formed to harass the enemy, seizing strategically located houses as sniper stations. Nine black men occupied a building overlooking a major street-car line on the edge of the inner city, and with rifle fire stopped traffic for nearly an hour before retreating. Near downtown a group attacked the Inman Park trolley before a much larger police force gained control. By one o'clock in the morning motormen were refusing to go into black residential sections, as a half-dozen white motormen had driven through sniper fire making their rounds.[10]

Sunday morning Atlanta was quiet. At least twenty blacks lay dead, with scores more wounded. Walter White recalls a particularly grim scene: "Like skulls on a cannibal's hut the hats and caps of the victims of the mob the night before had been hung on the iron hooks of the telephone poles. None could tell whether each represented a dead Negro. But we knew that some of those

---

8. Atlanta *Georgian*, Sept. 24, 1906; New York *Times*, Sept. 23, 1906.

9. Interview with Mrs. M. G. Wartman, Mar. 19, 1974, Atlanta.

10. Savannah *Morning News,* Sept. 23, 1906; Crowe, "Racial Massacre in Atlanta," 165–66.

who had worn the hats would never again wear any."[11] White Atlantans experienced a range of emotions, but dominant was fear of black reprisal. Rumors abounded. A mob of 500 armed blacks reportedly was moving to burn the white residential area of West End. Police rushed to guard the city water works after a story circulated that blacks planned to cut water mains, then burn the city. Armed whites patrolled residential areas, awaiting attack.[12]

The city's black community also guarded against renewal of hostilities. W. E. B. Du Bois was out of town on September 22, but he hurried back to Atlanta to stand guard, shotgun in hand, on the front porch of his home. Walter White's family lived near "Darktown," the city's worst and toughest slum. On Sunday afternoon word leaked that a white mob planned to march on Darktown to "clean out the niggers." Shortly after midnight the vanguard of a torch-bearing crowd reached White's home and stopped, determined to burn the house "too nice for a nigger to live in." White's father quietly instructed his thirteen-year-old son not to shoot "until the first man puts his foot on the lawn and then—don't you miss." At that moment blacks barricaded in a brick building two doors away opened fire and scattered the intruders.[13]

Darktown was prepared. Residents shot out all street lights to hamper invaders, and most men were armed. Earlier they reportedly sent word to the governor, "Don't send the militia; we want the mob!"[14] When the mob came, blacks repulsed each attack with gunfire. The importance of the defense of Darktown is difficult to assess. Perhaps whites were not really serious about invading black neighborhoods. William H. Crogman, soon to become president of Clark College, believed Darktown's resistance prevented a second bloodbath. Reflecting on the irony, Crogman told Mary White Ovington: "Here we have worked and

11. White, A Man Called White, 10.

12. Atlanta Georgian, Sept. 24, 1906.

13. White, A Man Called White, 11–12; Herbert Aptheker, introduction to Booker T. Washington and W. E. B. Du Bois, The Negro in the South (New York, 1970), x.

14. Mary White Ovington, The Walls Came Tumbling Down (New York, 1947), 65; W. E. B. Du Bois, "The Tragedy of Atlanta," World Today, 11 (1906), 1174.

prayed and tried to make good men and women of our colored population, and at our very doorstep the whites kill these good men. But the lawless element in our population, the element we have condemned fights back, and it is to these people that we owe our lives." Tensions remained high in Darktown, and on Monday snipers still shot at whites venturing into the area.[15]

Action shifted on Monday from the Darktown slum to the middle-class neighborhood of Brownsville in south Atlanta. "The most orderly and law abiding community in the state" was the home of Clark College and Gammon Theological Seminary. During the riot the colleges offered sanctuary to hundreds of frightened citizens, and Gammon president J. W. E. Bowen asked for troops to protect the colleges. Instead, on Monday evening a boisterous squad of county police, augmented by white vigilantes, marched into Brownsville and began arresting residents for possessing weapons. At the end of a narrow street blacks ambushed the force, whose leader, James Heard, was shot out of his saddle and died instantly. Three other officers and several blacks were wounded in the initial exchange before the outgunned troops fled, leaving Heard's body behind. Police sealed off Brownsville until Tuesday morning, when they searched each house and arrested everyone with firearms, netting enough guns and ammunition to fill three large wagons. Nearly three hundred blacks were arrested and marched through city streets, flanked by police and guarded from the rear by a machine gun. College students and professors, including President Bowen, were among the arrested. Some won quick release; fifty-nine were charged with Heard's murder, but eventually all but one prisoner would be freed.[16]

The black community saw little difference between the mob and the police. Where the mob dared not go the militia went, invading residential areas and disarming citizens. Four blacks

15. Atlanta *Georgian*, Sept. 25, 1906. Anti-white feeling was running so high in Darktown that a light-skinned Negro doctor had to do some fast talking to convince an angry group of blacks that he was one of them. Interview with Mrs. Grace Towns Hamilton, Mar. 18, 1974, Atlanta.
16. O. C. Fuller to Baker, Nov. 5, 1906, Baker Papers; Du Bois, "Tragedy of Atlanta," 1174; Baker, *Following the Color Line*, 11–14; Atlanta *Georgian*, Sept. 25, 1906; Atlanta *Evening News*, Sept. 25, 1906; Savannah *Tribune*, Nov. 10, 1906. Alex Walker was found guilty and sentenced to life imprisonment. Atlanta *Georgian*, Nov. 2, 1906.

died in Brownsville during the police search: a grocer, a seventy-year-old Civil War pensioner, a brickmason, and a carpenter. None was resisting arrest. The *Voice* summed up bitterness over Brownsville, commenting that after the real riot was over, "THEN comes the militia, the defenders of society, and disarms the Negroes whom the mob had feared to attack."[17] The Atlanta *Journal* expressed the gratitude of whites to the militia and urged the troops to "Keep up the work . . . and with the negroes unarmed Atlanta can retire to a night of peace and quiet rest."[18] The Brownsville affair was the last major incident, and by Thursday a troubled calm returned. By then many blacks had fled the city, some permanently.

According to official reports twenty-five blacks had died during the days of rioting, with six times that number seriously wounded. Only one white, Officer Heard, was listed as killed during the riot. Black Atlantans, then and now, dispute these statistics. Writing shortly after the riot, Du Bois stated that at least a hundred persons died, "most of whom were Negroes, although a large proportion of both the dead and maimed were white, the exact number on either side being unknown."[19] In this connection the reminiscences of a prominent black Atlantan, Mrs. H. S. Murphy, are of interest. Referring to a conversation she had many years ago with mortician David T. Howard, Atlanta's most respected black citizen, Mrs. Murphy recalls: "You know what he told me? He said, 'You have no idea how many white people I was forced to bury in the Negro cemetery because they didn't want the white people to know who was getting killed by the Negroes in the riots.' Now he told me that himself. 'Darling, you know I had to bury them where they told me. I had to live. I had to go out at night and bury them.' "[20]

It would have been in the interest of white leaders to minimize Caucasian casualties, if only to prevent further exacerbation of racial tensions. On the other hand, it is likely that the story of the riot has been embellished in the retelling over the years. But given

17. *The Voice*, 3 (Nov., 1906), 488; Baker, *Following the Color Line*, 13–14.
18. Atlanta *Journal*, Sept. 25, 1906.
19. Crow, "Racial Massacre in Atlanta," 168, 172; Du Bois, "Tragedy of Atlanta," 1173.
20. Interview with Mrs. H. S. Murphy, July 6, 1972, Atlanta.

the detailed accounts of race violence in the Atlanta press, the official figures for riot fatalities appear low. Although blacks were unable to offer effective resistance when trapped downtown or caught in white sections of the city, they did fight back successfully when the mobs invaded their neighborhoods. In light of these facts, the Atlanta authorities' statement that Officer Heard was the only white person killed during the four days of rioting must be viewed with skepticism.

A white investigating committee blamed the riot on the inflammatory journalism of the three evening newspapers. In a campaign to rid Atlanta of alleged black rapists, the papers had exploited white frustrations. Five weeks before the riot the *Georgian's* lead editorial recommended castration for all black rapists. While reader response was enthusiastic, some believed the editorial did not go far enough: "Let's continue to kill all negroes who commit the unmentionable crime," wrote one reader, "and make eunuchs of all new male issues before they are eight days old." Another writer, believing that black women seduced white men to have mulatto children, suggested sterilization of Negro baby girls. Although these letters were representative of the lunatic fringe, they indicate the state of near-hysteria that had seized the white community. *Georgian* editor John Temple Graves, a personal friend of Theodore Roosevelt, printed without editorial comment these letters advocating genocide.[21]

Whites were obsessed with the black man's sexuality. Four days before the riot the *Evening News* criticized white women who sat next to their black chauffeurs: "To see a big black negro sitting alongside of and touching the body of a white woman makes the blood in every white man's veins boil. . . . They get in these narrow seated buggies and take a big black buck up by their side, and it is utterly impossible for the woman to keep from touching the body of the negro. This is a horrible sight for white people to witness."[22] The image of the black man as a sexually superior savage lusting after white women tormented the white male. Concern over alleged rapes moved the *Evening News* to advocate lynching any black man committing a sexual assault and to call for revival of the Ku Klux Klan. For this, *News* editor

21. Atlanta *Georgian*, Aug. 16, 25, 1906; clipping from Macon *Telegraph*, Sept. 12, 1906, in Smith scrapbooks, Hoke Smith Collection.
22. Atlanta *Evening News*, Sept. 18, 1906.

Charles Daniels was made a special deputy sheriff. In
the award the Fulton County sheriff declared, his voic
with emotion: "Gentlemen, we will suppress these g
nities upon our fair wives and daughters if we have to
negro in a thousand miles of this place."[23]

Incendiary rhetoric had a profound effect on lower-class whites,
many recently moved to Atlanta and competing with blacks for
jobs. For them the black man was also an economic threat, and
the Atlanta riot provided opportunity for poor whites to work out
their frustrations. Many whites were genuinely shocked by the
murder of innocent blacks, and biracial committees sprang up to
prevent another tragedy. Yet the white majority probably agreed
with Mayor Woodward, who, when asked how future riots might
be avoided, replied: "The only remedy is to remove the cause.
As long as black brutes attempt rape upon our women, just so
long will they be unceremoniously dealt with."[24]

The worst racial clash in Georgia since Reconstruction, the Atlanta riot was an urban response to the buildup of interracial
tensions. In the countryside, white animosity toward blacks often
culminated in lynchings. Between 1882 and 1923 Georgia led the
nation with 505 recorded lynchings. In almost every other state
this practice hit a peak between 1880 and 1900 and remained
steady or declined thereafter; however, Georgians lynched more
blacks between 1900 and 1920 than they had in the previous
twenty years.[25] Many white southerners defended lynching as a
deterrent to rape, and most assumed that the vast majority of
lynch victims were rapists. Both assumptions were incorrect. An
NAACP study showed that of 2,522 blacks lynched nationally between 1889 and 1918 fewer than 30 percent were charged with
attacks on women and only 19 percent of these were specifically
accused of rape.[26] Lynchings did not stop would-be rapists, and
quite possibly publicity given to sex crimes increased attacks.

23. *Ibid.*, Aug. 26, 15, 25, 1906.
24. Atlanta *Journal*, Sept. 23, 1906.
25. Walter White, *Rope and Faggot* (New York, 1929), 254–58. Lynching
figures are deceiving, for many lynchings were covered up by explanations such
as "shot while resisting arrest" or "shot while attempting to escape." See Charles
E. Wynes, *Race Relations in Virginia, 1870–1902* (Charlottesville, Va., 1961),
143.
26. NAACP, *Thirty Years of Lynching in the United States, 1889–1918* (New
York, 1919), quoted in White, *Rope and Faggot,* 252–53.

Over a third of all lynchings involved men charged with murder; the remainder were accused of a variety of crimes or, in many cases, no crimes at all.[27]

Blacks were lynched all over Georgia in every season of the year, but if there were such a thing as a typical lynching it took place in a rural south Georgia county during the summer. Small southern towns were not, as a rule, lively places; rather, they provided little recreation for residents. The pace was slow during the long, hot summer days before cotton-picking season, and many welcomed a lynching to break the monotony. There is truth in H. L. Mencken's statement that lynching often replaced the merry-go-round, theater, brass band, and other diversions found in the city.[28] Lynching was, however, more than sport. A bulwark of the caste system, it was tolerated and at times encouraged by the white ruling class. Lynching also reflected the white man's fear of his black neighbor, and a number of hangings and burnings occurred after particularly gruesome crimes.

Statesboro, county seat of Bullock County, is about seventy miles from Savannah. Founded in the early nineteenth century, the town did not thrive until the 1890s, when industrialists discovered wealth in turpentine forests. Seven of every ten residents were church members; the town had no saloon. In all, it was a quiet, prospering community.[29] About six miles from Statesboro lived the family of Henry Hodges, a successful white farmer about forty years old. His wife, Claudia, was a tall, thin, attractive woman of twenty-five. The Hodges had an eight-year-old daughter, Kitty, a two-year-old son, and a five-month-old baby boy. On the afternoon of July 29, 1904, Hodges went to a neighbor's house to bring Kitty back from school. The two arrived home at dark. As he went to the barn to put the buggy away, at least two assailants attacked and beat him to death with a stone and a buggy brace. Hearing the commotion, Mrs. Hodges rushed to the barn, where she met the same fate. Supposedly the attackers were thieves who searched the house, found no money, and left. Later that evening they returned to the farm to hide evidence of their crime and dragged the bodies into the house, where they

27. White, *Rope and Faggot*, 57, 252–53.
28. *Ibid.*, 9–10, quoting H. L. Mencken.
29. Baker, *Following the Color Line*, 177–78.

found Kitty hiding. After killing her they set fire to the house; the two youngest children perished in the blaze.[30]

Statesboro residents were shocked and angered by the Hodges tragedy. Immediately a dozen blacks were arrested—it was assumed that only blacks would perpetrate such a crime—and lynching rumors filled the town. The list of prime suspects narrowed to Paul Reed and Will Cato, illiterate turpentine workers employed in a camp near the Hodges farm. To prevent a lynching, officials took them to the Savannah jail until their trial two weeks later. When Cato and Reed returned to Statesboro, feeling was running so high that local officials called out a company of the state militia. On the first day of the trial many strangers flocked to Statesboro, some well supplied with whiskey and guns.[31] The court tried Cato first. He pleaded innocent, accusing Reed of the murders. Evidence against Cato was circumstantial at best, yet the jury deliberated only eight minutes before finding him guilty. The judge sentenced him to hang.

By the second day the crowd had greatly increased, converging on Statesboro from all directions. Railroads put on extra coaches to accommodate passengers. The Savannah company of the state militia also arrived, but the force of 68 men was hardly capable of handling the estimated 10,000 spectators.[32] Paul Reed's trial proceeded swiftly. Both Cato and his wife testified against Reed, and officers claimed to have found Reed's footprints at the scene of the crime and his blood-soaked clothes in his cabin. Reed maintained innocence. The jury verdict was guilty, and after cheering died down the judge sentenced Reed to the gallows. The trial verdicts surprised no one: Reed and Cato were to pay for the Hodges murders.

The crowd outside was in no mood to let the law take its course. After finding out the militiamen were carrying unloaded weapons, angry spectators led by the court bailiff stormed the courthouse, breaking into the room where Cato and Reed were with their families. Sheriff J. Z. Kendrick proved helpful by pointing out

30. The account of the Hodges murders comes from Savannah *Press*, Savannah *Morning News*, and Atlanta *Constitution*, Aug. 30–Sept. 2, 1904. See also Baker, *Following the Color Line*, 179–81.

31. Savannah *Morning News*, Aug. 16, 1904.

32. Atlanta *Constitution*, Aug. 16, 1904.

the prisoners—"There is that son of a bitch Reed"—and offering no resistance as the mob dragged them away.[33] The militia remained in town. Determination to lynch the two at the scene of the crime wilted in the heat, and the march ended in a turpentine forest a mile out of town. There, after being allowed to pray, Reed and Cato were chained together to a seven-foot stump. The brother of the slain farmer, Reverend H. H. Hodges, pleaded in vain to save them, but the crowd had decided upon death by fire. A wagonload of pine wood was hauled to the spot and piled waist high around them. Someone climbed to the top of the stump and poured twenty gallons of oil, followed by liberal quantities of pitch, over the victims. As a final preliminary the mob stepped aside to let a photographer take several pictures. Reed and Cato were now ready for burning.

The executioners had done their job well. A lighted match turned the stump into an inferno, causing frenzied cheers from thousand of onlookers. Paul Reed died first, losing consciousness within three minutes. Will Cato was not so fortunate. The flames fastened on his oil-soaked hair; the hemp rope became a collar of fire around his neck. Screaming and begging to be shot, Cato was left to writhe in agony while some in the crowd threw chunks of wood at his head. Finally someone mercifully leaned over and knocked him unconscious with a club. As the mob began to disperse some stayed behind, feeding the fire until little remained of the two bodies. Late that afternoon souvenir hunters combed the area, picking up charred bones and other remnants. Conspicuous among lynchers and later crowds were a number of small boys in knee pants.[34]

Cato's and Reed's deaths triggered more violence. Throughout the region night riders assaulted blacks indiscriminately, forcing many from their homes. At least two black men were killed, neither suspected in the Hodges murders.[35] The Statesboro affair

33. Robert M. Hitch to A. J. Scott, Acting Attorney General, Aug. 17, 1904, photo copy from Correspondence of the Adjutant General, Georgia Department of Archives and History. Later, when asked why he cooperated with the mob at the courthouse, Sheriff Kendrick replied: "Well, they were going in there anyhow; what was the use of letting them break up state property?" *Ibid.*

34. Descriptions of the Statesboro lynchings are found in Savannah *Morning News,* Savannah *Press,* Atlanta *Constitution,* and Atlanta *Journal,* Aug. 16–17, 1904.

35. Atlanta *Constitution,* Aug. 18, 1904.

attracted national attention. Northern papers featured mob atrocities, while the southern press emphasized the original crime. Labeling lynching "a grievous offense against law and morality," the Atlanta *Journal* went on to ask: "Where is the man who can wholly condemn those who on yesterday avenged the cruel murder of the Hodges family?"[36] The citizens of Statesboro apparently agreed, for they convicted no one for the lynching of Cato and Reed, despite the fact that practically all the mob leaders were well known to city and county officials.[37]

A major cause of the Statesboro violence was an atmosphere of fear permeating the white community after the Hodges murders. This was no new development. Antebellum plantation owners had worried that their slaves might follow the example of Nat Turner, and for a time after the Civil War the black man became a political as well as a physical threat. The plantation system still predominated in the early twentieth century, leaving white farmers isolated and outnumbered by blacks. (The Hodges family lived three-quarters of a mile from the nearest house, which was inhabited by a black man.) Immediately after the Hodges killings a false rumor circulated that blacks had organized "Before Day Clubs" to execute whites. One state officeholder said he and his wife would never return to their south Georgia home:

> The Hodges murder showed what the negro is capable of. . . . Take a white family living on a plantation with forty or fifty negro families and the nearest white neighbor two or three miles away, and men, women, and children are at the mercy of the blacks. My wife says that when the people vote me out of office I must hunt another job, for she is not going back to her old home.[38]

White women occasionally let their racial fantasies run wild. One April Fools' Day two white boys blackened their faces and set out across Cordelia to scare their married sister. They succeeded, and she shot one of them dead. And in Madison the town's white ladies became hysterical when they saw yellow flags em-

36. Atlanta *Journal,* Aug. 17, 1904.
37. Hitch to Scott, Aug. 17, 1904, Adjutant General's Correspondence.
38. Savannah *Press,* Aug. 22, 1904.

blazoned with the word "SURRENDER," certain it was the signal for a black uprising. Extra police were put on duty before a business firm admitted the flags were part of an advertising scheme.[39]

Frightened whites had exaggerated but not wholly unfounded fears of blacks. The belief that racial violence during the progressive era consisted entirely of whites attacking and killing defenseless Negroes is misleading. In any racial confrontation whites had advantages, including control of all law enforcement, yet black people were not always intimidated. At times whites were victims of black criminals. Often black violence was a spontaneous reaction of poor farmers against such authority figures as landlords and sheriffs. Urban interracial clashes were more likely to occur in black neighborhoods between unemployed men and white police. The black man who killed a white person was, if caught, either lynched or legally executed, and his family might suffer reprisal. Despite the almost unlimited power of whites, a surprising number of black men and women fought back.

Violence was frequent in rural areas, where the master-slave relationship was still evident. Prosperity for a white plantation owner depended on control over a cheap labor supply, and he often used intimidation and force. The black tenant protesting working conditions did so at his peril. Shootings sometimes resulted from wage disputes. An owner who killed his tenant pleaded self-defense and went free (often without even a trial). If a black farmer shot his landlord, legal and extra-legal forces combined to capture and kill him, for he posed a threat to the economic system and white supremacy. In such cases lynchings and court sentences served the same purpose: upholding the system. Frustrated over lack of legal recourse, blacks did react violently to injustice. When a young sharecropper named Sam Conley saw his mother beaten senseless by their landlord, he killed the white man and fled. That evening a mob abducted Conley's mother, shot her to death, and left her body on a public highway.[40] Minor disagreements had tragic consequences. Two black sharecroppers killed their landlord, ostensibly because he

39. Atlanta *Constitution*, Apr. 12, 1916; Albert Bushnell Hart, *The Southern South* (New York, 1910), 164.
40. *Crisis*, 13 (Jan., 1917), 112–13; Atlanta *Constitution*, Oct. 5, 1916.

refused them permission to attend a funeral. A black minister named John Harvard was burned at the stake after a gun battle with a white man whose car had frightened Harvard's mules.[41]

Sexual attacks on black women also led to violence. Although retaliation for black assaults on white women made headlines, newspapers suppressed stories about black men defending their women against whites. When a black man, T. W. Walker, killed wealthy white planter C. S. Hollinshead, the local newspaper termed the murder unprovoked. A black Atlanta editor named Julius St. George White got himself convicted of libel for revealing that the planter had assaulted Walker's wife.[42] After three young white farmers "of good standing" murdered a black minister who had been defending his wife against their sexual advances, the official report stated that the men killed the minister "for some reason undisclosed." All three won acquittal despite positive identification by the minister's wife.[43] In Milan, located in the wiregrass county of Telfair, two young white men went to the black district at night and tried to rape the two daughters of Mrs. Emma McCollers, a widow. Their screams attracted Berry Washington, age seventy-two, an active member of the A.M.E. Church. Protecting the young ladies, Washington shot and killed one of the assailants, John Dowdy, and then turned himself in to the police. A mob took the old man from jail and hanged him from a post. The county commissioner asked local editors to suppress the story, and Georgia newspapers did not acknowledge the lynching until two months later, after NAACP investigators had released details to the northern press.[44] It is impossible to determine how many black men died defending their women, or the number of whites killed after assaulting black women, for white society was embarrassed by these incidents and tried to keep them quiet.

Poor law enforcement was responsible for much violence

41. Atlanta *Journal*, Dec. 4, 1904; Atlanta *Constitution*, Dec. 2, 1909.

42. Atlanta *Independent*, July 6, 1912. White was convicted; he lost his job as a mail carrier, and his paper, the *Georgia Broad Axe*, folded.

43. *Crisis*, 3 (Jan., 1912), 101; Savannah *Tribune*, Dec. 7, 1918.

44. "A Lynching Uncovered by the NAACP," pamphlet in NAACP Papers; Atlanta *Constitution*, July 25, 1919; Hugh M. Dorsey to Richard G. Knott, editor of the Louisville *Evening Post*, July 30, 1919, Hugh M. Dorsey Papers, Georgia Department of Archives and History. Governor Dorsey told the Louisville editor that the NAACP story was true, and that he had offered a reward for information leading to arrest and conviction of the lynchers. No one was convicted.

against blacks. With few exceptions police officers came from the lower socioeconomic class, lacked education, and shared the prejudice of their peers. Policemen enjoyed status and power denied them as sharecroppers or unskilled laborers. Many were corrupt and unreliable. Almost a quarter of the force on duty during the Atlanta riot was fired within the following three months, charged with drunkenness on the beat, neglect of duty, robbery, and other offenses.[45] More dismissals resulted from a 1910 investigation. These periodic purges did not noticeably improve law enforcement.[46] Black neighborhoods suffered from police lawlessness ranging from false arrests to the Atlanta murder of a ten-year-old boy carrying lunch to his brother. (The child ran when an officer ordered him to halt.[47])

Equally tragic was lack of police protection for blacks. As long as crimes involved whites against blacks or blacks against each other, police were lax in apprehending the guilty. When criminal activity was confined to black areas, most whites remained unaware or complacent. White Atlantans ignored "Jack the Ripper" murders of black women until their terrified maids refused to come to work. Only then did city officials press police to find the murderer.[48] And when the spirit of Judge Lynch was in the air, police all too frequently assisted the mob's work.

Given this adversary relationship, blacks at times struck back at police. Over a dozen Georgia sheriffs and town marshals, along with numerous policemen and constables, met death at the hands of black men during the first twenty years of this century. Most officers were shot attempting to make arrests. Although black leaders did not publicly condone these acts, there was little mourning for the dead lawmen in the black community.[49] Whites reacted to attacks on police as they did to rape. Symbolizing the

45. Crowe, "Racial Massacre in Atlanta," 157; Atlanta *Journal*, Oct. 10, 1906. See also Eugene J. Watts, "The Police in Atlanta, 1890–1915," *Journal of Southern History*, 39 (May, 1973), 165–82. Watts points out that Atlanta police were relatively well paid.
46. Atlanta *Constitution*, Dec. 7, 11, 12, 1910.
47. *Ibid.*, Jan. 4, 1912; Oct. 14, 1915.
48. *Crisis*, 2 (Sept., 1911), 186.
49. *Ibid.*, 2 (Oct., 1911), 233; 11 (Mar., 1916), 222; 15 (Apr., 1918), 300; Atlanta *Journal*, Jan. 10, 1904; Savannah *Tribune*, Aug. 30, 1902; Oct. 10, 1903; Atlanta *Independent*, Oct. 24, 1908; Atlanta *Constitution*, Apr. 6, 1909; Aug. 19, 1911; Jan. 21, 1916.

white southern way of life, the lawman was a caretaker of the color line and a defender of the caste system; to attack him was to assault the whole of white society. When Police Chief J. B. Williams of Monticello entered Daniel Barber's house to arrest him on a bootlegging charge, Barber and his family beat him up. After other police arrived and arrested the Barbers, 200 enraged townspeople stormed the jail and dragged Barber, his son, and two daughters to a tall pine tree half a mile away in the middle of the Negro district. There they hanged the family one by one. The last to die, Barber witnessed the execution of his children.[50]

With proliferation of small counties in Georgia, decentralized law enforcement also aided white mobs. The "good old boys" who elected the county sheriff and judge were the same men who did the lynching. No sheriff or judge lost·an election for failure ·to prevent a lynching or convict the lynchers. The member of the mob felt confident that no law officer would harm him, nor would any jury of his neighbors convict him. Judge Charles H. Brand of Lawrenceville, whose refusal to call for troops resulted in three lynchings, justified his failure to take action:

> I don't propose to be the engine of sacrificing any white man's life for all such Negro criminals in the country. I would not imperil the life of one white man to save the lives of a hundred such Negroes. I am opposed to lynching, but if I had called the military and some young man among the soldiers was killed or some of the citizens of Walton County were killed I would never forgive myself.[51]

Georgia senators filibustered federal anti-lynching proposals and state legislators never enacted a statute effectively proscribing local autonomy. As a result, lynchers continued to go free.[52]

50. Savannah *Tribune,* Jan. 23, 30, 1915; Atlanta *Journal,* Jan. 15, 1915; *Crisis,* 9 (Mar., 1915), 225–28.

51. *Crisis,* 2 (Aug., 1911), 142–43. There were some exceptions. In Valdosta a jailor faced down an angry mob of would-be lynchers with this threat: "We are not going to have any foolishness around here tonight . . . and if you don't move away from here, they'll have to haul some of you away in wagons. We have got rifles, pistols, and shotguns in here and we can kill at least half your crowd while you are breaking in that door. Hit another lick and we'll start the hell-raisin' right here yet, do you hear. . . ." Of course, the circumstances here were somewhat different—the lynch mob the jailor was addressing was black! Savannah *Morning News,* Aug. 31, 1906.

52. A bill introduced in the Georgia legislature in 1916 would have permitted the state to remove sheriffs who did not try to prevent lynchings. The House

Violent behavior was commonplace in Georgia throughout the progressive era. Victims of the white mob and the judicial system, black Georgians did not always remain passive. Armed resistance during the Atlanta riot was repeated on a smaller scale across the state in numerous racial skirmishes. The conciliatory rhetoric of Booker T. Washington was giving way to the Niagara Movement's militant voices, advising black people to "arm yourselves, and when the mob invades your home, shoot and shoot to kill."[53] While educated blacks advocated self-defense, others acted more impulsively, taking a toll of white sheriffs, landlords, and other authority figures. Most of these aggressive blacks were poor illiterates who usually paid in kind for the death of their antagonists. Few had stated ideological concerns; most never heard of Du Bois and knew little about Washington. They probably did not see their acts as revolutionary. They did not stop white violence; perhaps they increased it. Leading members of their own race denounced them. Yet these "crimes" bear testimony to the racist character of society, and to the desperation of those who risked death rather than live imprisoned in Georgia's caste system.

defeated this measure, 113–29. A.M.E. Church, Ga. Conf., *Minutes*, 1st sess., Nov. 22–26, 1916.

53. *Horizon*, 4 (Sept., 1908), 1–3.

The Politics of Education

THE CONVICTION that formal education was the key to the good life drew thousands of newly freed slaves to schools opened by northern philanthropists. The sight of black children and their parents attending classes taught by New England missionaries in makeshift school buildings became common throughout the South. Nearly half of Georgia's black population was literate in 1900, proof of the remarkable progress made since slavery. Despite the increased number of blacks receiving some schooling, the earlier view of education as a panacea gave way to realities of the caste system, where a high school diploma or a college degree could even be a handicap.[1]

Georgia provided no operative public school system until 1858, and the Civil War destroyed this initial effort. Illiteracy among whites soared during the 1860s: at the end of the decade 125,000 white people over age ten could neither read nor write. Public schools began recovery in the mid-1870s and the state constitution of 1877 established free public elementary schools and a state university. High schools did not receive state funds, and as late as 1903 there were only seven four-year high schools producing ninety-four graduates. The gap between elementary school and university existed long after a 1912 law made the high school part of the public school system.[2] The state's poor financial position retarded public education, but almost as dam-

1. W. E. B. Du Bois, ed., *The Negro Common School*, Atlanta University *Publications* No. 6 (Atlanta, 1901), 18; *Twelfth Census, Population*, II, pt. 1, cxv; Gaston, "Negro Wage Earner," 26.
2. Dorothy Orr, *A History of Education in Georgia* (Chapel Hill, 1950), 173, 176, 207, 224–25, 263–64.

aging was the taxpayer's failure to realize the importance of schools. Lack of a compulsory attendance law kept Georgia lagging behind the nation in public school development.

The *Plessy* v. *Ferguson* decision of 1896 had given legal sanction to separate schools for blacks and whites. Georgia officials ignored the separate *but equal* clause. Some whites saw value in teaching reading, writing, and industrial arts to black children; most were suspicious of anything beyond a bare elementary education. Former governor Allen D. Candler wrote in 1901: "I do not believe in the higher education of the darky. He should be taught the trades, but when he is taught the fine arts he gets educated above his caste and it makes him unhappy."[3] Clark Howell complained to philanthropist George Foster Peabody that although Atlanta had more than 40,000 Negroes, it was almost impossible to find good domestic help. "It is an easy enough matter to go out and get a Greek or Latin graduate," wrote Howell, "but they do not want domestic work." The Atlanta editor called for more Negro schools devoted to "turning out well-equipped household servants, coachmen, gardeners, farm laborers and the like."[4]

Some school officials showed hostility toward all black education. A delegate to a 1906 meeting of county commissioners in south Georgia introduced a resolution that a commissioner should hire the least qualified of two or more black applicants for a teaching position. The resolution failed, but received strong support, and Atlanta University researchers believed this in fact was the practice in many rural districts.[5] Afraid that college-educated black teachers could not be trusted "to teach the Negro his place," a number of school authorities preferred to hire half-trained graduates from industrial schools at low wages for four-month school terms. These same officials often complained that their Negro teachers lacked education and "culture."[6]

Several movements began in the early 1900s to divide the school fund on the basis of taxes paid by each race. Proponents

3. Atlanta *Constitution*, Apr. 25, 1901.
4. Clark Howell to George F. Peabody, Nov. 10, 1906, copy in Baker Papers.
5. W. E. B. Du Bois and A. G. Dill, eds., *The Common School and the Negro American*, Atlanta University *Publications* No. 16 (Atlanta, 1911), 101.
6. *Ibid.*, 106.

claimed that, because blacks paid little property tax, whites assumed the burden of educating both races. To counter this pressure Du Bois, John Hope, and other black educators petitioned the Georgia legislature in 1900, contending that ownership was an unfair criterion for tax separation, because it was not the owner but the one working the land who generated the tax revenue.[7] Blacks also contributed their share of taxes on liquor, fertilizer, and other revenue sources comprising nearly 45 percent of the school fund. A white school superintendent analyzed the state superintendent's fiscal report for 1907 and showed that blacks were not merely supporting their own schools; they were paying for educating white children as well.[8] The school fund was never divided. Arguments of blacks and white moderates did have some effect, but the status quo was maintained by black belt legislators satisfied with the existing means of state distribution (based on all school-age children in each county) and local allocation (based on race). All superintendents in black belt counties awarded white schools a grossly disproportionate share of state funds. The following table shows per capita expenditures for Georgia counties in 1910, grouped according to percentage of black population.[9]

Percent of blacks in population	Per capita for white child	Per capita for black child
Under 10%	$ 4.20	$2.39
10-25%	5.77	2.42
25-50%	10.06	2.20
50-75%	12.34	1.50
75% and over	19.23	1.61

Black teachers were paid less, school facilities were inferior, and school terms were usually shorter than for whites. Libraries and four-year high schools for blacks were nonexistent.

The Georgia Commissioner of Education lamented that day

7. Du Bois, ed., *Negro Common School*, 93–95.
8. Charles L. Coon, "Public Taxation and Negro Schools," quoted in Du Bois and Dill, eds., *The Common School*, 120, 125–26; Silas X. Floyd, "The Georgia School Fund," *Independent*, 54 (Jan. 16, 1902), 160–61.
9. Thomas Jesse Jones, *Negro Education. A Study of the Private and Higher Schools for Colored People in the United States*, Dept. of the Interior, Bureau of Education, Bulletin 1916, No. 39, II (Washington, 1917), 187.

laborers on the street were receiving higher pay than the average
district schoolteacher.[10] A white teacher in 1905 earned an average monthly salary of $42.85, while the black instructor averaged
$19.88.[11] In rural areas teachers sometimes signed contracts stipu-
lating payment of a few cents a week for each pupil taught. And
in some places students had to pay part of the cost of their
"public" education: Mrs. Ella Daniels recalls paying her tuition
to the teacher in eggs.[12] Given these salaries it was inevitable
that many teachers, black and white, lacked adequate training.
Throughout the early twentieth century seven of every ten black
teachers had less than an eighth-grade education. Those with
college training usually worked in better urban areas like Atlanta,
where three-fourths of the city's black teachers had attended
Atlanta University.[13] The following note from a rural teacher
indicates how poorly trained some were:

my 12, 19011

Prof. —— I drop yo this card to let yo know that I will be in on
that early train munday morning tell mrs. markos to meet the train.

This woman taught more than a hundred students at the largest
school in the county, for which she was paid fourteen dollars each
working month. Since state funds were seldom available on time,
she may have had to discount her salary claim to a loan shark or,
like many rural teachers, kick back part of her salary to the
county superintendent.[14] Her economic situation made further
educational training unlikely.

Since their schools received less than 10 percent of the total
allocation for buildings, equipment, libraries, and maintenance,
many Negro communities had to provide facilities in churches,

10. *The Twenty-ninth Annual Report from the Department of Education to the General Assembly of the State of Georgia for 1900* (Atlanta, 1901), 13.
11. Orr, *Education in Georgia*, 317; Dept. of Education, *Report*, 1920 (Atlanta, 1921), 11.
12. Teaching contracts for George A. Towns, George A. Towns Collection, Negro Collection, Trevor Arnett Library, Atlanta University; interview between Henry Williams and Mrs. Ella M. Daniels, Aug. 14, 1973, Albany.
13. Jones, *Negro Education*, No. 39, II, 188; Du Bois and Dill, eds., *The Common School*, 61.
14. Du Bois and Dill, eds., *The Common School*, 106; Du Bois, ed., *Negro Common School*, 99; Dept. of Education, *Report*, 1900 (Atlanta, 1901), 13.

lodge halls, or deserted cabins.[15] For many rural children a typical school day meant walking five or six miles to the church where classes met, sitting on benches without backs, and often working by candlelight in unheated rooms without blackboards. As late as 1915 county boards owned only 208 Negro schoolhouses worth an average of $116; blacks owned 1,544 public school buildings valued at $106 each.[16] Had communities not furnished buildings, many children would have been without schools. Noting that blacks had financed and built five public schools in 1909, Fulton County's school superintendent asserted that they *preferred* to put up their own buildings! Some districts financed new buildings for blacks by shutting down their old schools for a year and using teacher salaries to purchase building materials. As late as 1930 three-fourths of Georgia's Negro public schools were shabby, one-room affairs in remote rural areas.[17]

Short school terms, irregular attendance, and lack of educational facilities beyond the elementary level frustrated efforts to educate black children. The term was shortest in rural areas, where it was divided to coincide with cotton planting and picking seasons.[18] In Twiggs County, a cotton belt area with heavy black population, Amy Renfroe taught 131 students from all eight grades (for fifteen dollars a month). Holland Grove School in the same county had only four students reading on a fourth-grade level, although eighteen were above age twelve.[19] Educational opportunities in the state were so limited that a 1911 Atlanta University study concluded: "It is certain that of the Negro children 6 to 14 years of age not 50 percent had a chance today to learn to read and write and cipher correctly."[20]

15. Du Bois and Dill, eds., *The Common School*, 121.
16. *Ibid.*, 59; Dept. of Education, *Report*, 1920 (Atlanta, 1921), 84; Orr, *Education in Georgia*, 314, 318.
17. Du Bois and Dill, eds., *The Common School*, 58; Raper, *Tenants of the Almighty*, 138; Orr, *Education in Georgia*, 335.
18. NAACP files, Atlanta branch, 1919–21, NAACP Papers; Thomas Jesse Jones, *Negro Education. A Study of the Private and Higher Schools for Colored People in the United States*, Dept. of the Interior, Bureau of Education, Bulletin 1916, No. 38, I (Washington, 1917), 35.
19. Twiggs County Board of Education, *Annual Report*, 1905, 1907, Twiggs County Board of Education Papers, Special Collection, University of Georgia Library.
20. "Resolutions of the Sixteenth Annual Conference," in Du Bois and Dill, eds., *The Common School*, 7–8.

Public education was a dead end for ambitious black youths. No public four-year high school existed, and only a handful of cities offered them any high school courses at all. Atlanta, Augusta, and Savannah had a combined black population of over 100,000, yet these cities not only failed to provide black secondary schools, they even eliminated the eighth grade from Negro elementary schools. The General Assembly passed a bill in 1906 to create eleven white agricultural high schools, one in each congressional district, to be supported by revenues from a fertilizer tax. Although black farmers paid the tax, there were to be no black agricultural schools.[21] The only route to secondary education for blacks lay through the seventeen four-year private high schools, enrolling about 2,000 students. Concentrated in urban areas, especially Atlanta, these schools were inaccessible to most children.[22]

From selecting the teachers to buying the chalk, whites ran black public schools. Superintendents hired tractable instructors and often made short shrift of those who thought independently. (A capable teacher in Palmetto, for example, lost his job for voicing approval of Booker T. Washington's dining with whites.[23]) President of the Chatham County Board of Education George A. Mercer required black schoolchildren to memorize and sing his composition "Goin' Back to Dixie," a defense of the caste system which praised the white South and condemned the North, where Negroes reportedly froze to death. Protests against Mercer's demand were unsuccessful, and continued agitation by local leaders for some community control led the General Assembly to pass a law reaffirming the Chatham County school board's authority over black education.[24] Blacks petitioned for more schools, higher pay for teachers, longer terms, and public high schools in other cities—usually without success.

Black efforts to improve public schools were more profitable in Atlanta, the state's largest system. A 1913 Russell Sage Foundation investigation of Atlanta public schools found slightly more

21. Orr, *Education in Georgia,* 275, 319; Du Bois and Dill, eds., *The Common School,* 127–29.

22. Jones, *Negro Education,* No. 39, II, 190.

23. J. H. Adams, "Rough Sketches," *The Voice,* 4 (June, 1907), 240.

24. George Anderson Mercer Papers, 1904–7, Georgia State Historical Society; *Georgia Laws,* 1907, pp. 975–76.

than half of 10,000 black school-aged children enrolled. For its
17,000 white children Atlanta provided thirty-eight grammar
schools, a boys' high school, a high school and commercial school
for girls, and five night schools. Black children were allotted but
eleven grammar schools. Most black teachers taught double shifts
in overcrowded classrooms; an instructor frequently met sixty
children from nine until noon, and another sixty from one until
four in the afternoon. Two-thirds of the classes were on double
shifts, yet hundreds of children were turned away for lack of
room. Conditions in most schools were unsanitary, with classrooms adjoining open toilets. At Summer Hill School children
huddled in a corner on rainy days to keep dry, and in the Roach
Street School pupils in basement rooms studied by candlelight
on cloudy days. Superintendent of Schools William Slaton admitted that some schools were "a disgrace to civilization and unfit
for cattle to be herded in."[25]

Black Atlantans protested. A group of women led by Mrs.
Lugenia Hope organized a civic improvement committee in 1914,
achieving limited results. More effective was the young Atlanta
NAACP's staunch opposition to a 1917 plan to provide funds for
a new white junior high school by abolishing the seventh grade
in black schools.[26] Two years later the same group organized the
black community to defeat a citywide bond referendum. (While
the disfranchisement law and the poll tax had eliminated black
voting potential in most areas of the state, Atlanta remained a
city where the black vote could be decisive in any election not
governed by the white primary and of significant interest to the
black community.) Atlanta blacks had previously supported
school bond issues, supplying the winning margin in a 1903 referendum and contributing to passage of a 1910 issue. Both times
white leaders failed to deliver on promises to provide better educational facilities for blacks.[27] The NAACP quietly began voter
registration in 1919, adding over a thousand voters in a campaign
so tightly organized that one daily newspaper reported the regis-

25. *Crisis*, 5 (Feb., 1913), 165; (Mar., 1913), 279; 9 (Feb., 1915), 182;
Atlanta *Constitution*, Oct. 10, 1913.
26. Walter F. White to Roy Nash, Mar. 3, 1917, Branch File, NAACP Papers.
See also Edgar A. Toppin, "Walter White and the Atlanta NAACP's Fight for
Equal Schools, 1916–1917," *History of Education Quarterly*, 7 (1967), 3–21.
27. Atlanta *Independent*, Jan. 30, 1904; Sept. 23, 1911.

tration drive was *for* the bonds. When the black vote defeated the
bond issue the Atlanta *Georgian,* considered one of the South's
leading progressive dailies, charged that "The Negroes—stupidly
in the light of their own real interest, but led by shrewd white
men ready to use them to the limit—voted solidly against every-
thing."[28]

The NAACP proved blacks had taken it upon themselves to
defeat the issue, and listed eight grievances to be met before the
black community would support more bonds. White authorities
did not respond, and blacks twice defeated the next bond issue.
Finally, after the city administration specifically pledged $1,250,-
000 for black schools, the issue passed.[29] In 1924 the first four-
year public secondary school in Atlanta, Booker T. Washington
High School, opened its doors.

This successful attempt to gain more school funds did not alter
the policy of giving a disproportionate share of local and state
money to white schools. However, Atlanta's blacks proved that
organization and voter strength could wring concessions from an
unsympathetic government. Elsewhere in the state there was less
progress, and as late as 1930 no more than half the black population had reached the third grade. On the other hand, the first two
decades of the century saw renewed interest and progress in educating whites. Their public high schools increased in number
from 12 in 1905 to 169 in 1920; in 1921 the state appropriated
over $1,000,000 for white colleges and only $25,000 for two sub-
standard black schools. The gap between public school opportunities for whites and blacks, already wide in 1900, continued
to grow. Frustrated by the inadequacies of public education,
blacks turned to private schools.[30]

In 1913 the seventy-eight private schools enrolled over 11,500
black students. Of these, about 9,300 attended elementary
schools, 2,100 went to secondary schools, and 150 enrolled in the
six black colleges. Private elementary schools, at times an alterna-

28. Quoted in *Crisis,* 18 (June, 1919), 90–91.
29. Bacote, "Negro in Atlanta Politics," 342.
30. Louis R. Harlan, *Separate and Unequal, Public School Campaigns and
Racism in the Southern Seaboard States, 1901–1915* (Chapel Hill, 1958), 259;
Orr, *Education in Georgia,* 275, 327; Willard F. Range, *The Rise and Progress of
Negro Colleges in Georgia, 1865–1943,* Phelps-Stokes Fellowship *Studies* No. 15
(Athens, Ga., 1951), 180.

tive to public education, often were the only schools available. Of the thirty-two schools offering some secondary work, seventeen had full four-year programs. (Black colleges also offered high school work, with classes taught by college faculty.) Training elementary teachers was an important function of secondary schools, and normal programs were established to meet that need.[31]

Private schools often included both elementary and secondary programs. Northern organizations, usually white church denominations, operated a number of these institutions, while others were founded, staffed, and administered by Georgia blacks. An example of the former was St. Athanasius School in Brunswick, near the coast, run by the American Church Institute of the Protestant Episcopal Church. Its principal, William Augustine Perry, was a Yale man. St. Athanasius emphasized academic rather than industrial training, and its curriculum resembled that of northern white schools: high school freshmen read Dickens's *Christmas Carol* and Cooper's *Last of the Mohicans,* while upperclassmen studied the essays of Emerson, Addison, and Bacon. Half the St. Athanasius faculty members were Fisk and Atlanta University alumni, but some denominations preferred to staff their schools with white teachers. In nearby Savannah, for example, the American Missionary Association of the Congregational Church established Beach Institute after the Civil War, and as late as World War I its faculty consisted entirely of white northerners.[32] In contrast were the institutions founded by Georgia blacks. Although financial exigencies doomed some operations to failure, thousands of black children were educated in these schools.

Probably the best private elementary and secondary school in the state was Haines Institute in Augusta, whose guiding spirit was its founder, Miss Lucy Craft Laney.[33] Born in Macon in 1854 of parents who had once been slaves, Miss Laney was a member

31. Jones, *Negro Education,* No. 39, II, 14, 188, 190; Orr, *Education in Georgia,* 295.

32. *Worth, A Monthly Publication of St. Athanasius School,* Nov., 1915–May, 1918, microfilm, Georgia Department of Archives and History; Jones, *Negro Education,* No. 39, II, 197.

33. Edward T. Ware to Walter Fleming, Dec. 7, 1911, Edward Twichell Ware Papers, Atlanta University Archives, Negro Collection, Trevor Arnett Library, Atlanta University.

of Atlanta University's first graduating class in 1873. After teaching in the public schools for a decade she launched the institution
she would lead for the next half-century. Named after a northern
Presbyterian philanthropist, Haines Institute began in one room
with Miss Laney and a few students. By 1915 its city-block
campus served 860 students, taught by a faculty of twenty-eight.
As in most elementary programs, students at Haines concentrated on the three R's, along with some history and geography.
The secondary program required four years of English and math-
ematics and three years of history. Students could choose such
electives as chemistry and physics, psychology and sociology,
French and German.[34]

Lucy Laney was a no-nonsense administrator who would not
brook foolishness. Haines students wore uniforms, and drill was
part of the routine. She believed in corporal punishment and did
not hesitate to "take a young man of eighteen years of age down
into the basement, throw him across a barrel and paddle him
until he could feel it." A former pupil summed up Miss Laney's
administrative philosophy when he said: "If you went to her
school it was to get an education, and if you stayed there she saw
that you got some education."[35] Her campus was both an educational facility and a sanctuary for its residents. Her niece, Miss
Louise Laney, recalls that as a first-grader at her aunt's school she
and her classmates lined up to be vaccinated against smallpox by
two white city doctors. When their methods and demeanor
frightened the children, Principal Laney ordered the physicians
off her campus, telling them the children's own doctors would
give the shots. For this she and one of her teachers were hauled
into court, charged with violating the city vaccination ordinance
and resisting arrest.[36] On another occasion, when a policeman
chased a suspect onto the Haines campus, Miss Laney chased the
officer away (sans suspect).[37]

Lucy Laney provided sound academic training for three gen-

34. Brawley, *Negro Builders and Heroes*, 280–81; Jones, *Negro Education*, No.
39, II, 237.
35. Wright, *87 Years Behind the Black Curtain*, 32.
36. Interview with Miss Louise Laney, July 17, 1974, Augusta. Reports of the
incident were also recorded in the Atlanta *Independent*, Dec. 7, 1907, and
Horizon, 2 (Dec. 7, 1907), 15–16.
37. Interview with Miss Louise Laney, July 17, 1974.

erations of students, but she also did much more: her courage, wisdom, and dedication inspired thousands of boys and girls growing up black in Georgia. "I am as good as anybody else," she once said. "God had no different dirt to make me out of than that used in making the first lady of the land."[39] Today her portrait stands in the Georgia capitol, alongside those of Bishop Henry McNeal Turner and Dr. Martin Luther King, Jr. It is only fitting that she be in such company.

The private colleges also represented the strength and hope of Black Georgia. Men like W. E. B. Du Bois, John Hope, and Benjamin Brawley taught and influenced hundreds of black youths, who became leaders of the state's black educational, religious, and business community. Aside from Paine College in Augusta, all colleges with four-year programs were located in Atlanta. In 1865 the American Missionary Association started Atlanta University in an old boxcar. Supported and controlled by the A.M.A. during its early years, A.U. became independent in the 1870s.[39] The American Baptist Home Mission Society founded Atlanta Baptist College for men (later changed to Morehouse College) in 1867, and Spelman Seminary for women in 1881. Clark University opened its doors in 1870, launched by the Freedmen's Aid Society of the Methodist Episcopal Church, which also supported Gammon Theological Seminary, a small but well-endowed institution devoted to training ministers. Morris Brown University, founded in 1881, was the only black-operated college, owned, maintained, and managed by the African Methodist Episcopal Church. White southern Methodists ran Paine College, founded in 1884, in cooperation with the Collored Methodist Episcopal Church. Although all six of these institutions offered college subjects, only Atlanta Baptist College and Atlanta University had the faculty, facilities, and enrollment to justify the name "college." Their alumni competed successfully with graduates of southern white colleges on standardized tests and in advanced work at northern universities.[40]

38. *Crimson and Gray*, 22 (Feb., 1939), 6.

39. Bacote, *Story of Atlanta University*, 5, 121.

40. *Scroll*, 7 (Apr., 1903), 76; W. E. B. Du Bois and A. G. Dill, eds., *The College-Bred Negro American*, Atlanta University *Publications* No. 15 (Atlanta, 1910), 22. W. E. B. Du Bois, ed., *The College-Bred Negro*, Atlanta University

Northern whites closely associated with leading academic centers controlled all the black colleges except Paine and Morris Brown. At the turn of the century the black college curriculum was still traditional, with heavy emphasis upon ancient languages. Thus the Atlanta University freshman could look forward to a year with such required courses as Xenophon's *Anabasis* and Cicero's *De Senectute* and *De Amicitia*. Until at least 1910 each A.U. student took a third of his courses in foreign languages, while undergraduates at Clark wrestled with languages in nearly half their classes. College preparatory students at Morris Brown took four years of Latin and three of Greek.[41] Black colleges retained the traditional curriculum longer than northern white schools, where the liberalizing trend away from ancient languages toward more emphasis on the social and physical sciences had begun in the late nineteenth century. Atlanta University was the first black college in Georgia to break out of the old pattern, stressing modern rather than ancient languages. By 1920 A.U. students could take but a year and a half of foreign language, and they could choose French or German over Greek and Latin. Influenced by Du Bois, the college also gave increasing attention to sociology and history, offering 19 percent of its courses in that area in 1910 (compared with 13 percent at Fisk and 10 percent at Howard). And along with Morehouse, A.U. provided a more flexible curriculum by increasing student electives and offerings in the physical and social sciences.[42]

Along with this liberalization in academic requirements, black studies became part of the curriculum. The Atlanta colleges were

---

Publications No. 5 (Atlanta, 1900), 17. It was not uncommon for graduates of black and white schools in the South to enroll in undergraduate programs of Ivy League colleges, usually as juniors or seniors. Atlanta University was proud that its graduates competed so well against southern whites. When an A.U. graduate, James T. Gates, took his A.B. degree at Harvard in 1912, Atlanta University officials were quick to note that Cates "graduated with distinction. . . . Of the twelve graduates from Georgia, he was the only colored man and the only man to get honors." *Crimson and Gray*, 3 (Oct., 1912), 1.

41. Atlanta University *Catalogue*, 1899–1900, p. 7; Jones, *Negro Education*, No. 39, II, 213, 216, 219, 221, 238; Du Bois and Dill, eds., *The College-Bred Negro American*, 20; for excellent material on the role of whites in the development of black colleges, see James M. McPherson, *The Abolitionist Legacy: From Reconstruction to the NAACP* (Princeton, 1975).

42. Atlanta University *Catalogue*, 1920, p. 10; Du Bois and Dill, eds., *The College-Bred Negro American*, 20.

first to respond to the growth in racial consciousness and pride. Already by 1905 Benjamin Brawley had introduced a course in Negro American history at Spelman and Morehouse, while Du Bois began promoting African and Afro-American studies when he joined the Atlanta University faculty in 1897. A.U. juniors took required courses from Du Bois in African history and the "Economic History of the Negro American," while seniors enrolled in Sociology II, the "Social Condition of the Negro American."[43] Of particular significance were the Atlanta University *Publications*, a series of twenty monographs on the condition of blacks in America, published between 1896 and 1920. Director of sixteen of the studies, Du Bois at first believed that scientific investigations of the Afro-American experience would alleviate the race problem by exposing racist myths. The plan, to investigate a different aspect of Negro life each year and to repeat the same research topic every ten years, would compile "a continuous record of the condition and development of ten to twenty millions of men."[44] Du Bois noted in 1904 that few whites saw the necessity and significance of the work, and he later observed that, although they were widely read, the studies were not treated seriously by academicians. "We rated merely as Negroes studying Negroes," he concluded, "and after all what had Negroes to do with America or science?"[45] Nonetheless, Atlanta University was one of the first colleges in the South to engage in sociological research, particularly in the area of urban studies, and investigations of black Americans provided A.U. students with an excellent learning opportunity.[46]

If black students were beginning to learn more about their own past, their collegiate environment was still that of puritan New England. Schoolmasters were rigid disciplinarians. Rules regulating student conduct were strict, though tempered by paternalism. Students attended "daily prayers" and church on Sunday, in addition to special evening meetings of such organizations as the Social Purity Society and Christian Endeavor. Drinking,

43. Atlanta University *Catalogue*, 1909–10, p. 13; 1905–6, p. 7.
44. W. E. B. Du Bois, "The Atlanta Conferences," *Voice of the Negro*, 1 (Mar., 1904), 88; Bacote, *Story of Atlanta University*, 135–39.
45. W. E. B. Du Bois, *The Autobiography of W. E. B. Du Bois* (New York, 1968), 228; Du Bois, "Atlanta Conferences," 88.
46. Bacote, *Story of Atlanta University*, 136.

smoking, gambling, fighting, loud talk, and tardiness were punishable offenses.[47] Spelman girls were carefully regimented. Awakened at 5:45, they marched to the dining room an hour later, where at the tap of a bell they sat down and sang a blessing. The girls performed house-cleaning tasks after breakfast until classes began at 8:15; instruction lasted all day with a short lunch break. Dinner was promptly at 5:00; a short chapel service followed at 6:15. Students spent weekday evenings in study hall, except for Fridays, when a lecture or concert brought diversion. A bell at 9:00 signaled the "goodnight song" and retirement. On Sunday mornings the girls could sleep fifteen minutes extra.[48]

Regimentation was not peculiar to black institutions, for the Spelman routine followed that of Vassar, Mount Holyoke, and Oberlin; however, officials in black schools were radically changing the lifestyle of their students. Dancing, a popular pastime in the black community, was pronounced immoral and outlawed. At dinner students received instruction on the "correct" way to handle themselves and their food. Church services, reflecting the puritan spirit, lacked the enthusiasm of black worship, and black music, except for spirituals, was banned. Puritan discipline carried to the drab clothes required for daily wear. Men and women were kept apart as much as possible. In Atlanta University's early days a male student had to get a pass signed by the president or dean in order to visit a young lady for twenty minutes a month.[49]

The paternalism of college administrators at times gave way to heavy-handed authoritarianism. When several Atlanta University baseball players walked off the field in the middle of a game to protest the substitution of a player they regarded as incompetent, President Edward T. Ware was shocked at the "breach of loyalty to Atlanta University which could not be overlooked."[50] Ware called a faculty meeting which resulted in expulsion of six of the offenders from the team—and from the university. Although angry alumni protested this action, Ware and his faculty held fast. Even Du Bois agreed with the punishment, warning his

---

47. Range, *Negro Colleges in Georgia*, 128, 137–39.
48. Florence Matilda Reed, *The Story of Spelman College* (Princeton, 1961), 155.
49. Range, *Negro Colleges in Georgia*, 127, 129, 140–41.
50. Ware to Edward Mickey, Apr., 7, 1910, Ware Papers.

president: "This is a time for unfaltering firmness. The suspended boys should leave the campus *today* and other boys should leave or go to their duties. Unless this firm stand is taken we shall have trouble."[51] And at Morehouse Du Bois's close friend John Hope followed the principle that "We ought to tell the young people what to do; and if more emphasis is given to positive commands and instructions, rather than prohibitions, we might make greater headway."[52] During the progressive era black and white administrators agreed on a narrow definition of student freedom. And while succeeding decades would bring gradual liberalization, the principle of absolute administrative authority would not be easily discarded on black college campuses.

Black colleges had serious financial problems and operated on limited budgets. Most students were from poor families and could pay only nominal tuition. The state gave no support to black colleges; few white Georgians made contributions. Under the Morrill Act of 1890 the federal government supported selected black schools, but in Georgia federal funds went only to Georgia State Industrial College in Savannah, an inadequate state-controlled elementary and secondary school.[53] Since black colleges in Georgia had to rely upon northern philanthropy, their presidents spent much time on the road soliciting donations. Sponsoring churches supplied major financial support in early postwar years, continuing as an important source of funds well into the twentieth century. Dependent on the American Baptist Home Mission Society, Morehouse and Spelman received additional money from John D. Rockefeller, who was especially interested in developing the latter school. Church sponsors provided three-fourths of Paine's $23,000 budget, Clark received over half its $16,000 income from the Freedmen's Aid Society, and Morris Brown raised 75 percent of its operating funds from various A.M.E. Church conferences throughout the state. Only Gammon Theological Seminary had a large endowment, which put it in the pleasantly embarrassing position of having an annual financial surplus.[54]

51. Du Bois to Ware, Mar. 29, 1910, Ware Papers. See also Ware to A. L. Tucker, Mar. 24, 1910, and Tucker to Ware, Mar. 29, 1910, *ibid.*
52. John Hope, in *A.M.E. Church Review,* 22 (Oct., 1915), 104.
53. Range, *Negro Colleges in Georgia,* 190–92.
54. Jones, *Negro Education,* No. 38, I, 333–38; *Negro Education,* No. 39, II, 212–23, 238–39.

An independent college, Atlanta University had the largest budget and the greatest financial problems. With three-fourths of its income from general donations, the college budget in 1900 was nearly $40,000 (compared with only $47,000 for the University of Georgia, the state's largest white college). A.U.'s reputation as one of the best southern schools had won influential northern friends, but its controversial position on race relations threatened its survival.[55] From its inception the college stood publicly for racial equality; unlike most black colleges, it enrolled white students, the children of professors. Failure to expel these white students in 1887 resulted in loss of an annual $8,000 appropriation from the state.[56] By the turn of the century, when the financial picture was bleak, fund-raising efforts were set back further when two Atlanta University professors publicly criticized Booker T. Washington.

The most influential man in black America, Washington could be a valuable ally or a powerful enemy. His concept of industrial education for the black masses struck a receptive chord among northern philanthropists. A Washington admirer, John D. Rockefeller organized the General Education Board in 1902 to aid education in the South. It quickly became "a sort of clearinghouse for southern education," influencing the Slater, Peabody, and Southern Education boards. Assisting Negro industrial schools such as Tuskegee and Hampton, these boards ignored academic institutions like Atlanta University.[57]

Leading the opposition to Washington was W. E. B. Du Bois. His chapter "Of Booker T. Washington and Others" in *The Souls of Black Folk* brought earlier disagreements into the open, and the Atlanta University study of *The Negro Artisan,* published in 1902, included a carefully written attack on industrial schools.[58] Du Bois did not oppose the idea of industrial education, but he did protest whites employing Washington's philosophy to strangle higher education for blacks. Upset by Du Bois's hostility

55. Range, *Negro Colleges in Georgia,* 101; W. E. B. Du Bois, "The Cultural Mission of Atlanta University," *Phylon,* 3 (Second Quarter, 1942), 108–9.
56. Bacote, *Story of Atlanta University,* 86–90.
57. Harlan, *Separate and Unequal,* 85–88; Horace Mann Bond, *The Education of the Negro in the American Social Order* (New York, 1934), 149.
58. Du Bois, ed., *The Negro Artisan,* 79–83.

toward Washington, New York financier and philanthropist George Foster Peabody (a native of Columbus, Georgia) complained to Atlanta University officials, who asked Du Bois to write Peabody explaining his position.[59] Both Du Bois and A.U. leaders were aware that his opinions were endangering the college's financial position. In 1908 President Ware wrote Harvey Fisk to learn why the General Education Board had frozen out Atlanta University that year. In his reply Fisk said that Dr. Wallace Buttrick, executive secretary of the G.E.B., "feels that Du Bois unconsciously is conveying to his students a feeling of unrest, which is not helpful to them." Buttrick would not change his mind about supporting the college.[60] Shortly before he resigned in 1910 to become editor of the *Crisis* Du Bois wrote: "I insist on my right to think and speak; but if that freedom is made an excuse for abuse or denial of aid to Atlanta University, then with regret I shall withdraw from Atlanta University." Du Bois's academic reputation kept school officials from seriously interfering with his work, but his last years at A.U. were marked by conflict with President Ware, who became increasingly concerned about the high price the school was paying for tolerating Du Bois's militant ideas.[61]

If Du Bois was above open administrative recrimination, his protégé, George A. Towns, was not. A young professor who had graduated from Atlanta University in 1894, Towns wrote a letter of support to Monroe Trotter, the radical black Boston *Guardian* editor jailed in October 1903 for disrupting a meeting addressed by Washington. Towns also expressed opposition to Washington, and the irrepressible Trotter published the letter. At that, Presi-

59. Herbert Aptheker, *Afro-American History: The Modern Era* (New York, 1971), 137–38. Du Bois's letter to Peabody is reprinted in Herbert Aptheker, ed., *A Documentary History of the Negro People in the United States,* I (New York, 1951), 881–83.
60. Harvey E. Fisk to Ware, Apr. 6, 1908, Ware Papers.
61. Du Bois, *Autobiography,* 229; Francis L. Broderick, *W. E. B. Du Bois: Negro Leader in Time of Crisis* (Stanford, 1959), 57; Ware to Horace Bumstead, Dec. 2, 10, 1909; Oct. 5, 1911; Du Bois to Ware, Jan. 25, 1912; Ware to Du Bois, Jan. 27, 1912, Ware Papers. Ware was less sympathetic with Du Bois's "extra-academic propaganda" than was his predecessor, Horace Bumstead. Du Bois's blasts at the white establishment upset Ware more than he would admit publicly. And Du Bois's "Litany at Atlanta" was, for the A.U. president, "nothing short of blasphemous." Ware to Bumstead, Mar. 13, 1908, *ibid.*

dent Horace Bumstead, in Boston at the time raising money, angrily wrote Towns that

> the publication in the *Guardian* of your letter to Mr. Trotter is making serious trouble for me and I fear will work considerable injury to the University and its cause. I can hardly believe that you wrote it for publication or consented to have it printed . . . it is one thing to express to Mr. Trotter sympathy with the general principle for which he is contending, and quite another thing to seem to endorse his intemperate utterances or condone his illegal action.[62]

A month later the college's board of trustees recorded "great astonishment and profound regret that such a letter could have been written, much more allowed to be published by a professor in Atlanta University. . . ." Perhaps Trotter was correct when he wrote Towns that "Booker was setting the white millionaires onto Bumstead to get after you for your letter to me."[63] Whatever the case, Atlanta University was in no position to countenance an attack on Washington by an upstart professor.

John Hope was another Washington opponent. Born in Augusta and educated first by Lucy Laney and then at Brown University, where he graduated with distinction, Hope became Atlanta Baptist's first black president in 1906. Two months after taking office he and other black radicals met at the annual convention of the Niagara Movement at Harpers Ferry, where he joined in a barefoot pilgrimage to the site of John Brown's last stand. Hope was the only president at Harpers Ferry and also the sole college head at the organizational meeting of what would become the NAACP. He took pride in his militancy and later wrote to Du Bois: "I have dared to live up to my views even when they threw me in the midst of the most radical." Then he added, "Furthermore, every man on our faculty does the same and will as long as I am head of the institution." Because of his strong political views and opposition to Washington, Hope found white philanthropists ignoring the appeals of his college. Only after he reluctantly permitted a friend to intercede with Wash-

---

62. Bumstead to Towns, Nov. 5, 1903, Towns Papers.
63. Bumstead to Towns, Dec. 5, 1903; Monroe Trotter to Towns, Jan. 2, 1904, *ibid*. Towns recovered from this censure, and he remained politically active while teaching with distinction at A.U. for thirty-four years.

ington did Atlanta Baptist begin to get the northern money it needed. But Hope remained consistent in his philosophy, and under his firm leadership Atlanta Baptist and Morehouse made consistent progress.[64]

Morehouse and other black colleges survived Booker T. Washington and industrial education. All schools offered some industrial training, but by the turn of the century most colleges were moving away from the industrial concept.[65] In fact, aside from Tuskegee and Hampton, industrial education was probably never successful—the program was too expensive, and most blacks who had the opportunity for education wanted more than industrial training. By 1900 the industrial revolution had convinced many educators that the machine had made industrial education obsolete. Yet more than a few institutions advertised ambitious but non-existent programs in order to snare northern dollars.[66] Atlanta Normal and Industrial Institute combined a hat-in-hand approach with promises of sound industrial training. Its principal, Richard D. Stinson, who started the school after being fired as vice-president of Morris Brown College, solicited funds across the country by glorifying industrial education for black people "yet ashamed of honest hard work." Stinson's school was a fly-by-night operation whose industrial training program consisted of a class in sewing.[67]

By the turn of the century blacks had begun to protest white control of their colleges. They did not question the sincerity or motives of the first white educators who came south when few blacks were qualified to teach. As the number of black college

64. Ridgely Torrence, *The Story of John Hope* (New York, 1948), 149–51; Hope to Du Bois, Jan. 17, 1910, in Aptheker, ed., *Correspondence of W. E. B. Du Bois*, I, 165–67. This letter is a poignant attempt by Hope to explain to Du Bois his reasons for accepting Booker T. Washington's assistance in obtaining a $10,000 gift from Andrew Carnegie. Hope assured his friend, "I would not yield a *principle* for the benefit of myself or my school." Du Bois replied with a kind letter stating that he hated to see Hope "in Washington's net," but went on to "say frankly I do not see any other course of action before you but the one you took." Du Bois to Hope, Jan. 22, 1910, *ibid.*, 167.
65. Reed, *Story of Spelman College*, 190; Jones, *Negro Education*, No. 39, II, 223. For its efforts in the industrial area, Spelman received support from the General Education Board and the Slater Fund.
66. Bond, *Education of the Negro*, 124.
67. Letter to Atlanta *Constitution*, Oct. 12, 1914; Jones, *Negro Education*, No. 39, II, 255.

graduates rose, blacks began to resent white influence. Black
Baptists first raised the issue after the predominantly white board
at Atlanta Baptist College failed to increase its black membership.
The leading black minister from Savannah, E. K. Love, charged
that white teachers were incapable of understanding black students' social needs, were less dedicated than their predecessors,
and were racists who induced hopelessness and defeat in their
students. Furthermore, white control of Atlanta Baptist and Spelman deprived blacks of opportunities to promote racial self-
reliance and self-confidence.[68] His arguments ignored, Love
founded Central City College near Macon to rival Atlanta Baptist,
but most black Baptists remained loyal to the Atlanta schools.
Love's rebellion may have influenced Atlanta Baptist trustees,
who in 1906 appointed John Hope as the school's first black
president and increased the number of black faculty. By 1914
seventeen of nineteen Atlanta Baptist teachers were black, as
were two-thirds of the Clark and Paine faculties, with Morris
Brown continuing its tradition as an all-black institution.[69]

Other black schools faced more difficult racial problems. Soon
after 1900 Clark appointed a distinguished black professor, William H. Crogman, to the presidency, and its sister school, Gammon Theological Seminary, named black educator and author
J. W. E. Bowen as its head. Trouble between white and black
faculty at Clark and dissatisfaction at Gammon led the M.E.
Church (white) to remove both black presidents, naming a white
minister to run both schools. Blacks protested the action, to no
avail.[70] At Paine the racial situation was often tense, for there
southern white presidents and faculty—usually ministers and
missionaries—often adopted a patronizing, if not racist attitude

68. E. K. Love, *Annual Address to the Missionary Baptist Convention of
Georgia* (Nashville, 1899), 19–27, quoted in Range, *Negro Colleges in Georgia*,
109–11; see also James M. McPherson, "The Liberals and Black Power in Negro
Education, 1865–1915," *American Historical Review*, 75 (June, 1970), 1372–74.
69. Range, *Negro Colleges in Georgia*, 110–11; Jones, *Negro Education*, No.
38, I, 316, 326, 329–30, 348.
70. Ware to Bumstead, Jan. 30, 1909, Ware Papers. Atlanta *Independent*, Sept.
10, 1910. *The Foundation*, 1 (Jan., 1911), 4. Crogman and Bowen stayed on as
professors. After 1910 Crogman again took on administrative duties, as his white
successors proved unable to solve Clark's problems. *The Foundation*, 5 (Dec.,
1915), 2.

toward their black students and colleagues.[71] Atlanta University and Spelman remained firmly under northern white control, and while A.U. escaped severe censure because of its leadership in racial matters, Spelman was more vulnerable.

Under the presidency of Miss Lucy Hale Tapley, Spelman stressed industrial education, or "instruction in the house-wifely arts," at the expense of intellectual training, and seemed willing to tolerate southern mores. (As late as the 1920s Spelman's chapel had a designated section for "white guests" at certain events.) Moreover, the campus housed MacVicar Hospital, which for a time barred black physicians and admitted only patients referred by white staff doctors.[72] Spelman administrators frowned on student political activity. Dean Edith V. Brill answered an NAACP request to establish a student chapter by saying, "It is impossible for us to consider any more organizations than we now have at Spelman. Every tiny space is full and it is impractical for us to plan for any more at present." After the NAACP renewed its request three years later President Tapley declined, adding that "the hardest thing we have to do is select the most necessary things . . . the girls need to enjoy their girlhood which at best passes so rapidly."[73]

Student life did have its lighter side. With the passage of time administrators began to relax some of their regulations. Fraternities sprang up—sometimes illegally—with secret societies competing for the brightest pledges. Athletics, particularly football and baseball, were popular on the campuses. Students also participated in debate and dramatics. Atlanta University put on excellent productions of Shakespeare, and its Cosmopolitan Orchestra gave concerts and played for dances.[74] As the second decade of the century came to a close, life on black campuses was becoming less rigid, more secular. Students enjoyed life behind the college

71. Floyd to Ware, Dec. 23, 1912, Ware Papers; Alandus C. Johnson, "The Growth of Paine College: A Successful Interracial Venture, 1903–1946" (Ph.D. dissertation, University of Georgia, 1970), 315, 367, 372.

72. Interview with Mrs. Grace Towns Hamilton, Mar. 18, 1974, Atlanta; Reed, Story of Spelman College, 192, 138–39.

73. Edith V. Brill to Catherine D. Lealtad, Oct. 19, 1920; Lucy Hale Tapley to Robert W. Bagnall, Feb. 23, 1923, Branch File, NAACP Papers.

74. Bacote, Story of Atlanta University, 128–29, 210–15, 220–35, 243; Scroll, 14 (Jan., 1910), 46.

gates, where they could fashion a society to their liking, somewhat removed from the pressures and realities of the world outside.

Looking backward on black education in Georgia, one is impressed not so much by its shortcomings as by its achievements against overwhelming odds. Whether from habit or design, white politicians and school administrators thwarted black educational opportunities at every turn: schools were inadequate, teachers were overworked and underpaid, and many children were denied even basic elementary education. Still, in the years before World War I black Georgia schools produced educators of the caliber of John Hope and George Towns and future leaders like James Weldon Johnson and Walter White, along with hundreds of doctors, ministers, lawyers, and businessmen. Their success is tribute to their determination, to sacrifices by their parents, and to the dedication of their teachers. One can but speculate as to how the face of Georgia and America would look today had black children enjoyed anything resembling equal educational opportunity a century, or even a half-century ago.

Black Thought

THE BLACK RESPONSE to white supremacy varied from acceptance of the status quo to militant protest to African emigration. The different philosophies of leaders like W. E. B. Du Bois, Booker T. Washington, and Bishop Henry McNeal Turner did not prevent their followers from working together in a common effort to improve local conditions. What united these men and women—their blackness, the caste system—often transcended ideological differences. All agreed on the need for race pride, self-help, black enterprise, and education for the masses. The question of allegiance was, however, a major divisive factor: alignment with Washington demanded loyalty in return for political and economic favor, while to challenge him invited retribution. This system of reward and punishment created jealousy and animosity, diverting energy from more pressing problems. After Washington's death in 1915 his followers and critics joined forces in the NAACP chapters which sprang up across the state. Throughout his lifetime, though, Booker T. Washington was extremely powerful, and race leaders in Georgia usually preferred to stay within Tuskegee's protective shadow.

Most black newspaper editors aligned with Washington, with notable exceptions.[1] The editors of the state's leading black weeklies, Sol C. Johnson of the Savannah *Tribune* and Benjamin Davis of the Atlanta *Independent*, were both active in Republican politics and fraternal orders and generally supported the Tuskegee position. Johnson praised Washington in his columns, yet at the

1. Georgia had over a dozen black weekly newspapers during the progressive era, but the files of only two, the Atlanta *Independent* and the Savannah *Tribune*, are extant. Many weeklies were short-lived, shoestring operations.

same time he was a political activist who strongly supported movements like the streetcar boycotts. If he did not attack racism with the fervor of a Monroe Trotter, he stood for justice and did not court white favor. As noted earlier, Davis defied categorization. He could condemn his people with such comments as "The Negro is a child race . . . the average Negro leader is as ignorant as a bat," and denounce lynching and racism with unmatched severity. Leading Atlanta blacks despised Davis's opportunism and flamboyant lifestyle (the editor had a taste for flashy cars and fast women) and would not permit the Atlanta *Independent* to be read in their homes. An admirer of Washington, Davis criticized the Tuskegean's protégés and in later years became less hostile to the protest movement. During World War I he became an officer in the Atlanta NAACP, but continued to be a maverick.[2]

The *Voice of Missions* and the *Georgia Baptist* were monthly newspapers of black religious denominations, but with a difference: each bore the stamp of one individual. Organ of the mission department of the African Methodist Episcopal Church, the *Voice of Missions* became the personal voice of editor Henry McNeal Turner, who from 1893 to 1900 filled his columns with attacks on racism, good news from Africa, and plans for black emigration. Turner started his own paper, the *Voice of the People*, in 1901. It appeared monthly for six years, devoted to promotion of "African emigration and the manhood of the race."[3]

Published in Augusta, the *Georgia Baptist* reflected the radical views of William Jefferson White, long-time educator and political leader. The son of an antebellum planter, White began his career during Reconstruction. A foe of Washington, he was at odds with both Augusta's black conservatives and the city's white leadership. His outspoken editorials often got him into trouble. As noted, an editorial in 1900 denouncing a local lynching brought a mob of angry whites to his office to threaten his life. Then, in the fall of 1906, White responded to an Augusta *Chronicle* editorial be-

2. Atlanta *Independent*, Sept. 12, 1908; Mar. 2, 1907; interview with Dr. Homer Nash, July 4, 1972, Atlanta; interview with Mrs. Grace Towns Hamilton, Mar. 18, 1974, Atlanta; White to James W. Johnson, Dec. 5, 1917, Branch Files, NAACP Papers.

3. The *Voice of Missions* and the *Voice of the People* are available on microfilm at the Interdenominational Theological Center Library, Atlanta. For more on Turner's emigrationist views, see pp. 175–78.

moaning the declining quality of kitchen help with this audacious observation: "Jim Crow laws have caused many of Augusta's good cooks, nurses, and chambermaids to leave Augusta for northern cities. . . . It would be a good idea for Southern aristocrats to get white women servants from the North who have been discarded in favor of colored servants."[4] The inference that white domestic workers were inferior to blacks did not sit well with white Augustans, and on September 22 the *Chronicle* growled, "Negroes like White ought to be made to leave the South." That same day the Atlanta riot broke out, sending its shock waves down to Augusta. An ad hoc Ku Klux Klan group threatened White's life, but the editor took friends' advice and fled the city. Undaunted, White soon returned to Augusta, continuing his crusade for black equality in the columns of the *Georgia Baptist* until his death seven years later at the age of eighty-two.[5]

The nation's most distinguished black periodical was Jesse Max Barber's *Voice of the Negro*, begun in Atlanta in 1904 as a forum for such black spokesmen as Kelly Miller, Archibald Grimké, Mary Church Terrell, Du Bois, and Washington. Designed to protest "against anything short of manhood recognition of our people," it promised to be an outlet for differing political views.[6] The twenty-six-year-old editor needed Tuskegee approval to get his magazine off the ground, and Washington wanted an editorial voice on the new national periodical, so Barber hired Washington's aide, Emmett J. Scott, as assistant editor. Barber's militancy upset Washington so much that he complained to the magazine's owner. This intervention angered Barber, who reminded Scott that "there is much talk of Mr. Washington's trying to dictate the policy of every colored interest in this country. . . ."[7]

Deteriorating relations between Tuskegee and Barber in the summer of 1904 led to Scott's resignation, and thereafter the magazine began criticizing Washington personally. When the

4. Augusta *Chronicle*, June 3, 4, 1900; Sept. 22, 1906; Savannah *Tribune*, June 9, 1900.

5. Augusta *Chronicle*, Sept. 22, 26, 29, 1906; Atlanta *Constitution*, Sept. 26, 1906; Savannah *Tribune*, Apr. 19, 1913; Meier, *Negro Thought in America*, 156, 221. Unfortunately, no complete files of the *Georgia Baptist* exist. See above, p. 17, on the threat to lynch White.

6. *Voice of the Negro*, 1 (May, 1904), 208.

7. Jesse Max Barber to Scott, Apr. 18, 1904, Washington Papers.

black leader told an audience of whites in Philadelphia that accumulation of wealth was important because "The black man who is the largest contractor in his town and lives in a two-story brick house is not likely to be lynched," Barber denounced the Tuskegean's "pusillanimous speech" as "downright soulless materialism."[8] In a confidential letter to his friend J. W. E. Bowen, nominally senior editor of the magazine, Washington had accused Barber of using his columns to "cast unwarranted slurs on me and the organizations with which I may be affiliated." He went on:

> Do you know a single Negro in the history of the whole South, who has for two years, borne the curses of the entire Southern white people for standing up for a principle and asserting his rights as a citizen in accepting the hospitality when offered, of a gentleman with whom he had a right to dine? . . . Do you know of any other colored man who has stood up for the political rights of the Negro amid the abuse and curses of the Southern white people to the extent that I have during the past two years? My checkbook will show that I spent at least four thousand dollars in cash out of my own pocket during this same period, in advancing the rights of the black man.[9]

Barber continued to criticize this man "of profound political ability, but who lacks sound political ideas," while at the same time he tried to persuade the Tuskegean to write for the *Voice*. Washington declined.[10]

Barber's primary concern was not Tuskegee so much as the racial climate in Atlanta during and after the 1906 gubernatorial campaign. The week after the Atlanta riot he wrote anonymously to the New York *World* blaming the riot on the yellow journalism of the white newspapers, a judgment later confirmed by a white investigating body. When local whites learned of his authorship the young editor was summoned before Governor Terrell's chief of staff, Colonel James English, and given three choices: retract his charges, leave town, or face a chain gang sentence. Since he

8. *Voice of the Negro*, 2 (Mar., 1905), 194–96.
9. Washington to Bowen, Dec. 27, 1904, Washington Papers. Here Washington was obviously referring to the controversy which erupted over his dining with President Theodore Roosevelt.
10. *Voice of the Negro*, 3 (May, 1906), 318; Barber to Washington, Nov. 29, 1905; Washington to Barber, Dec. 1, 1905, Washington Papers.

would not recant and did not "care to be made a slave on a Georgia chaingang," Barber left Atlanta and tried to reestablish his magazine in Chicago. The abrupt uprooting, together with financial problems exacerbated by Washington's opposition, led to the *Voice*'s demise in 1907. Throughout its four-year existence it spoke directly to the needs of American blacks, and was the ideological forerunner of the *Crisis*.[11]

For every Max Barber there were many moderate and conservative spokesmen, especially among the clergy. One of the state's most civic-minded ministers was H. H. Proctor, minister of Atlanta's First Congregational Church. A friend of both Washington and Du Bois, Proctor called for race pride and self-help, although he did solicit funds from whites to assist his community efforts. Proctor saw his political role as a mediator between black and white, and his most notable work here was as catalyst for the interracial committee formed after the Atlanta riot. Proctor shows his middle-class orientation in the following letter to Booker T. Washington: "I am preaching a series of sermons to young men on lessons of inspiration from careers of men who have attained eminence. The three names chosen are President Roosevelt, Mr. John D. Rockefeller, and yourself." When Proctor accepted the pastorate of a church in New York City in 1919, the mayor of Atlanta was among those expressing regret at his departure.[12]

Another popular minister, Charles T. Walker, was a spellbinding orator with Baptist congregations in both New York and Augusta. Like Proctor, Walker believed blacks should work together without alienating the "best" white people. A staunch Washington ally, Walker was active in Georgia politics, belonging to the conservative faction of the local Republican party. During World War I, when Lucy Laney and a few other black Augustans were starting an NAACP chapter, one organizer singled out Walker as leader of "some of the most reactionary Negroes in this

11. "Why Mr. Barber Left Atlanta," *Voice of the Negro*, 3 (Nov., 1906), 470–72. Washington's opposition to Barber continued after the *Voice* folded, and the Tuskegean's influence was so strong that Barber eventually left journalism and became a dentist. Louis Harlan, Comments, "Beyond Booker T. Washington: Black Leadership, 1880–1920," American Historical Association, Atlanta, Dec. 29, 1975.
12. H. H. Proctor to Washington, Dec. 2, 1901, Washington Papers; Proctor, *Between Black and White*, 96, 97, 120; Atlanta *Constitution*, June 3, Dec. 13, 1908; Jan. 1, 1911; Savannah *Tribune*, Oct. 18, 1919.

country. They cater openly and unabashed to Bourbon white sentiment." Yet Walker stood publicly for race solidarity and self-help, and his book *Appeal to Caesar* was a call for citizenship rights for blacks.[13]

Aside from radicals like Du Bois, Hope, and Lucy Laney, most black educators were in the Tuskegee camp. William H. Crogman began his academic career teaching Greek and Latin at Clark College. During the midst of the national debate about the innate capacities of blacks, Crogman interjected this note of common sense: "The Negro is just as good and just as bad as anybody, just as dull and just as bright as anybody, just as industrious and just as indolent as anybody. He is man, and whatever pertains to man pertains to him physically, mentally, morally." Crogman spoke out strongly for full rights for blacks in the late nineteenth century, but threw in with Tuskegee after he became president of Clark. Radicals like Du Bois and George Towns had much respect for this witty, urbane man, who refused to ride a streetcar after the Jim Crow law was passed and walked the five miles to town and back "as long as he was able to walk at all."[14] Washington influenced administrators like Henry A. Hunt, Atlanta University graduate and president of the industrial school at Fort Valley, and J. W. E. Bowen, who with Washington's assistance was selected president of Gammon. Du Bois had hopes that Bowen would repudiate Tuskegee, but his conservative speeches after the Atlanta riot led Du Bois to dismiss him as a "renegade and copperhead of the most dangerous character."[15]

Typical of those black educators forced to accommodate to white authority was Richard R. Wright, Sr., of Savannah. Born in Dalton in 1855, Wright began a long career as a public school administrator after graduating from Atlanta University. He be-

13. Wilson Jeffers to Roy Nash, Apr. 11, 1917, Branch Files, NAACP Papers; Meier, *Negro Thought in America*, 156, 221–22, 260. The term "radical" in this chapter means what it meant then: a person who publicly advocated immediate abolition of all discrimination based on race. Usually radicals identified with Du Bois and the Niagara Platform and opposed Washington and his accommodationist philosophy.

14. George A. Towns, "Wm. Henry Crogman," p. 4, undated MS in Towns Collection; Du Bois, "Looking Backward on Seventy-five Years," 243; William H. Crogman, *Talks for the Times* (Atlanta, 1896), 156–57.

15. Atlanta *Evening News*, Sept. 27, 1906; Atlanta *Georgian*, Sept. 26, 1906; W. E. B. Du Bois, "Has J. W. E. Bowen Gone Crazy?" *Horizon*, 1 (Feb., 1907), 15–16; Meier, *Negro Thought in America*, 211–12.

came the first president of Georgia State Industrial College, remaining there for the next thirty years. Financed by state and federal funds, Georgia State was not a college at all, though Wright at times tried to "bootleg" college courses into his secondary curriculum.[16] Wright ran his school with an iron hand, took a conservative position in Savannah politics (and was blasted in Sol Johnson's *Tribune* for his views), and promoted an annual Negro State Fair which drew thousands of blacks from south Georgia. But beneath the facade of the "good Negro" there was a proud, angry man. In 1921, when a Savannah bank teller refused to call his daughter "Miss Wright" and in the ensuing altercation struck her, Wright promptly filed suit against the bank. When he lost the case Wright quit his job at Georgia State and moved to Philadelphia, where he vowed to "organize a bank where anybody may come and be treated like a lady or a gentleman." He did just that, remaining president of the prosperous Citizens and Southern Bank of Philadelphia until his death in 1947.[17]

At the turn of the century most black leaders either supported Booker T. Washington or kept their opinions to themselves. The Tuskegean influenced the Negro press, controlled such racial uplift organizations as the Afro-American Council, and founded a large body devoted to his principles in the National Negro Business League. Black radicals, opposed to Washington's philosophy and alarmed by rapid consolidation of his power, formed the Niagara Movement in hopes of reversing the accommodationist trend.

The twenty-nine men answering Du Bois's call "for organized determination and aggressive action on the part of men who believe in Negro freedom and growth" met on the Canadian side of Niagara Falls from July 11 to 13, 1905, and agreed upon what was for the times a radical program which took issue with Washington at every turn. Where he told blacks to eschew political rights, the Niagara platform called for full manhood suffrage; where Washington counseled patience with the Jim Crow South, Niagara de-

16. Interview with Mr. R. W. Gadsden, July 20, 1974, Savannah.
17. Wright, *87 Years Behind the Black Curtain*, 15–16; Range, *Rise and Progress of the Negro College in Georgia*, 139–40; Elizabeth Ross Haynes, *The Black Boy of Atlanta* (Boston, 1952), 177–82.

manded immediate abolition of all caste distinctions. And in a
thinly veiled attack on the Tuskegee machine, the Niagara
document called for "freedom of speech and criticism" and "an
unfettered and unsubsidized press." Max Barber afterward wrote:
"If Mr. Washington can subscribe to the principles promulgated,
he will be welcomed as a member of the movement. If he cannot,
it is his business."[18] Four Georgians signed the call for the first
conference: Dr. L. B. Palmer; George A. Towns; Monroe Work,
later a distinguished scholar at Tuskegee; and John Hope. Atlanta
businessman Alonzo F. Herndon attended the founding meeting.[19]

The Niagara Movement's most prominent figure was its leader,
W. E. B. Du Bois, who at thirty-seven already enjoyed an international reputation, having written over fifty articles and three
major books on the race question, including his most widely read
work, *The Souls of Black Folk*. Born in New England and educated at Fisk, Harvard, and Berlin, Du Bois had come to Atlanta
University in 1897. In his autobiography he explains the significance of this period of his life: "My real work was begun at
Atlanta for thirteen years, from my twenty-ninth to my forty-
second birthday. They were years of great spiritual upturning, of
the making and unmaking of ideals, of hard work and hard play.
Here I found myself. I lost most of my mannerisms. I grew more
broadly human, made my closest and most holy friendships, and
studied human beings."[20]

At first Du Bois saw his role in Atlanta as that of scholar and
teacher. He would help train the "talented tenth" of black America and demonstrate to whites that their racial beliefs and policies
were based on lies and distortion. By the time he left Atlanta
University in 1910 he had been disabused of the idea that "the
cause of the problem was the ignorance of people; that the cure
wasn't simply telling the people the truth, it was inducing them
to act on the truth. . . ."[21] Moreover, while maintaining the necessity of higher education for blacks, Du Bois was moving away
from his vision of an elitist, college-educated petite bourgeoisie of

18. *Voice of the Negro*, 2 (Sept., 1905), 600–603; Aptheker, ed., *Documentary History of the Negro People*, I, 901–4; Aptheker, *Afro-American History*, 154–55; Du Bois, "A Pageant in Seven Decades," 22–23.

19. Aptheker, *Afro-American History*, 154.

20. Du Bois, *Autobiography*, 213.

21. Du Bois, OHC, 146.

black professionals and businessmen toward a socialistic view which brought the black worker to the forefront of the struggle. All the while he continued to emphasize racial solidarity and to agitate for complete citizenship rights.[22] Living and working in the South, Du Bois "became widely acquainted with the real condition of my people." His years at Atlanta University were important to the development of his thought.[23]

Du Bois as an Atlanta University scholar seems to conjure an image of a recluse, unapproachable and austere, contemplating the future of the race from deep within his study. Part of this stems from Du Bois's own self-deprecating comments in later years, and part comes from his imposing appearance on the A.U. campus. Nearly three-quarters of a century later a Du Bois student would retain this vivid impression: "I can see him right now, coming across the campus to his breakfast with his head high, his step quick, but dressed right, from the top of his head to the soles of his feet. He was immaculate!"[24]

Once students got to know their distinguished professor they found him outgoing. Mrs. H. S. Murphy fondly recalls Saturday night faculty-student parties where Du Bois would enthusiastically participate in singing old college songs, and the student newspaper noted that at the annual Christmas party "The distribution of refreshments was under the personal supervision of professors Webster and Du Bois, who by repeated inroads upon their storehouse of wit and humor filled the room with merriment." Du Bois seemed to thrive on campus life, attending the dramatic productions directed by his close friend Adrienne Herndon and bringing nationally known speakers to campus. He made small contributions to such worthy campus organizations as the A.U. football team, was active in the faculty governing body, and lobbied with his president for more work room by drawing up floor plans for Stone Hall alterations.[25] A demanding instructor, he became one

22. W. E. B. Du Bois, *The Conservation of the Races*, American Negro Academy Occasional Papers No. 2 (1897), 7; *Horizon*, 6 (Nov., 1909), 1; 3 (Feb., 1908), 18; Meier, "Negro Racial Thought," 577–96. Du Bois's plea for racial solidarity is a consistent theme in his Atlanta University studies.

23. Du Bois, *Autobiography*, 213.

24. Interview with Mrs. H. S. Murphy, July 6, 1972, Atlanta.

25. *Ibid.; Scroll*, 7 (Jan., 1903), 42; 6 (Feb., 1902), 52; "Proposals to President Ware on Alterations in Stone Hall," MS in Du Bois folder, Ware Papers.

of the most popular teachers. When Du Bois spoke at prayer meetings the attendance was unusually large, perhaps because while reading from the prayer book "I used to improve upon the prayers now and then."[26]

Nor did Du Bois shun the world outside the campus gates. Contemptuous of "car window sociologists," he made detailed federal investigations of several black belt areas in Alabama, Virginia, and southwest Georgia, and in 1900 headed a team of census takers working in Georgia's Atlantic coastal counties. Du Bois spoke before black audiences across the state, lecturing on Frederick Douglass, John Brown, and other important figures, and was the author of protests against Jim Crow laws and bills to divide the educational fund by race.[27] Rarely in close contact with southern whites, he was particularly suspicious of white moderates, and although he initially participated in the interracial meetings following the Atlanta riot, he later dismissed the movement as "gotten up primarily for advertising purposes."[28]

The Atlanta riot had dramatically illustrated the failure of Booker T. Washington's accommodationist philosophy. Eleven years earlier Du Bois had approved Washington's Atlanta Compromise speech in the belief that "if the South accepted it, I thought that was going to be a great step ahead, and lead away from the physical violence and lawlessness." The intervening decade saw attempts by Tuskegee to enlist Du Bois's services, but the two men were headed in different ideological directions, and the publication of *The Souls of Black Folk* in 1903 "ended the whole business."[29] Du Bois and Washington did attempt to reconcile differences in the following two years, but the founding of the Niagara Movement made the break permanent.[30]

Membership in the Niagara Movement was small, especially in the South. Washington's opposition, the movement's uncompromising attitude toward racial injustice, and Du Bois's growing

26. Du Bois, OHC, 137; Bacote, *Story of Atlanta University*, 132.
27. Aptheker, *Afro-American History*, 152–53; Savannah *Tribune*, Mar. 3, 1900; Mar. 10, 1906; Feb. 12, 1910; Du Bois, *Autobiography*, 219.
28. Du Bois to Baker, May 6, 1909, Baker Papers; "Conversation between W. E. B. Du Bois and Rev. C. B. Wilmer," *ibid.*
29. Du Bois, OHC, 157, 159.
30. Herbert Aptheker, "The Washington–Du Bois Conference of 1904," *Science and Society*, 13 (1949), 344–51; Aptheker, *Afro-American History*, 118–26.

interest in socialism frightened some black southerners and angered others. Ben Davis believed the Niagara leaders were "as hurtful to the race in the main as Tom Watson and Hoke Smith." He thought Du Bois "simply one of those over-educated theorists. . . . In fact, the poor devil is crazy and ought not to be taken seriously."[31] But many did take Du Bois and Niagara seriously, and it became the militant voice of black protest at a time when repression was at its peak. Despite its small size it challenged Washington's power; and it set the stage for the founding of its ideological successor, the National Association for the Advancement of Colored People. The first modern civil rights organization, the Niagara Movement initiated the twentieth-century drive for recognition of black equality in America.[32]

Inspired by the Niagara Movement, a number of Georgia blacks called the Equal Rights Convention to protest white injustice. Under William Jefferson White's leadership several hundred teachers, clergymen, professionals, and farmers met in February 1906 in Macon. Conservatives (and Washington's spies) attended, but the conference reflected the radical spirit of the Niagara declarations.[33] Speakers denounced peonage, the convict lease system, exclusion of blacks from juries, and unequal distribution of state school funds. Convention president White told his audience that to improve their condition they must "buy land and homes. We must encourage Negro businessmen. And at the same time we must agitate, complain, protest, and keep protesting against the invasion of our manhood rights . . . and above all organize these million brothers of ours into one great fist which shall never cease to pound at the gates of opportunity until they shall fly open."[34] The angriest words, however, came from the

31. Atlanta *Independent*, Jan. 28, Aug. 5, 1905; Apr. 21, 1906.
32. Aptheker, *Afro-American History*, 153–57. For selected documents relating to the Niagara Movement, see Aptheker, ed., *Documentary History of the Negro People*, I, 897–915.
33. Washington told C. T. Walker to attend the convention to keep an eye on the radicals. Walker stayed only a day, but arranged to "put a number of men on guard to watch affairs." Washington to Walker, Feb. 11, 1906; Walker to Washington, Feb. 14, 1906, Washington Papers; Bacote, "Negro in Georgia Politics," 435.
34. "The Georgia Equal Rights Convention," pamphlet in Moorland Collection, Howard University Library; *Voice of the Negro*, 3 (Feb., 1906), 90; (Mar., 1906), 163–64, 175–77.

vice-president of the convention, Bishop Turner, who was quoted
as saying, "To the Negro in the country the American flag is a
dirty and contemptible rag. . . . I wish to say that hell is an
improvement upon the United States when the Negro is involved."[35] Despite its enthusiastic beginning, the Equal Rights
Convention did not become a permanent organization. Du Bois
reflected on the odds against all-black protest groups succeeding
when he later spoke of the decline of the Niagara Movement:
"Well, it was difficult to do anything as a Negro organization.
What influence could we have on white public opinion? What
openings with papers and magazines? . . . How could we get a
chance to lecture? We had to have some white people at least
friendly to us, and it would be a great deal better if we had one
organization."[36]

That "one organization," of course, would be the NAACP, and
its founding would result in Du Bois leaving Atlanta for New York
and the editorship of the *Crisis,* the NAACP organ. After more
than a decade at Atlanta University, Du Bois was ready to depart.
Frustrated at the failure of his research and writing to initiate
social change, he was feeling increasing pressure from the A.U.
administration to tone down his protests. And there was the
matter of the region itself. Several years earlier Du Bois had
noted how "A certain sort of soul, a certain kind of spirit finds
the narrow repression, the provincialism of the South almost
unbearable."[37] Closing the door on the Atlanta stage of his career,
Du Bois left for New York, where in the *Crisis* he would have a
monthly national forum for his ideas.

The NAACP did not take hold in Georgia until the war years.
Opposition from local whites, the NAACP's northern base, and
the absence of experienced organizers in the field were all factors.
But perhaps most important was Booker T. Washington's angry
opposition to the new organization, which he correctly perceived
as a threat to his power. For the first time in this century the
forces of black protest had influential white support, and this at a
time when the Tuskegean's influence in the white community
(certainly in the White House) was slipping. Washington found

35. Atlanta *Independent,* Feb. 24, 1906.
36. Du Bois, OHC, 154.
37. Quoted in Savannah *Tribune,* Mar. 8, 1902.

most of the whites and blacks who set up the NAACP "either
without sincerity or without stability. . . . There are few colored
men in this organization of any real standing in their own communities. . . . What they want is nonsense."[38] NAACP chapters
proliferated in Georgia in the years after Washington's death, for
by then pro- and anti-Washington forces were able to develop a
degree of unity around the NAACP program. In Atlanta, for example, Ben Davis would serve on the branch's executive committee with John Hope and George Towns. Yet all was not
harmonious, and the combination of internal and external pressures took their toll on the fledging NAACP chapters.[39]

Disillusioned Georgia blacks who rejected the programs of
both Washington and Du Bois might look to African emigration
or racial separatism within the United States as realistic solutions
to the American race problem. The prophet of emigration between Reconstruction and World War I was Bishop Henry
McNeal Turner. After his political career ran aground during
Reconstruction, Turner used his influential position within the
A.M.E. Church as a forum, urging blacks to move to Africa. Like
Marcus Garvey, whom he resembled in several ways, Turner
contrasted his glowing accounts of life in Africa with indictments
of white America. Unlike Garvey, the bishop was not solely
occupied with emigration; he devoted much time to church business and conventional protest activities.[40]

The high tide of Back-to-Africa interest in Georgia was reached
in the 1890s. Promising cheap transportation to Liberia, in 1891
the Congo Company drew over 1,000 blacks to Atlanta; there they
awaited a trip to Savannah, the port of embarkation. When the
Congo Company could not obtain ships the scheme collapsed.
The company finally sent 42 emigrés in 1894, and over 200 left
for Liberia a year later, but the decade was marked by failure of
agents to make good on their promises. A confidence man collected a dollar apiece for steamship tickets from an estimated

38. Washington to Baker, May 24, 1910, Washington Papers.
39. White to Nash, Mar. 3, 1917, Branch Files, NAACP Papers; NAACP
branch files for Atlanta, Augusta, Savannah, Athens, and Macon, 1917–21, *ibid.*
For more on the work of the NAACP in Georgia, see pp. 206–7.
40. Edwin S. Redkey, *Black Exodus, Black Nationalist and Back-to-Africa
Movements, 1890–1910* (New Haven, 1969), 24, 295.

3,000 Hancock County farmers before he disappeared. Such operations were common.[41]

Emigration enthusiasm had died down by the turn of the century. The frustrated Bishop Turner fumed: "If a law was passed telling the colored people of the United States to either return to Africa or select masters, millions would choose masters before they would leave the country."[42] The bishop made one last major effort to promote African settlement, organizing the Colored National Emigration Association in 1901 to raise $100,-000 to buy a used steamship for emigration and commercial purposes. President of the association was William H. Heard, former United States minister to Liberia and pastor of an Atlanta A.M.E. Church. The following year Turner wrote his son from Liberia, telling him to ask Senator John T. Morgan of Alabama (who had long supported deportation of blacks) to "use his great influence to have the United States government to aid this enterprise." Nothing positive developed from this contact, and Turner's new organization attracted so little financial support over the next four years that he refunded what money subscribers had invested.[43]

If economic factors and lack of transportation discouraged emigration, tales of misery and death brought back by returning African colonists further dampened enthusiasm. Of a group of fifty-three black colonists from Irwin County who paid their own way to Liberia in 1903, twenty died from fever before the year was out, and the rest were reported to be "ragged, starving, and homeless." Their attempts to return to Georgia received a big play in the southern white press, and no doubt their experience dissuaded some black people from making emigration plans.[44]

41. *Ibid.*, 150–62, 208, 215–18; Bacote, "Negro in Georgia Politics," 27.
42. *Voice of the People,* July 1, 1901.
43. Turner to John P. Turner, M.D., Apr. 25, 1902, Justice Dept. Records, Record Group 94, National Archives. After talking with John Turner, Senator Morgan tried to convince Secretary of War Elihu Root to send Turner and a black colonizing group to the Philippines, where presumably they would be of assistance in pacifying the rebellious Filipinos. Nothing came of this scheme, and no doubt Turner would have rejected it had he known of it, for the bishop was a strong supporter of the Filipino insurrection against the Yankee invaders. Morgan to Elihu Root, Apr. 17, 1902, *ibid.;* Root to Morgan, July 8, 1902, *ibid. Voice of Missions,* Oct. 1, 1900.
44. Columbus *Enquirer-Sun,* Nov. 7, 14, 1903; Redkey, *Black Exodus,* 273–74.

Stories of terrible living conditions in Liberia turned some blacks to thoughts of establishing a separate colony or state within the American continent. Leader of the separatist movement was another Georgian, Lucius H. Holsey, an important bishop in the Colored Methodist Episcopal Church. Like Turner, Holsey despaired of the races coexisting in the United States; he wanted the federal government to establish a Negro state in part of the Indian territory, New Mexico, or some other western region. Blacks would exercise full control over the affairs of this state, with whites ineligible for residence except through marriage. Not so aggressive as Turner, Holsey made no serious attempt to advance his program after 1903, but he continued to believe that separatism was the only viable alternative for black Americans.[45]

Bishops Turner and Holsey were respected black clergymen, and if their ideas did not receive endorsement by most blacks, neither were they often dismissed out of hand.[46] Of the two men, Bishop Turner was by far the more active in promoting his program, and he remained a controversial figure until his death. An intellectual, proud and arrogant, Turner insisted on having his way, and his biting attacks on ideological enemies hampered efforts toward accommodation among black leaders. His personal lifestyle also alienated some blacks, as when at age seventy-three he married a divorcée, against the objections of A.M.E. churchmen.[47] His Back-to-Africa movement held little appeal for successful blacks, unwilling to give up what they had gained in this country for an uncertain fate abroad. Moreover, his glowing accounts of life in Africa did not always jibe with the facts, as Turner well knew. Still, no black leader in Georgia was more courageous or audacious in his denunciation of racism. And while middle-class blacks embraced the positions of Washington or Du Bois, Turner awakened the aspirations of the poor and uneducated, who had little concern for philosophies of accommodation or protest. Bishop Turner's African dream remained just that, but the enthusiasm of its acceptance by thousands of black

---

45. Lucius H. Holsey, "Race Segregation," in Willis B. Park, ed., *The Possibilities of the Negro in Symposium* (Atlanta, 1904), 100, 113–19; John B. Cade, *Holsey, the Invincible* (New York, 1964), 116, 118.

46. Savannah *Tribune*, Nov. 15, 1902.

47. Atlanta *Independent*, Dec. 7, 1907.

Georgians says much about both the nature and extent of white racism and the development of black nationalism.

Black nationalism in America grew up alongside the republic. It developed strength in the post-Reconstruction period, in part due to increasing white violence and proscription, in part because of a growing racial consciousness among blacks. By the turn of the century black nationalism provided some common ground for agreement among Washington accommodationists, Turner emigrationists, and Du Bois egalitarians. Earlier chapters have examined two manifestations of black nationalism in Georgia: the emphasis on self-help, exemplified in groups like the Neighborhood Union; and the movement to develop strong, independent economic institutions, with blacks urged by leaders to patronize their own businessmen and professionals.[48] To these must be added a third component, the development of racial pride.

While teaching at Atlanta University, Du Bois wrote "The Song of the Smoke," which included the following verse:

> I am the smoke king,
> I am black.
>> I am darkening with song,
>> I am heartening to wrong;
>> I will be black as blackness can,
>> The blacker the mantle the mightier the man,
>> My purpling midnights no day dawn may ban.
> I am carving God in night,
> I am painting hell in white.
> I am the smoke king,
> I am black.[49]

Anticipating the Harlem Renaissance by over a decade, this poem symbolizes the early twentieth century emphasis on black consciousness and pride. Du Bois also took a series of lectures to the black community of Atlanta on "The History of the Negro Race," a third of which were devoted to the African past, while Benjamin Brawley at Morehouse was advancing cultural nationalism with his theory of the "Negro Genius" in the arts and his concept of a race soul. Throughout the state interest in black history and

48. See the chapters on "Working" and "Community" for discussion of economic nationalism and self-help.
49. *Crisis*, 7 (Jan., 1914), 132. The poem originally appeared in *Horizon*.

culture awakened.[50] Black editors met racist arguments of pseudo-scientists and polemicists head on, urging readers to be proud of their heritage. Sol Johnson turned down advertisements for skin bleaches and hair straighteners in the *Tribune,* and a Savannah minister told his congregation that if he caught his wife "bleaching her black skin or straightening her kinky hair I would sue her for divorce and my allegation would be immorality."[51] The black ministry was perhaps the greatest single force in developing race pride. Bishop Turner casually announced that "God is a Negro," while book agents in the black community made huge profits on illustrated Bibles portraying Christ, the angels, and other scriptural characters as black.[52]

These facets of black nationalism—race pride, self-help, economic chauvinism—came together in attempts to establish all-black communities in Georgia. A few small villages such as Burroughs and Harrisburg had only black residents, but none rivaled Mound Bayou, Mississippi, in size and organization. Several groups purchased tracts and advertised for residents, appealing to the racial pride of their clientele. A secret society began "Odd Fellow City" in Middle Georgia, "owned, controlled, and governed by Negro people," and claimed that "The Negroes of Georgia will make Odd Fellow City the same thing that Mound Bayou is to Mississippi." A Booker T. Washington colony was planned for Irwin County in the wiregrass section, and a land developer named R. D. Cornish put up a hundred acres for sale near Bushnell, advertising for a doctor and promising a school and drugstore.[53] Plans for black towns were no more successful than the more ambitious emigrationist and separatist ventures. Still, the idea of living in a totally black environment was appealing. While young men, Du Bois, Hope, Proctor, and their circle of Atlanta friends discussed the possibility of moving down to the Georgia coast near Brunswick and starting a black colony there. From that point south on the coast there would be a black belt extending through the West Indies clear to southern Brazil, and

50. Circular in Du Bois Collection, Fisk University Library; Meier, "Negro Racial Thought," 871–72.

51. Savannah *Tribune,* Jan. 11, 1902; May 2, 1903; Nov. 6, 1909.

52. *Voice of Missions,* Feb. 1, 1898; Atlanta *Constitution,* Feb. 12, 1911.

53. *Crisis,* 19 (Apr., 1920), 340; Atlanta *Independent,* Oct. 2, 1909; Dec. 27, 1913; Sept. 12, 1914; Savannah *Tribune,* Sept. 4, 1909.

they could not be surrounded by whites. "Now's the time to do it," remarked John Hope, "before we get settled in our jobs." But the project remained a dream.[54]

The first decade of the twentieth century witnessed a black intellectual flowering in Georgia unmatched anywhere. Du Bois was compiling his Atlanta University studies, writing *The Souls of Black Folk,* and inaugurating the Niagara Movement. Max Barber was editing the best black periodical in America, the *Voice of the Negro;* Bishop Turner was compiling his monthly analysis of Africa and the world; and over in Augusta William J. White was filling the columns of the *Georgia Baptist* with demands for radical social and political change. More moderate voices—Sol Johnson in the Savannah *Tribune,* J. W. E. Bowen at Gammon, and H. H. Proctor at the First Congregational Church—were also being heard, as was Booker T. Washington himself, who took a strong personal interest in the affairs of Georgia blacks.

The primary theme of black intellectual life was that of survival in a hostile, racist environment. Some thinkers preferred the Tuskegean's manner of talking softly and working with the white moderates, while those at the opposite pole rejected all white society and pressed for emigrationist or separatist solutions; but by the outbreak of World War I the forces of protest embodied in the Niagara Movement and the Georgia Equal Rights Convention were ascendant. Both Bishop Turner and Booker T. Washington died in 1915, a year when Du Bois's voice in the *Crisis* was growing ever stronger. His message was clear: blacks must demand full equality before the law, while never forgetting the need for political, economic, and cultural unity. It was a message that would not be stilled by the sounds of war across the seas.

54. Torrence, *Story of John Hope,* 135; Du Bois, OHC, 161.

The War Years

ELECTION OF a Virginian to the presidency in 1912 drew a mixed reaction from Georgians. Whites hailed Woodrow Wilson as the first southern President since the Civil War, while blacks waited to see if Wilson made good his campaign promise to give them fair treatment. Indication of Wilson's policy came only a month after inauguration, when his Georgia-born wife toured the Bureau of Printing and Engraving and was shocked to find black and white women dining together in the lunchroom. Shortly thereafter a supervisor "requested" that blacks eat in a separate section.[1] Between April and September 1913 the Wilson administration quietly segregated working, eating, and toilet facilities in the Treasury, Post Office, and Navy departments. When office routine prevented moving blacks from work rooms, the government put up screens to isolate them. Wilson also replaced black Republican appointees with whites and permitted the Civil Service Commission to require photographs of all job applicants.[2] In November 1914 the President curtly dismissed a protest delegation led by Monroe Trotter. Du Bois, who supported Wilson in 1912, told Henry Morgenthau that "a campaign pledge has never been more persistently and thoroughly broken than this splendid word of Mr. Wilson."[3]

The presidential election of 1912 had broad implications for Georgia politicians, both at home and in Congress. Federal patron-

1. Morton Sosna, "The South in the Saddle: Racial Politics During the Wilson Years," *Wisconsin Magazine of History,* 54 (Autumn, 1970), 33.
   2. *Ibid.,* 23–24.
   3. Du Bois to Henry Morgenthau, Apr. 10, 1916, Du Bois Collection, Fisk. For a good account of the Wilson-Trotter encounter, see Stephen R. Fox, *The Guardian of Boston, William Monroe Trotter* (New York, 1970), 168–87.

age returned to the Democratic party after a sixteen-year absence. Atlanta's new postmaster segregated office workers, then dismissed thirty-five black employees whom he claimed were not covered by civil service.[4] The state's new collector of revenue justified similar actions by saying, "There are no government positions for Negroes in the South; a Negro's place is in the cornfield."[5] In Congress, southern Democrats assumed most committee chairmanships and introduced a flood of bills segregating federal employees and prohibiting interracial marriages. After heavyweight champion Jack Johnson's marriage to a white woman, Georgia representative Seaborn A. Roddenbery introduced a resolution to ban interracial marriages by constitutional amendment. "No brutality, no infamy, no degradation in all the years of southern slavery," he said, "possessed such villainous character and such atrocious qualities as the provisions of state laws . . . which allow the marriage of Jack Johnson to a woman of the Caucasian strain."[6] Representative Thomas M. Hardwick fulfilled a campaign pledge by offering two resolutions for repeal of parts of the Fourteenth and all of the Fifteenth Amendments, and Congressman Carl Vinson sought to segregate the races in all civil service jobs. Other southerners introduced bills segregating streetcars in the District of Columbia.[7] None of these measures became law, but their number and the intensity with which they were pursued reflected the change in Washington's political climate.

While their representatives promoted southern values in Washington, Georgians became less provincial. They were fascinated by the automobile, which became a familiar sight in larger

4. Savannah *Tribune,* Sept. 20, 1913; Atlanta *Independent,* Sept. 27, 1913; Sidney S. Tobin, "Debates on Negro Problems in Congress, 1907–1921" (Master's thesis, Howard University, 1961), 87.

5. Tobin, "Debates on Negro Problems," 87; Charles Flint Kellogg, *NAACP: A History of the National Association for the Advancement of Colored People, Vol. 1, 1909–1920* (Baltimore, 1967), 171.

6. *Cong. Record,* 62nd Cong., 3rd sess., p. 502 (Dec. 11, 1912), quoted in Tobin, "Debates on Negro Problems," 49.

7. *Cong. Record,* 62nd Cong., 1st sess., p. 184 (Apr. 12, 1911); 65th Cong., spec. sess., p. 299 (Apr. 4, 1917); Tobin, "Debates on Negro Problems," 68. See also August Meier and Elliott Rudwick, "The Rise of Segregation in the Federal Bureaucracy, 1900–1930," *Phylon,* 28 (Summer, 1967), 178–84; Kathleen L. Wolgemuth, "Woodrow Wilson's Appointment Policy and the Negro," *Journal of Southern History,* 24 (Nov., 1958), 457–71; Ann Firor Scott, "A Progressive Wind from the South," *Journal of Southern History,* 29 (Feb., 1963), 53–70.

cities. The glamour of urban life attracted thousands of rural residents to the cities, and Atlanta became the urban center of the South with its expanding population and economy. There was something of a cultural awakening. Thousands heard Enrico Caruso and Geraldine Farrar when the Metropolitan Opera Company made its annual week-long visits to Atlanta. As for the vaudeville and theater circuit, the capital city played host in 1911 to the queen of the stage, Madame Sarah Bernhardt, performing in *Camille* and *Jeanne d'Arc*.[8] By 1914 blacks in Atlanta and Savannah were supporting theaters and vaudeville houses. There were also innumerable sporting events. A Savannah promoter advertised "the only Colored Motorcycle Club in existence" and drew crowds to races at Woodlawn Park.[9] Under Richard R. Wright's leadership blacks organized and financed a Negro state fair, held annually in a different south Georgia town.

The new motion picture industry revolutionized the world of entertainment, for in the movie house residents of small towns could enjoy the same performances available to their city cousins. Film crews even came to Georgia to shoot on location, taking advantage of the climate in the southern part of the state. One film shot in Augusta and released for national distribution in 1915 had race relations as its theme. Based on an Edward Sheldon play, *The Nigger* concerned a southern governor who discovers his Negro ancestry, eventually deciding to disclose this racial heritage to his constituency rather than submit to political blackmail. NAACP officials found the subject matter "not objectionable," but white Augustans came in with a different review.

Invited to assist in the shooting of a film supposedly called *The New Governor* and kept in the dark about its plot, starstruck Augustans poured on the southern hospitality, opening their beautiful homes and gardens to theatrical people. Local citizens acted in the film—the town's mayor had a part—and the moviemakers even got permission to use Georgia's National Guard in staging mob scenes. When *The Nigger* was released, outraged whites saw they had been duped into helping produce "one of those disgusting and libelous pictures of the race problem." Al-

8. Atlanta *Journal*, May 5, 1910; Atlanta *Constitution*, Mar. 23, 1911.
9. Savannah *Tribune*, Aug. 8, Sept. 12, 1914.

though furious at being so deceived and disapproving the film's message, 195 of 200 Augustans interviewed believed the picture should be shown. History does not record just how many of these champions of the First Amendment had roles in the film.[10]

One of the most popular forms of recreation was the religious revival, and no tent meeting created more excitement than a crusade featuring the Reverend Billy Sunday. The ballplayer-turned-evangelist had a fanatical following in the South. At the end of the week-long revival where he had preached to capacity audiences of Atlanta whites, Sunday announced a special service for Negroes. Not all black leaders endorsed this meeting, but some ministers did, and several thousand blacks turned out to hear the evangelist. Sunday was in fine form as he praised his audience for their progress over the past fifty years, pointed out that southern whites were their best friends, and suggested the way to obtain equal rights was to "strive to make yourselves more worthy of them." When the service concluded, some in the audience pressed near the stage, where the evangelist lay flat on his belly to greet them. As he reached down to shake their hands, Billy looked up at a group of reporters and beamed, "Boys, ain't it great!"[11]

Religious fervor, technological innovation, and more leisure activity did not improve race relations. Lynchings continued, only now the victim often rode to his execution on the floor of a Model T Ford. The most widely publicized hanging of the era was that of Leo M. Frank, a Jewish pencil manufacturer accused of murdering a young employee, Mary Phagan. An Atlanta jury convicted Frank on the flimsiest of evidence, much of it supplied by the factory's black janitor, who was also a prime suspect. Here anti-Semitism won out, and the janitor's conflicting testimony led to Frank's death sentence. As the injustice attracted national publicity, pressure mounted on Governor John Slaton to commute the sentence to life imprisonment, which he did the day before he left office. Tom Watson, leader of the public outcry against Slaton's action, used this headline for his *Weekly Jeffer-*

10. Augusta *Chronicle*, Mar. 18, 13, 23, 24, 1915; Atlanta *Journal*, Mar. 22, 1915; Mary Childs Nerney to Mrs. Val Do Turner, Apr. 13, 1915, Administrative File, NAACP Papers.
    11. Atlanta *Constitution*, Nov. 7, 15, 19, 1917.

sonian magazine: "Our Grand Old Empire State HAS BEEN RAPED!"[12] The once-popular governor had to flee the state. On the night of August 16, 1915, less than two months after the commutation, twenty-five armed men walked into the state penitentiary at Milledgeville, removed Frank, drove 175 miles to Marietta (the slain girl's home), and hanged him from a tree. The next day an estimated 15,000 people filed past Frank's body in an Atlanta mortuary, on display at the mob's insistence. Pictures of Frank's hanging body sold widely, and the "Ballad of Mary Phagan" became a folk classic. Blacks did not appear overly concerned about the injustice to Leo Frank. For them the story—and its ending—were familiar.[13]

During the furor over the *Frank* case Tom Watson suggested reviving the Ku Klux Klan. On Thanksgiving night, 1915, an Atlanta preacher and salesman named William J. Simmons led thirty-four Georgians to the top of Stone Mountain; there, amid flaming torches and a burning cross, the Klan was reborn. Simmons's followers included the speaker of the Georgia House of Representatives and a future congressman.[14] At first it was largely a social club confined to the Atlanta area, and one observer remarked that until 1920 the Klan had less strength in Atlanta than did the B'nai B'rith.[15] Klan recruiting got a boost from David W. Griffith's film, *The Birth of a Nation,* which romanticized the post–Civil War KKK as defender of white supremacy and depicted the black man as a brute. *Birth of a Nation* opened its Atlanta run to cheering audiences on December 6, 1915, breaking all attendance records, even with a two-dollar ticket price. Not since *Uncle Tom's Cabin* had a work of fiction created such furor. NAACP chapters demanded that the film be banned, and in

12. *Weekly Jeffersonian,* June 24, 1915.

13. For a good brief summary of the *Frank* case, see Woodward, *Tom Watson,* 435–50. Harry Golden, *A Little Girl Is Dead* (Cleveland, 1965), is an interesting journalistic account. Leonard Dinnerstein, *The Leo Frank Case* (New York, 1968), is the best historical study.

14. *Weekly Jeffersonian,* Sept. 2, 1915; Woodward, *Tom Watson,* 446. David M. Chalmers, *Hooded Americanism: The First Century of the Ku Klux Klan, 1865–1965* (New York, 1965) 29, 35; Atlanta *Constitution,* Dec. 7, 1915; Charles O. Jackson, "William J. Simmons: A Career in Ku Kluxism," *Georgia Historical Quarterly,* 50 (Dec., 1966), 351–65. See also Kenneth T. Jackson, *The Ku Klux Klan in the City, 1915–1930* (New York, 1967).

15. Ward Greene, "Notes for a History of the Klan," *American Mercury,* 5 (June, 1925), 241.

Chicago Mayor William Thompson did intervene to prohibit its showing. But white ministers in Savannah refused to sign petitions condemning the film, and Griffith's classic had four runs to capacity audiences in Atlanta during the war years.[16]

Revival of the Ku Klux Klan and the tremendous appeal of *Birth of a Nation* were symptoms of nostalgia among a growing number of Georgians who longed for simpler days when the good guys all wore white hoods. For now war had broken out in Europe, the price of cotton had hit rock bottom, the boll weevil was marching through Georgia, and the black man was beginning his flight north.

The Great Migration began as early as 1914, with the departure from Savannah of five Pennsylvania Railroad trains packed full of black laborers bound for work on railroad lines. It marked the onset of a movement which would relocate a half-million southern blacks during the war years, the most important event in black America since emancipation. Its cause was the demand for skilled and unskilled labor in the North, brought on by decreasing migration from Europe.[17] Blacks went north both to obtain higher wages and to escape southern repression. In 1915 farm laborers were earning less than a dollar a day in Georgia, while shops and factories paid only $1.25. Northern wages were from two to four times as high.[18] Blacks also wanted to escape white violence, and an investigation in south Georgia showed a direct correlation between lynching and migration. The denial of legal rights, which

16. Atlanta *Constitution*, Dec. 7, 19, 1915; Atlanta *Journal*, Dec. 7, 1915; Savannah *Tribune*, Apr. 24, 1915; Jan. 29, 1916; Thomas R. Cripps, "The Reaction of the Negro to the Motion Picture *Birth of a Nation*," in Meier and Rudwick, eds., *The Making of Black America*, II, 159; Julius Wayne Dudley, "A Brief Study of Three Subversive Organizations in Atlanta, Georgia, 1915–1946" (Master's thesis, Atlanta University, 1969), 7–8. After a private White House showing Woodrow Wilson reportedly praised the film as "history written in lightning." Cripps, "The Reaction of the Negro," 153.

17. Savannah *Tribune*, Feb. 3, 1914; U.S. Dept. of Labor, *The Negro at Work During the World War and During Reconstruction* (Washington, 1921), 10; Dewey H. Palmer, "Moving North: Negro Migration During World War I," *Phylon*, 28 (Spring, 1967), 52; Emmett J. Scott, *Negro Migration During the War* (New York, 1921), 52.

18. U.S. Dept. of Labor, *Negro Migration in 1916–17* (Washington, 1919), 11–12, 86–87; Scott, *Negro Migration During the War*, 13–25; Palmer, "Moving North," 53.

affected almost all blacks, caused many to leave the South.[19] In short, emigrating blacks hoped to leave the caste system behind.

Long subject to social, economic, and political inequities in the South, blacks had endured these conditions because of limited opportunities elsewhere. Reports that the North was the "promised land" spread through black communities. Labor agents first brought the news, but their presence declined after white authorities made recruiting conditions unpleasant. The Chicago *Defender*, a radical black weekly edited by native Georgian Robert S. Abbott, urged its growing southern constituency to move north; the newspaper was so persuasive that several southern towns banned both its sale and possession. The most effective emigration agent was the United States mail, which brought encouraging letters from friends and relatives in the North, often accompanied by money for train tickets to Philadelphia, Chicago, and other northern centers.[20]

Blacks migrated from all parts of Georgia, but the exodus was greatest in southwestern areas where the boll weevil, "a cross between a termite and a tank," had entered and badly damaged cotton crops in twenty counties. For farmers ruined by the boll weevil, northern employment was a godsend. Over 4,500 people left the Albany area in a ten-month period beginning in June 1916. Americus reported that 3,000 blacks had migrated and that thousands of acres of land were abandoned. Thomasville, Bainbridge, and other small towns were also affected. Early in 1917 the Southwest Georgia Conference of the A.M.E. Church reported its offerings sharply down, attributing the decrease "to the fact that within the past few months more than a thousand of our best paying members had migrated to the North."[21]

On the coast, Savannah's good rail and ship connections made it the South's leading migration center. Georgia migrants settled in the New York–Newark area, in Pennsylvania, Ohio, Michigan, and as far west as Chicago. They worked in Connecticut tobacco

19. Dept. of Labor, *Negro Migration in 1916–17*, 88; Scott, *Negro Migration During the War*, 22; W. E. B. Du Bois, "Migration of Negroes," *Crisis*, 14 (June, 1917), 65.

20. Scott, *Negro Migration During the War*, 30, 33, 34.

21. *A.M.E. Church Review*, 33 (Jan., 1917), 171; Atlanta *Constitution*, Mar. 21, 1917; Du Bois, "Negro Migration," 63.

fields, on railroads, in foundries, steel mills, slaughterhouses, and later in munitions plants. All sorts of people joined the exodus. Skilled tradesmen quickly found jobs, and black professionals followed their clients north. Factories furnished transportation for the unemployed and unskilled; wealthier blacks paid their own fares.[22] Migration was light in north Georgia, where black population was sparse. Few blacks left the black belt, partly because whites had them bound by contract or indebtedness; those in peonage were even more tied to the soil. Some did escape, stealing away from their cabins at night while leaving lights burning.[23]

As the war in Europe deepened and cotton prices rose, the labor shortage became so acute that intimidation and legal repression were used to deter migration. First to be harassed were labor agents. The General Assembly in 1917 passed a law requiring each agent to obtain a license, post a thousand-dollar bond, and pay whatever tax local authorities imposed.[24] The Macon City Council set its license fee at $25,000, further requiring each agent be recommended by ten local ministers, ten manufacturers, and twenty-five businessmen! Other cities merely set prohibitive license fees. Faced with this opposition, labor agents either worked clandestinely, operated in rural areas, or left the state.[25]

Police moved against the migrants, arresting scores at train stations. Albany lawmen tore up tickets of departing blacks, while Americus officers took a large group of migrants from a train, charged them with misdemeanors, and released most of them after the train had left. The Macon City Council approved the police chief's request for forty magazine rifles which, he explained, were needed to control blacks angered over the city's efforts to discourage migration.[26]

22. Atlanta *Constitution*, Oct. 31, 1916; Mar. 21, 1917; Emmett J. Scott, ed., "Letters of Negro Migrants of 1916–1918," *Journal of Negro History*, 4 (July, 1919), 290–340; Scott, *Negro Migration During the War*, 38–39, 74; Ray Stannard Baker, "The Negro Goes North," *World's Work*, 34 (July, 1917), 315.

23. H. A. Hunt, "Report to Tenth Annual Conference of the NAACP," June 24, 1919, NAACP Papers.

24. *Georgia Laws*, 1917, p. 90.

25. Scott, *Negro Migration During the War*, 73–74; Dept. of Labor, *Negro Migration in 1916–17*, 86; *Crisis*, 12 (Oct., 1916), 297.

26. Savannah *Tribune*, Aug. 19, 1916; Atlanta *Constitution*, Oct. 31, 1916; Dept. of Labor, *Negro Migration in 1916–17*, 110; Scott, *Negro Migration During the War*, 73–74.

The worst harassment occurred at Savannah, where the mayor at first complained to black leaders that the mass exodus was crippling local industry. When black spokesmen refused to help stop the movement, stronger measures resulted. A group of seventeen college students waiting to board a steamer for New York, where the Urban League had summer jobs for them, were arrested, held without charge, and released after the vessel's departure. Several weeks later police cordoned off the Negro section of the train station and arrested every black person in sight, including the managing editor of the Savannah *Tribune*, there to investigate the disturbance. One hundred twenty-five were booked for violating a loitering ordinance, though many had train tickets and others were at the station on business. In dismissing the charges the next day the city recorder reminded arresting officers that Negroes "have certain inalienable rights guaranteed under the Constitution of the United States which give them the privilege of going to Pennsylvania, Kamchatka, Russia or any place they desire and whenever they please."[27]

The Negro Business League of Savannah responded immediately by establishing a defense fund to cover future arrests, an action endorsed by forty-two black businessmen. League president L. E. Williams, also president of the Wage Earners Savings Bank, led a delegation to a city council meeting where the mayor defended police actions and denied there were any efforts to prevent blacks from leaving the port city. Soon thereafter a Savannah judge sentenced two men to thirty days on the county farm for reading a subversive poem, "Bound for the Promised Land."[28]

As the northern exodus continued, white leaders shifted to a strategy of conciliation. In his inaugural address on July 1, 1917, Governor Hugh M. Dorsey noted with alarm that during the preceding year 50,000 blacks had left the state. He then praised "law-abiding, faithful, and respectable" Negroes and asked for increased state aid to black schools. A month later the legislature established a normal school for training black teachers and increased appropriations for the industrial school at Savannah.[29]

27. Savannah *Tribune*, Nov. 4, Aug. 19, 1916.
28. *Ibid.*, Nov. 4, Dec. 9, 1916; Scott, *Negro Migration During the War*, 37.
29. Atlanta *Constitution*, July 2, Aug. 1, 13, 14, 1917.

The Atlanta *Constitution* called for fairness toward the Negro, admitting that "we have not shown that fairness in the past, nor are we showing it today, either in justice before the law, in facilities accorded for education or in other directions." The Albany *Herald* observed that "the Negro is leaving because he thinks he is not getting a square deal; and he is not." Also blaming whites for the exodus was the Tifton *Gazette*:

> Whites have allowed Negroes to be lynched, five at a time, on nothing stronger than suspicion . . . they have allowed them to be whitecapped and their homes burned, with only the weakest and most spasmodic efforts to apprehend or punish those guilty— when any efforts were made at all. Has not the Negro been given the strongest proof that he has no assured right to live, to own property, or to expect justice in Georgia?[30]

Interracial meetings occurred in towns like Thomasville and Waycross, where white leaders pledged to improve conditions for blacks. The annual meeting of the Georgia Federation of Women's Clubs condemned lynching for any cause, and seventy-five black representatives met with state officials in August 1918 to adopt a resolution calling for better schools, improved housing and sanitation facilities, and equal job opportunities for blacks.[31]

Talk of positive change did not stop migration, which continued until job openings in the North declined at the end of the war. Black leaders, gratified that thousands were striking a blow for freedom by leaving, at the same time felt the loss of many of Georgia's strongest black people. Negro ministers watched as congregations melted away, and other race "leaders" saw "followers" taking off without notice.[32] Once enthusiastic about the movement, the Savannah *Tribune* later had second thoughts, complaining that migration was depleting churches, reducing deposits in

30. *Ibid.*, Dec. 10, 1916; Dept. of Labor, *Negro Migration in 1916–17*, p. 102, quoting Albany *Herald;* Du Bois and Dill, eds., *Economic Cooperation Among Negro Americans*, 28, quoting Tifton *Gazette*. Although it is not possible to fathom the motives behind these editorial confessions, it is probably more than coincidence that they came at the height of migration and appear to have been forgotten once conditions returned to normal.

31. Scott, *Negro Migration during the War*, 80; Atlanta *Independent*, June 30, 1917; Dept. of Labor, *The Negro at Work during the War*, 66–67.

32. Scott, *Negro Migration during the War*, 40; Dept. of Labor, *Negro Migration in 1916–17*, p. 95; Du Bois and Dill, eds. *Economic Cooperation among Negro Americans*, 28.

black banks and insurance companies, and cutting down business
of black doctors, lawyers, dentists, and merchants, who in turn
were forced to migrate. Over 50,000 blacks left Georgia during
the war years, and their departure set back efforts to build independent black institutions within the state.[33]

Migration also benefited blacks remaining in Georgia, for labor
scarcity in a time of war prosperity drove up wages in practically
all occupations. In Rome, interracial meetings led to adjustments
in the local wage scale which aided black workers. Especially
fortunate were farmers, for wartime demand drove up cotton from
seven cents a pound in 1914 to over thirty-five cents by 1919.
Farm owners paid off debts, and black farmers bought nearly
300,000 acres of land. The tight labor market helped farm workers and sharecroppers gain more freedom in negotiating wages
and tenant contracts. H. A. Hunt first claimed that "the migration
of Negroes from the South has pushed forward more than we
could have hoped to gain in the next fifty years." Tempering his
remarks, the Fort Valley educator then observed, "Things are not
quite as bad as before the war or before migration began."[34]
Progress as a result of migration was real, but for the most part
short-lived, for it was war that stimulated migration and created
prosperity, and the conflict's end saw Georgia resume its normal
pattern of economic and race relations.

While black spokesmen in Georgia scorned President Wilson
for his racial stand and disapproved of the Marine occupation of
the black republic of Haiti, they generally supported his foreign
policy.[35] When Europe went to war the Savannah *Tribune* had
reflected feelings of millions of Americans, deploring the "barbarous struggle," blaming all parties, and urging the President to
keep the United States out of the conflict. Late in 1914 Savannah

33. Savannah *Tribune*, Mar. 31, 1917.
34. Raper, *Tenants of the Almighty*, 371; Hunt, "Report to Tenth Annual
NAACP Conference"; Atlanta *Independent*, Oct. 7, 1916; Charles Lewis, "Thirty
Cent Cotton and the Negro," *Illustrated World*, 29 (May, 1918), 470; Gaston,
"Negro Wage Earner," 65; Francis T. Long, *The Negroes of Clarke County,
Georgia, during the Great War*, Phelps-Stokes Fellowship *Studies* No. 5 (Athens,
Ga., 1919), 49–55; Savannah *Tribune*, May 9, July 21, 1917.
35. James Weldon Johnson, *Along This Way* (New York, 1933), 349; Atlanta
Independent, June 24, 1916; May 29, 1915.

blacks could still debate the proposition "That Germany was
Justified in its Declaration of War Upon the Allies." As America
swung toward the Allies, so did most black leaders.[36] Georgians
generally supported Wilson's preparedness program in 1916, yet
whites in Atlanta and other cities refused requests by blacks to
join in patriotic parades and rallies.[37] Most Georgians also approved the declaration of war against Germany in April 1917.
That month veterans of the black Georgia State Troops, disbanded by the legislature over a decade earlier, volunteered for
duty, and the Atlanta NAACP chapter offered "the flower of the
race" for enlistment, asking for equality of opportunity in all
branches of service.[38] Included in most prowar endorsements
were declarations of loyalty, made necessary by exaggerated
stories that German agents were at work in the South to gain
sympathy among blacks.[39]

Not all Georgia blacks supported the war. In West Point a
white man was arrested for denouncing the war to assembled
Negroes after his efforts had met with some success. An official of
the Savannah Negro Business League wrote that blacks should
not be as concerned about the war in Europe as about discrimination and mob violence at home.[40] Some blacks held anti-war meetings in Atlanta. Other young black men got jobs in war-related
industries, such as the Brunswick shipyards, to avoid military
service. Most probably agreed with Savannah's Sol Johnson, who
warned the Wilson administration: "'We are with you,' as the
saying goes, but we are going to watch you to see whether our
efforts are as much appreciated as they appear to be desired."[41]

From April 1917 to November 1918 black businessmen and professionals, with support from schools, church groups, and fraternal

36. Savannah *Tribune*, Aug. 8, Oct. 31, 1914.
37. Atlanta *Independent*, July 8, 1916.
38. Savannah *Tribune*, Apr. 14, 21, 1917; Atlanta *Independent*, Apr. 7, 1917.
39. Atlanta *Independent*, Apr. 7, 1914; Emmett J. Scott, *Scott's Official History
of the American Negro in the World War* (Washington, 1919), 344–47.
40. Aptheker, *Afro-American History*, 165; Savannah *Tribune*, Apr. 14, 1917.
Some whites in Georgia also opposed American involvement in the war. Three of
the state's most important politicians, Hoke Smith, Tom Hardwick, and Tom
Watson, maintained their public opposition until the war's end.
41. Savannah *Tribune*, Dec. 29. 1917; Atlanta *Independent*, May 17, 1917;
interview with Dr. Miles Amos, Mar. 20, 1974, Atlanta.

orders, held parades in cities in connection with Liberty Bond drives to support the war. Officials like Governor Dorsey and Atlanta mayor Asa Griggs Candler reviewed black troops and exhorted audiences to buy bonds, while white newspapers praised the patriotism and fighting record of black troops.[42] To insure Negro support of the war the Committee on Public Information organized a "Committee of One Hundred" black leaders to deliver speeches across the country. Emmett J. Scott, now special assistant to Secretary of War Newton D. Baker, called a conference of black editors in Washington to hear government spokesmen, including the young Assistant Secretary of the Navy, Franklin D. Roosevelt. The editors pledged "every endeavor to keep these 12,000,000 people at the highest pitch, not simply of passive loyalty, but of active, enthusiastic and self-sacrificing participation in the war."[43] Such propagandizing was necessary because beneath the veneer of flag-waving and unity blacks were victims of discrimination not only in the civilian sector, but in the armed forces as well.

The first indication of trouble came in early 1917. The War Department began refusing Negro enlistees, stating that the four regular black military units had been brought to full strength. After passage of the Selective Service Act, fourteen officer training camps were established, exclusively for whites. Angered at the prospect of black draftees serving only under whites, Negro leaders demanded a separate camp for black officers. Endorsement of a segregated facility caused uneasiness, but the alternative of no black officers was the greater evil. The War Department designated Fort Des Moines, Iowa, as the Negro officer training camp in May 1917. The Seventh Company of recruits, made up of Georgia men, included lawyers, doctors, schoolteachers, letter

42. Savannah *Tribune*, Apr. 21, June 16, Oct. 6, 1917; Apr. 20, May 4, 11, 1918; Atlanta *Independent*, Apr. 20, 1918; *Crisis*, 15 (Jan., 1918), 141; 16 (June, 1918), 69; 16 (Aug., 1918), 188; Macon *Telegraph*, May 25, 1918; Atlanta *Constitution*, Apr. 15, 19, Oct. 13, 1918; Valdosta *Times*, July 12, 1918, clipping in NAACP Papers. The May 21, 1918, Atlanta *Constitution* headline read: "Two Negro Soldiers Beat Twenty Germans."

43. Scott, *Negro in the World War*, 355–56; New York *Post*, July 1, 1918, clipping in NAACP Papers; Atlanta *Independent*, July 6, 1918; *Second Report of the Provost Marshal General to the Secretary of War on the Operations of the Selective Service System to December 20, 1918* (Washington, 1919), 196.

carriers, and students.[44] The first graduating class of officers met hostility from white enlisted men (who refused to salute them) and from white officers (who treated them as inferiors). About 1,200 black officers received commissions during the war. Emmett Scott later observed that had blacks received their proportionate share, 8,000 would have been commissioned.[45]

Black draftees bore the brunt of army discrimination. The situation varied from camp to camp, but training in the South was especially severe. Complaints reached the War Department that white officers were calling black soldiers "niggers," "coons," and other epithets. Other charges ranged from overwork under unsanitary conditions to assault. Singled out were the military police, accused of punishing blacks for trivial offenses and restricting their leisure activity. And of course this was a Jim Crow army. At Fort Oglethorpe, Georgia, for example, black enlisted men had to line up for mess and wait until white enlisted men had eaten. In crowded camps commanding officers moved Negro units to less desirable quarters, where they suffered from exposure and influenza.[46]

Camp Gordon, near Atlanta, was one of the largest training centers for Negro troops in the South, housing over 9,000 Georgia blacks by late 1917. While some southern state leaders opposed training black troops in the South, Georgia officials held that they should be stationed at Gordon along with white recruits.[47] Black troops there suffered the indignities common elsewhere, and

44. John B. Cade, *Twenty-two Months with "Uncle Sam"* (Atlanta, 1929), 18; Scott, *Negro in the World War*, 34, 82–91; *Crisis*, 14 (June, 1917), 59–61. Twenty Atlanta University students were in the first class of commissioned officers at Fort Des Moines. In 1918 a unit of the Army Officer Training Corps was set up at Atlanta University and Morehouse College, graduating sixteen officers. Savannah *Tribune,* Oct. 20, 1917; Du Bois, "Looking Seventy-five Years Backward," 246.

45. Savannah *Tribune,* Nov. 11, 1917; June 29, 1918; *Jim Jam Jems* June, 1919, p. 50, magazine copy in Du Bois Collection, Fisk; Emmett J. Scott, address before the Tenth Annual Conference of the NAACP, June 22, 1919, p. 4, MS, NAACP Papers.

46. NAACP, New York, to Secretary of War, Mar. 28, 1919, summary on microfilm reel no. 897, National Archives; Scott, *Negro in the World War*, 101–3; Charles H. Williams, *Sidelights on Negro Soldiers* (Norwood, Mass., 1923), 26. Williams investigated military life in America and France under the auspices of the Federal Council of Churches of Christ and the Phelps-Stokes Fund.

47. *Crisis*, 15 (Dec., 1917), 85; Atlanta *Constitution,* Oct. 16, 1917; Williams, *Sidelights on Negro Soldiers*, 20. After September, 1917, only blacks from Georgia were sent to Camp Gordon. Atlanta *Constitution,* Sept. 19, 1917.

absence of any black commissioned officers increased their problems. Most black recruits were assigned to engineer or labor service battalions, where they were to perform tedious, often back-breaking tasks, loading and unloading cargo on both sides of the Atlantic. Since these battalions would have no black officer above the rank of corporal, Camp Gordon officials recruited a number of white sergeants, "specially and carefully selected as having had actual experience in charge of gangs of colored laborers."[48] The white chain gang boss, then, would be an ideal man to oversee the work of black privates.

Blacks at Camp Gordon received inadequate health care. When several Negro service battalions, including the 539th, left Gordon for overseas duty, the Inspector's Office at the port of embarkation in New Jersey complained loudly that the men were physically unfit. Of the 941 men in the 539th Service Battalion, fewer than 45 had received the required typhoid vaccinations and none had been examined for tuberculosis. One-tenth of the men in the battalion were kept in the states for reasons of poor health; 53 of them had venereal disease.[49] The Camp Gordon command was particularly cynical in dealing with black venereal disease cases. Operating under the order that "Only those who cannot be utilized in any useful capacity whatsoever will be discharged from the service," recruits with venereal disease became part of the army. There was even a VD battalion, the 406th Reserve Labor Battalion, which had among its duties unloading food, clothing, and other equipment from troop trains and working in the camp warehouse and ice plant. The commanding officer did concede, though, that the physical disability would "render a large percentage of them unfit for constant daily labor."[50]

Interracial outbreaks occurred at Camp Gordon. Twenty-five

48. Memorandum from Brigadier General T. V. Abbott, Acting Chief of Engineers, to Chief of Staff, Feb. 18, 1918, file no. 8142–91, War Department, War College Division, National Archives (hereafter cited as War Dept. Records); memorandum from Brig. Gen. Henry Jervey to Adjutant General, Mar. 13, 1918, file no. 9796–149, *ibid.*

49. Memorandum from Inspector's Office, Port of Embarkation, to Commanding General, Port of Embarkation, Sept. 4, 1918, Record Group 407, AG 333.3, *ibid.*

50. Brig. Gen. Henry Jervey to Adjutant General, July 8, 1918, file no. 8689–248; memorandum from Brig. Gen. E. D. Anderson to the Chief of Staff, Sept. 26, 1918, file no. 8689–328, *ibid.*

black soldiers were arrested after a fight with guards who denied them passes, ostensibly because of the Spanish flu epidemic. When a military policeman arrested a black soldier on an Atlanta street-car on charges of drunkenness, civilians overwhelmed the officer and the man escaped.[51] Efforts of Atlanta blacks to furnish troops at Gordon with personal services and recreational facilities met with rebuffs from the Army and white YMCA and Red Cross officers. Only through persistent efforts by Mrs. Lugenia Hope, the Neighborhood Union, and the Phillis Wheatley branch of the Atlanta YWCA was a recreational center for black soldiers built outside the camp grounds shortly before the war's end.[52]

Perhaps the most obvious example of discrimination occurred in the selective service system. White reluctance to see blacks in uniform disappeared as involvement in the war increased. Local draft boards which gave 1-A classifications to black men with wives and children exempted single white males, and drafted black farmers while deferring white farmers. While some black farm owners with families received notices to report, single black sharecroppers working for white planters won deferments.[53] President Wilson dismissed three draft boards in December 1917, including the Fulton County Board serving the Atlanta area, which had exempted 85 percent of registered whites and drafted 97 percent of blacks called. The three-man board included a judge, R. F. Thompson, and a doctor, C. M. Curtis, the examining physician.[54] A glance at draft statistics for Georgia shows state-wide discrimination, as a 40 percent black population supplied over half the state's conscripts. This induction rate was well above

51. *Crisis,* 15 (Mar., 1918), 242; Atlanta *Constitution,* Oct. 8, 14, 1918; Atlanta *Independent,* Oct. 19, 1918; Scott, *Negro in the World War,* 94.

52. Williams, *Sidelights on Negro Soldiers,* 89; Shivery, "The Neighborhood Union," 144–45; Atlanta *Constitution,* Feb. 5, 1918; Torrence, *The Story of John Hope,* 209. The Atlanta Red Cross chapter was particularly uncooperative. Blacks were thwarted in their efforts to set up a Negro branch and were even discouraged from contributing to Red Cross fund-raising drives. In Savannah, where there was a Negro chapter, the "white" Red Cross chapter received $25,000 from the local War Chest Fund, but the black branch got nothing. See Williams, *Sidelights on Negro Soldiers,* 123–24; Savannah *Tribune,* Nov. 9, 1918.

53. Savannah *Tribune,* May 26, 1917; Mar. 9, 1918; Atlanta *Independent,* Mar. 30, 1918; Scott, *Negro in the World War,* 428; Williams, *Sidelights on Negro Soldiers,* 21.

54. Atlanta *Constitution,* Dec. 16, 1917. Of 618 white men called in Fulton County, 526 were exempted; only 6 of the 202 blacks were deferred.

the percentage of blacks drafted nationally.[55] Scott pointed out the primary defect of the draft, telling an NAACP audience that "black men had no part in the matter of administering an organization which was to call their men to the colors and send them forward to service." Georgia blacks protested, comparing conscription with disfranchisement, and asked for representatives on local boards. They would have to wait a half-century to see a black man so appointed.[56]

In some areas of the South, lawmen and draft board officials collaborated in a scheme reminiscent of bounty hunting in the Old West. Throughout late 1917 and 1918 the War Department classified a significant number of blacks (nearly 9,000 in Georgia) as "deserters." That is, these men had failed to obey orders of the local board to report for military duty. The Army believed most were "non-willful deserters." Illiteracy, ignorance of the draft, frequent movement—all explained the large number of black deserters, most of whom lived in rural areas.[57] Unscrupulous sheriffs and local board members exploited this situation, for the War Department offered a reward of fifty dollars for each "deserter" brought into camp. In a six-month period in 1918 rewards went out for 1,287 deserters delivered to Camp Wheeler in south Georgia. Only 31 of these "slackers" were white. Among those arrested were black men "who have been lame for 15 years," and men beyond the age of forty or physically unfit. One black Floridian coming to Georgia on a visit was shanghaied as he stepped off the train in Milledgeville and dragged off to the local board meeting, where his captor received the reward. Several blacks were arrested before they were supposed to have reported for induction, and another man received his draft notice while in the Army stockade![58]

55. *Report of the Provost Marshal*, 459; Scott, *Negro in the World War*, 429.
56. Scott, "NAACP Address," 3; Savannah *Tribune*, Sept. 21, 28, 1918. The first black appointment to a local board was made by Governor Lester Maddox.
57. *Report of the Provost Marshal*, 205, 461.
58. Paul T. Murray, "Blacks and the Draft: An Analysis of Institutional Racism, 1917–1971" (Ph.D. dissertation, Florida State University, 1972), 65–66; memorandum from Capt. J. E. Cutler, Camp Wheeling, Ga., to Provost Marshal General Crowder, Oct. 18, 1918, Selective Service Files for World War I, Record Group 163, National Archives (hereafter cited as Selective Service Files); memorandum from National Inspector W. S. Nash to Crowder, Sept. 27, 1918, *ibid.*; memorandum from Col. Allen Crenshaw to the Commanding Officer, Camp Wheeling, Ga., Sept. 7, 1918, *ibid.*

Three separate Army investigations into bounty hunting in
south Georgia arrived at the same conclusion: sheriffs in at least
five counties "have reaped a harvest by fraudulently arresting
colored men and turning them over to the local boards as slackers,
for the sole purpose of getting the reward of $50 offered by the
government."[59] Cooperation of local draft board members was
essential in this racket, for the Selective Service Act placed entire
responsibility for paying the bounty upon them. Despite protests,
this provision remained. Before the war some Georgia sheriffs
arrested blacks on trumped-up charges and sold them into
peonage. Now the lawmen reaped further rewards, performing
their patriotic duty by selling poor blacks into military service.[60]

Other southern whites took advantage of the national emer-
gency to force blacks into civilian servitude. To insure a labor
supply the Provost Marshal issued a "work-or-fight" order that
every able-bodied man between draft ages engage in some
necessary employment. The Georgia General Assembly attempted
to extend coverage to women because of the shortage of domestic
help, but opposition by Atlanta blacks thwarted this effort.[61] The
work-or-fight measure enacted by the legislature went beyond the
Provost Marshal's order, covering able-bodied males between
sixteen and fifty-five. Resembling the vagrancy laws, the act differed in one important respect: possession of money, property,
and income was not a defense against prosecution.[62] The town of
Pelham carried this to such an extreme that the local marshal
arrested the agency director for the Standard Life Insurance
Company, Rufus G. McCrary, who had a personal income of $225
a month and twenty-five agents working under him. The marshal
told McCrary he must change jobs, for selling insurance was
not an essential occupation for a Negro.[63]

Since neither federal order nor state law covered female labor,
Georgia towns passed ordinances to force the black woman into

59. Memorandum, Cutler to Crowder, Oct. 18, 1918, Selective Service Files;
memorandum, Nash to Crowder, Sept. 27, 1918, *ibid.*
60. Murray, "Blacks and the Draft," 66.
61. Walter F. White, " 'Work or Fight' in the South," *New Republic*, 18 (Mar.
1, 1919), 144; J. P. Bryant of Atlanta, "Report to Tenth Annual Conference of
the NAACP," June 24, 1919, NAACP Papers.
62. *Georgia Laws*, 1918, p. 278.
63. White, "Work or Fight," 145.

the white man's kitchen. A Wrightsville law required both men and women to work at least fifty hours a week and carry a card signed by the employer to prove compliance; the ordinance was enforced only against black women. A Macon woman arrested for not working explained to the judge that her husband earned enough to support their family. She was fined $25.75 and told she must work as a domestic or face a jail sentence, for marriage did not exempt her from the law.[64] A Bainbridge ordinance was more specific: women whose duties were only those of their homes must find work. Black housewives were arrested, fined $15.00 apiece, and told to get jobs. Black residents held a meeting and informed city authorities that if arrests continued they would resist "to the last drop of blood in their bodies." No further arrests were made.[65]

At first the national NAACP office was reluctant to oppose these work-or-fight laws, "lest the organization be characterized as disloyal in so doing." However, as the intent of these statutes became obvious, local NAACP chapters and ad hoc black civic groups went into action.[66] NAACP attorneys won acquittal for a black woman arrested in Macon for leaving domestic service for a better position. A black civic league in Thomasville stopped enforcement of the local ordinance and, encouraged, formed an NAACP branch. And in Atlanta blacks prevented local prosecutions under the state law. It is impossible to tell how widespread was the impact of work-or-fight laws, for they were most likely to be enforced in small towns which lacked an organized black citizenry.[67]

From the beginning of American participation in the war, blacks tempered patriotism with skepticism that the war to make the world safe for democracy might not make Georgia safe for

64. John R. Shillady to White, Sept. 25, 1918, Administrative File, NAACP Papers; White, "Work or Fight," 145.

65. *Crisis*, 18 (June, 1919), 97.

66. Shillady to O. A. Toomer of Atlanta, Aug. 3, 1918, Branch File, NAACP Papers.

67. *Crisis*, 17 (Apr., 1919), 281; A. B. Johnson, president of Thomasville NAACP branch, to James Weldon Johnson, Dec. 1, 1918, Branch File, NAACP Papers; "Report of Thomasville Branch to Tenth Annual Convention of the NAACP," June 24, 1919, NAACP Papers; Bryant, "Report to Tenth Annual NAACP Convention."

black people. As early as September 1917 the Savannah *Tribune* protested that the nation was forcing the Negro to "die for a fiction called Democracy. The Negro soldier all but knows that, though he wins or helps win the war, he can know no real freedom when he returns home."[68] Throughout the war years blacks suffered setbacks both at home and on the European front.

Aside from the inequities in the draft and instances of prejudice in camps, the first blow to hopes for racial justice in the armed forces came in Texas in December 1917, when thirteen black soldiers were executed for their alleged part in a Houston race riot which left seventeen white persons dead, including five policemen. Army response to the Houston riot appeared to be avoidance of sensitive contacts between black soldiers and white civilians, even if rights of black troops were abridged. In Kansas after a Manhattan theater manager refused admittance to a black sergeant, the commanding officer of the black 92nd Division, General C. C. Ballou, issued his Bulletin No. 35 ordering all troops to "refrain from going where your presence will be resented." Ballou made things worse by reminding his troops that "white men had made the Division, and they can break it just as easily if it becomes a trouble maker." Black Americans protested Ballou's action, but the order stood.[69]

Jim Crow was also a passenger on ships carrying American fighting men to Europe. Black soldiers were segregated on troop transports, in camps and mess halls, and at the front. The French people welcomed blacks in uniform, angering enough white American soldiers to cause General James Ervin to forbid blacks to associate with French women or to attend social functions. General John J. Pershing's headquarters circulated a memorandum, "Secret Information Concerning Black Troops," to warn French officers not to fraternize with black officers. The French continued to befriend black soldiers.[70] Of 200,000 black troops sent to France, 80 percent served behind the lines as stevedores. Those who saw combat fought well.[71] Some white officers at-

68. Savannah *Tribune*, Sept. 15, 1917.
69. Scott, *Negro in the World War*, 97–101; Savannah *Tribune*, Apr. 20, 1918; Atlanta *Independent*, Apr. 27, 1918.
70. *Crisis*, 18 (May, 1919), 16–18; Aptheker, *Afro-American History*, 168; Savannah *Tribune*, Jan. 26, 1918; Scott, *Negro in the World War*, 297–99, 442–43.
71. Scott, *Negro in the World War*, 256–70.

tempted to discredit the combat record of troops led by black officers. Throughout the 92nd Division black officers were transferred or dismissed, often without cause, and replaced by whites. Despite the machinations of Army politics, black soldiers won high praise from the allies, the American public, and the Army high command.[72]

Back in the United States, race violence increased during the war years. In East St. Louis, Illinois, at least forty blacks were killed in a riot growing out of employment of black workers in a factory holding government contracts.[73] Georgia again led the nation in lynchings. The murder of Hampton Smith, a white farmer with a reputation for cruelty toward tenants, led to a five-day orgy in Brookes and Lowndes counties. Among eleven blacks lynched was Hayes Turner, taken from officers who were holding him in custody. Turner's wife, Mary, then in her eighth month of pregnancy, proclaimed his innocence and warned that if she learned the identity of his murderers she would swear out warrants against them. For this, several hundred men and women seized her and took her to a nearby stream, tied her ankles and hanged her head downwards, soaked her clothes with gasoline and set them afire. After her clothes burned off, and while she was yet alive, a man slit open her abdomen. Her unborn child fell from her womb, gave two cries, and was then crushed under the heel of a member of the mob. Fathers held children up in their arms to witness this brutality. Mary Turner and her child were buried about ten feet from the stream, their graves marked by an empty whiskey bottle with a cigar stump placed in the neck. NAACP investigator Walter White supplied Governor Dorsey with the names of fourteen lynchers, including the ringleaders. No one was brought to trial.[74]

72. *Ibid.*, 15–16, quoting Secretary of War Newton D. Baker and General John J. Pershing; Savannah *Tribune*, Jan. 12, 1918. The first two Americans to receive the French Croix de Guerre were black, and later four black infantry regiments were similarly decorated.

73. President Wilson declined to see a delegation of Maryland blacks about the East St. Louis riot, but he publicly denounced lynching for the first time in 1918. Kelly Miller, *The Disgrace of Democracy: An Open Letter to President Woodrow Wilson* (n.p., 1917). For a full account of the riot, see Elliott M. Rudwick, *Race Riot at East St. Louis* (Carbondale, Ill., 1964).

74. Memorandum for Governor Dorsey from White, July 10, 1918; Dorsey to Shillady, Aug. 27, 1918, White to T. W. Loyless, editor of the Augusta *Chronicle,*

Despite increasing violence at home and discrimination in the armed forces, black spokesmen in Georgia continued to support the war. Early optimism gave way to determination to see the war through, to defer payment on grievances until after the conflict's end. Many blacks agreed with W. E. B. Du Bois, who in July 1918 wrote his "Close Ranks" editorial in the *Crisis:* "Let us not hesitate. Let us, while the war lasts, forget our special grievances and close our ranks shoulder to shoulder with our own fellow white citizens and the allied nations that are fighting for democracy. We make no ordinary sacrifice, but we make it gladly and willingly, with our eyes lifted to the hills." Not until later, after the shooting in Europe had stopped and the troops had come home, would Du Bois and others reflect that the sacrifices made by black Americans during the war years had been largely in vain.[75]

Aug. 24, 1918, NAACP Papers; Savannah *Tribune*, May 25, 1918; Kellogg, *NAACP*, 230; Ovington, *The Walls Came Tumbling Down*, 152. White obtained names of the lynchers from George Spratling, himself a member of the mob.

75. W. E. B. Du Bois, "Close Ranks," *Crisis*, 16 (July, 1918), 111; 19 (Feb., 1920), 213; Du Bois, *Darkwater*, 34; Torrence, *The Story of John Hope*, 227.

Aftermath

SHOUTS OF JUBILATION after the Armistice faded
into silence as Americans, black and white, faced problems of
inflation and industrial unrest. Some blamed the nation's woes on
radicals, many foreign-born, who had opposed the war, supported
the Bolshevik Revolution, and were now fomenting labor unrest.
Attorney General A. Mitchell Palmer's campaign to rid the country of radical influence resulted in thousands of arrests and de-
portation of nearly 600 aliens.[1] This Red Scare of 1919 had
repercussions in black America, which was experiencing its own
postwar problems.

The first of 200,000 black troops stationed overseas returned
to enthusiastic receptions in New York and other ports. Several
thousand blacks paraded through Savannah in early May alongside 1,200 returning Georgia veterans, and speakers heralded a
new day. Such celebrations were short-lived, for the summer of
1919 ushered in the greatest interracial strife the nation had yet
witnessed.[2] Beginning on May 10 with a riot in Charleston, South
Carolina, this Red Summer lasted until the September 30 clash
in Elaine, Arkansas, between black sharecroppers and white
farmers. Some twenty-five American cities suffered riots, with the
most serious outbreaks in Chicago and Washington killing scores
of blacks and whites.[3] These episodes arose from a national mood
of uncertainty, economic competition in the North between

1. Robert K. Murray, *Red Scare, A Study in National Hysteria, 1919–1920*
(Minneapolis, 1955), 251.
2. Savannah *Tribune,* May 10, 1919; Atlanta *Constitution,* Feb. 18, 1919.
3. Arthur I. Waskow, *From Race Riot to Sit-In, 1919 and the 1960s* (New
York, 1966), 12–20; Johnson, *Along This Way,* 341.

whites and recently arrived blacks, militance among blacks, and
the revival of the Ku Klux Klan. Overshadowing these factors
were the social upheaval brought on by the war and attempts to
turn back the clock to "better" days.

Shortly after the armistice Georgia senator Thomas Hardwick
had asked: "What will be the result when tens of thousands of
Negroes come home from this war with a record of honorable
military service? I can conceive that a new agitation may arise as
strong and bitter as the agitation for Negro suffrage which swept
the North after the Civil War."[4] In Hardwick's home state whites
took steps to prevent "agitation" by returning black troops. When
a convalescent Negro soldier, Ben Herne, asked for a glass of
soda water in an Atlanta drug store an employee beat him senseless with a baseball bat. Later Herne said he had just returned
from France and was unaware that blacks were not served at
the fountain.[5] In February 1919 soldiers being discharged from
Camp Gordon were told that they should wear their uniforms
with pride. Less than two months later a group of whites in
Blakely, "the meanest town in Georgia," murdered veteran Wilbur Little because he had worn his uniform "too long." Some
areas of the state reported well over half the returning black
soldiers soon moving away to distant cities in the North—the
black veteran coming back to his home town became "just a nigger" again.[6]

Georgia had no outbreaks on the scale of Chicago or Washington, but was the scene of several racial clashes. Violence broke
out in the town of Berkeley after an attempted lynching, with
blacks killing four would-be assassins. In April, a disturbance
which began in a church in Millen, not far from the South Carolina border, led to the deaths of a white policeman and marshal.
Whites retaliated by killing five blacks and burning seven
churches and lodge halls. A minor dispute over class colors be-

    4. *Crisis,* 17 (Dec., 1918), 62, quoting Hardwick.
    5. Atlanta *Constitution,* Apr. 16, 1919.
    6. "Report of the Demobilization Inspector at Camp Gordon," Feb. 1, 1919,
AG 333.1, War Dept. Records; Atlanta *Independent,* Mar. 29, 1919; Kellogg,
NAACP, 235; John Hope Franklin, *From Slavery to Freedom: A History of
American Negroes* (New York, 1956), 480; Pittsburgh *Courier,* Aug. 23, 1919,
clipping in NAACP Papers; Towns to Shillady, Aug. 8, 1919; White to Shillady,
Apr. 15, 1919, NAACP Papers; Raper, *Tenants of the Almighty,* 148; *Crisis,* 18
(July, 1919), 155.

tween black and white high school seniors in Milledgeville threatened to get out of hand. Fearing that whites would disrupt their commencement program, Milledgeville blacks sent young men to Macon to buy guns and ammunition. As the exercises were going on in the First Baptist Church over a hundred armed men stood guard outside, "carrying their guns with as much calmness as if they were going to shoot a rabbit in a hunt." The whites stayed away.[7] When Walter White visited Atlanta in late July he saw white people crowding hardware stores and pawnshops to buy guns, afraid of outbreaks similar to those in the North. This witness to the 1906 Atlanta riot wrote to a friend, "Never before have I seen or felt such a widespread feeling of unrest here in Atlanta." In Savannah the police department requested, as a "precautionary" action, that stores refuse to sell guns and ammunition to blacks.[8]

Coming on the heels of the war to make the world safe for democracy, this increase in racial proscription and violence angered black spokesmen. Du Bois, whose *Crisis* editorials had supported Wilson's war policies, now wrote that blacks had been "Fools, yes that's it fools. All of us fools fought a long, cruel, bloody and unnecessary war and we not only killed our boys—we killed Faith and Hope."[9] The Justice Department investigated the *Crisis* and other black journals, including A. Philip Randolph's militantly socialist *Messenger*, and Attorney General Palmer commissioned young J. Edgar Hoover to prepare a report on radical activity among blacks.[10]

The hostile atmosphere that marked the postwar years united blacks in community self-help groups like the NAACP and the Urban League. The national office of the Urban League decided in 1919 to locate its southern regional headquarters in Atlanta, with Jesse O. Thomas, a Tuskegee graduate and professional so-

7. Waskow, *Race Riot to Sit-In*, 304–6; *Crisis*, 19 (Feb., 1920), 183–86; Baltimore *Daily Herald*, Aug. 29, 1919, clipping in NAACP Papers; New York *Times*, Oct. 7, 1919; Atlanta *Constitution*, Apr. 14, Aug. 29, 1919; Rev. Dr. James Arthur Martin to Du Bois, May 30, 1919, in Aptheker, ed., *Correspondence of W. E. B. Du Bois*, I, 233–34.

8. White to Ovington, July 30, 1919, NAACP Papers; Atlanta *Constitution*, Aug. 4, 1919.

9. *Crisis*, 19 (Feb., 1920), 213.

10. Broderick, *W. E. B. Du Bois*, 112; Waskow, *Race Riot to Sit-In*, 188.

cial worker, as field secretary. Thomas also founded the local
League chapter, and under his leadership the Atlanta branch
quickly gained city funds for two Negro nurses for the public
school system and for a black physician to serve indigents. That
same year it financed an extensive survey of living and working
conditions among blacks and was responsible for some improve-
ments in black schools. The Urban League had chapters in other
Georgia cities, most notably Savannah, but for a time only Atlanta would provide the combination of black initiative and white
money essential for a successful full-scale operation.[11]

Blacks in several Georgia communities had organized NAACP
chapters during the war, and by 1920 branches were active in
sixteen cities. Atlanta's membership increased from 700 to over
3,000 in eighteen months.[12] These branches lobbied with government officials for better schools and city services and investigated
lynchings and other cases of racial injustice. The Savannah
branch stalled a government-sanctioned plan to move the city's
red light district to a black residential area, and Lucy Laney
headed the Augusta NAACP drive to register black women to
vote, while the Atlanta chapter stopped efforts to drop the seventh grade in black schools and helped defeat two bond issues
detrimental to blacks.[13]

Pressure from whites curtailed NAACP activities in smaller
towns. A typical sentiment was expressed by a south Georgia
newspaper, the Dublin *Courier-Herald and Dispatch:* "This white
man's country . . . [will not tolerate] the interference of a nigger
society, breeding discontent with every hour of its existence."[14]
The Thomasville branch, at one time claiming 300 members, disbanded in 1920 after whites threatened to kill the president. The

11. Matthews, "Studies in Race Relations," 363–64; Jesse O. Thomas, *My Story in Black and White* (New York, 1967), 96–99, 111; National Urban League, *Annual Report, 1920* (New York, 1921), 5, 17, 19. Thomas was also a member of the faculty of the new Atlanta School of Social Service at Morehouse.
12. Shillady to Toomer, Sept. 26, 1918, NAACP Papers; *Crisis*, 19 (Mar., 1920), 246.
13. J. G. Lemon, Secretary of Savannah branch, to New York NAACP head-quarters, Jan. 30, 1918, NAACP Papers; Lucy Laney, MS, June 26, 1919, *ibid.*; Savannah *Tribune*, June 30, 1917; reports from Thomasville, Macon, Rome, and Brunswick branches, Branch Files, NAACP Papers.
14. Undated copy of Dublin *Courier-Herald and Dispatch* editorial, in NAACP Papers.

leader was not harmed, but he lost his job as a mail carrier as a result of NAACP work.[15] Enthusiasm to start local chapters waned under white opposition, for only a few black business and professional people could escape the threat of economic reprisal. By the early 1920s branches would have influence in few communities.[16]

While chapters in many cities were struggling to survive and the Justice Department was investigating the NAACP as a subversive organization, the city of Atlanta in a surprise move invited the NAACP to hold its eleventh annual national convention there.[17] Atlanta was using the conference to improve its racial image, but the move of local elected officials to invite and address such a gathering was noteworthy. Two hundred twenty-seven delegates from ninety-two branches in twenty-nine states attended. (Representation from northern cities was smaller than usual because some delegates were afraid to make the trip.[18]) In this first national meeting in a southern city NAACP speakers pressed for voting rights, federal suppression of lynching, and dismantling the Jim Crow system. A convention highlight was presentation of the Joel E. Spingarn medal, given annually to an outstanding leader; on this occasion the award went to a former Atlantan, W. E. B. Du Bois.[19]

One convention session discussed the "Atlanta Plan" of interracial cooperation. A group of southern white ministers, teachers, and professionals, concerned about the dangers inherent in the postwar era, had met in Atlanta in early 1919 to discuss ways of averting racial conflict. Out of these meetings grew the Interracial Commission, led by former Methodist minister and YMCA worker Will W. Alexander. By many standards a conservative group, from the outset it declared itself "absolutely loyal . . . to the principle of racial integrity," and never came to grips with

15. A. B. Johnson to Shillady, Dec. 1, 1918; Johnson to James W. Johnson, June 2, 1920, NAACP Papers.

16. Reports from Georgia chapters, Branch Files, NAACP Papers.

17. T. K. Gibson, Secretary-Manager of Atlanta NAACP, to White, May 20, 1920, NAACP Papers.

18. NAACP press release, June 12, 1920, copy in NAACP Papers; Johnson, *Along This Way*, 356–57.

19. NAACP press release, June 12, 1920, NAACP Papers; *Crisis*, 20 (July, 1920), 117.

the segregation issue.[20] And while the Interracial Commission's white leadership was no doubt the best the South had to offer, these men did not always invite the ablest black leaders to join their deliberations. Du Bois put it more bluntly in a letter to a Commission official when he stated that his "greatest objection to the Interracial Commission is the kind of Negro you pick to go on it." True, John Hope was an "excellent representative, but he stands almost alone. . . . You have favored too much the sort of Colored men that we call 'WHITE FOLKS' NIGGERS.' "[21]

For all its apparent timidity, the Interracial Commission was an innovation in the South, where whites and blacks had seldom worked together on other than an ad hoc basis. Interracial committees were formed in over a hundred Georgia counties just after the war, defusing a number of potentially explosive racial confrontations.[22] By threatening court action, the Atlanta committee prevented the city from reneging on a pledge to build a black high school. In the early 1920s the Georgia Commission helped get twenty-two indictments in lynching cases which led to four convictions, a feat unheard of before the war. One of the Interracial Commission's most interesting achievements was convincing Governor Hugh M. Dorsey to go public with his findings on mistreatment of blacks in Georgia.[23]

Elected to the state's highest office in 1916 as a result of publicity received from prosecuting Leo Frank, Dorsey at first displayed little interest in his black constituency, but later participated in efforts to improve Negro schools and recreational facilities. As his term neared its end he became increasingly concerned about white violence and his failure to persuade local officials to take action against mobs. Dorsey's *Statement . . . as to the Negro in Georgia* is probably the most candid and courageous attack on racial injustice issued by an American governor.

20. Quoted in Tindall, *Emergence of the New South*, 181.
21. Du Bois to Robert B. Eleazer, Mar. 12, 1926, Commission on Interracial Cooperation Papers, Negro Collection, Trevor Arnett Library, Atlanta University; "Report of the Interracial Program," 1920, *ibid.*
22. "Report of the Interracial Program," 1920, *ibid.*
23. Tindall, *Emergence of the New South*, 179; Torrence, *The Story of John Hope*, 230. See also Will W. Alexander, "*Phylon* Profile XI: John Hope," *Phylon*, 8 (First Quarter, 1947), 4–10. For a biography of Alexander, see Wilma Dykeman and James Stokely, *Seeds of Southern Change: The Life of Will Alexander* (Chicago, 1962).

The bulk of the statement was a summary of 135 cases of lynching, peonage, whitecapping, and other crimes against blacks. (Dorsey made no attempt to collect all cases, noting that if he had the number would have been much higher.) The governor minced no words: "To me it seems that we stand indicted as a people before the world. If the conditions indicated by these charges should continue both God and man would justly condemn Georgia more severely than man and God have condemned Belgium and Leopold for the Congo atrocities. But worse than that condemnation would be the destruction of our civilization by the continued toleration of such cruelties in Georgia."[24] The document proposed solutions, including publicity of facts relating to Negro mistreatment and establishment of state and local interracial committees. Dorsey asked for repeal of the state contract labor (peonage) law, and enactment of anti-lynching statutes which would give the governor powers of intervention to prevent lynchings and prosecute members of a mob.[25]

The Dorsey statement stunned Georgia. Black leaders applauded the governor's courage, and the NAACP reprinted and widely distributed the pamphlet.[26] A few whites endorsed Dorsey's action, but most reacted with hostility. The Macon *Telegraph* predicted that now "South-haters" would have "an official indictment by the highest official of the State," adding, "We won't get through denying this pamphlet for a long time to come." Whites went to mass meetings in Macon and other cities, there denouncing the governor as a traitor to his state. Governor-elect Tom Hardwick, whose long political career had been built on the rock of white supremacy, branded Dorsey's facts an "infamous slander."[27]

For blacks the white reaction against the governor's findings and recommendations came as the final blow to earlier hopes that the postwar era would bring relief. Although the last two

24. Hugh M. Dorsey, *A Statement from Governor Hugh M. Dorsey as to the Negro in Georgia* (Atlanta, 1921), 2; Atlanta *Constitution*, July 3, 8, 10, 1919.
25. Dorsey, *Statement*, 22–23.
26. Savannah *Tribune*, May 14, 1921; statement by White, Apr. 27, 1921, NAACP Papers.
27. Macon *Telegraph*, May 12, 20, 1921; Thomas Hardwick, quoted in "Trying to Stamp Out Peonage in Georgia," *Current Opinion*, 71 (July, 1921), 76.

years of the decade saw the beginning of an interracial movement and increased organizational efforts by the NAACP, the Urban League, and other groups devoted to racial advancement, the period was dominated by a rise in white violence and unwillingness among most state leaders to come to grips with Georgia's problems. In the presidential election of 1920 Americans opted for normalcy and Warren G. Harding, while Georgia voters voiced similar sentiments by electing Hardwick governor and sending Tom Watson to the Senate.

Blacks had made progress in Georgia during the first two decades of the twentieth century. Nearly 14,000 black farmers owned almost 2,000,000 acres of land in 1920, a figure not to be surpassed until the last years of the New Deal. Child labor dropped nearly 30 percent for blacks between 1900 and 1920, and the number of black industrial workers, professionals, and businessmen increased, even with migration.[28] The move to the cities continued—in 1920 almost one of every four Georgia blacks was an urban dweller—and black business districts sprang up to help serve this growing population. Though still inadequate, schools had improved since the turn of the century, particularly in the cities, and the illiteracy rate hit a new low.[29]

Yet Georgia blacks would face another half-century of violence and terror, of broken promises and dreams deferred. Economic depression and the spread of the boll weevil would in the 1920s call forth a northern migration greater than that of the war years. White supremacy outlasted both World War I and its aftermath, and for a time politics and race relations in Georgia would resume their familiar course. The Watsons and the Hardwicks would pass from the scene, only to be replaced by the Talmadges and the Maddoxes. But black perseverance and protest would survive. The legacy of W. E. B. Du Bois, John and Lugenia Hope, Bishop Turner, and Lucy Laney would be passed on to new gen-

28. Gaston, "Negro Wage Earner," 52–53; *Twelfth Census, Population,* II, 26–27; *Fourteenth Census, Population,* IV, 514–15, 903–6; *Twelfth Census, Special Report, Occupations,* 154–65. Between 1900 and 1920 the number of black industrial workers rose from 25,701 to 68,107, professionals increased from 4,879 to 7,662, and those involved in trade and transportation went up from 19,472 to 43,297.

29. *Negro Population,* 92; *Negroes in the U.S.,* 53; "Illiteracy Statistics, 1920, Georgia," in State Superintendent of Education, *Report,* 1920, p. 124.

erations who would press the fight for equality. Their achievements would be due in no small part to the courageous efforts
of those thousands of black men and women who kept the struggle for human dignity alive in Georgia during the early twentieth
century.)

Bibliographical Note

PRIMARY SOURCES

Manuscript Collections

The Booker T. Washington Papers (Manuscript Division, Library of Congress) show the widespread influence of the Tuskegean in Georgia, and are particularly valuable for their insights into black politics, business, and education. The collection includes Washington's early correspondence with Du Bois, his dispute with Max Barber of the *Voice of the Negro*, his correspondence with black leaders such as Henry L. Rucker and Reverend H. H. Proctor, plus information on the National Negro Business League and the Standard Life Insurance Company. The papers of the National Association for the Advancement of Colored People (Manuscript Division, Library of Congress) were important for the period 1910–20. Reports from local Georgia branches and investigations by the national office provide material on the racial struggle in Georgia. For study of race relations before 1910, the Ray Stannard Baker Papers (Manuscript Division, Library of Congress) should be consulted.

The Trevor Arnett Library, Atlanta University, contains a wealth of manuscript material. The Edward T. Ware Papers and the George A. Towns Papers, along with Atlanta University catalogs, newspapers, and alumni magazines, deal with the education of Georgia blacks. The Chautauqua Circle Collection was the best source on social clubs, and the Neighborhood Union Collection is valuable for its description of the state's most successful self-help organization. The Commission on Interracial Cooperation Collection contains interesting material but was of limited use for this study.

The Schomburg Collection (New York Public Library) was most helpful for its large collection of books, pamphlets, and manuscripts

212

on black fraternal orders, many of which dealt with lodges in Georgia. The Interdenominational Theological Center in Atlanta has a similar collection of materials on black religious life. The W. E. B. Du Bois Collection (Fisk University Library), though incomplete, includes some of Du Bois's correspondence and a number of pamphlets relating to race violence, lynching, and World War I. The bulk of the valuable Du Bois collection was at this writing being processed at the University of Massachusetts and was unavailable for this study. The first volume of Herbert Aptheker, ed., *Correspondence of W. E. B. Du Bois, Volume I, Selections 1877–1934* (University of Massachusetts, 1973), does contain some material on Du Bois's early years in Georgia. The Southern Labor Archives (Georgia State University Library, Atlanta) show evidence of anti-black activity among white Georgians in the labor movement.

White Georgia politicians could not avoid the race question, and their papers at times reflect their racial attitudes. The Tom Watson Papers (Southern Collection, University of North Carolina Library) and the Hoke Smith Collection (University of Georgia Library) contain much material but are disappointing in their coverage of racial activities from 1900 to 1920. The Henry P. Farrow Papers (University of Georgia Library) point out the frustrations of a white Republican politician who tried to keep his party biracial. The papers of a streetcar president, George Johnson Baldwin (Southern Collection, University of North Carolina Library), give management's reaction to a black boycott. A file on lynching in the gubernatorial papers of Hugh M. Dorsey (Georgia Department of Archives and History, Atlanta) shows both the governor's attempts to stop the practice and the procrastination of local law enforcement officials charged with preventing lynchings. The papers of the president of the Savannah school board, George Anderson Mercer (Georgia State Historical Society, Savannah) contain material on black schools, as do the Twiggs County Board of Education Papers (University of Georgia Library), a collection including salary scales and pupil loads for black and white teachers in this middle Georgia county. The Julian L. Harris Papers (Special Collection, Robert W. Woodruff Library, Emory University) are more complete for the period after 1920, but contain information on race and politics during the progressive era.

Government Documents and Publications

The reports of the Bureau of the Census from 1890 to 1930, particularly sections dealing with occupations, are useful. Two special volumes,

Negro Population in the United States, 1790–1915 (Washington, 1918) and *Negroes in the United States, 1920–1932* (Washington, 1933), supply a wealth of information on black America. The two-volume study directed by Thomas Jesse Jones, *Negro Education, A Study of the Private and Higher Schools for Colored People in the United States,* Department of the Interior, Bureau of Education, Bulletin 1916, Nos. 38 and 39 (Washington, 1917), contains reports of investigations made on Georgia's black schools. The emphasis on weaknesses in schools led black leaders to criticize this study. The Department of Labor sponsored two studies during the war years, *Negro Migration in 1916–17* (Washington, 1919) and *The Negro at Work During the World War and During Reconstruction* (Washington, 1921), which include material on black Georgians. Detailed statistical material on the draft in Georgia comes from the *Second Report of the Provost Marshal to the Secretary of War on the Operations of the Selective Service System to December 20, 1918* (Washington, 1919). The records of the War Department (National Archives) include some material on mistreatment of black soldiers in Georgia camps and on abuses in the selective service system.

In investigating the history of peonage in Georgia, the General Records of the Department of Justice, Record Group 60 (National Archives), were invaluable. The file, consisting of correspondence between the United States attorneys for North and South Georgia districts and the Attorney General, includes federal peonage investigations and testimony from black victims. Correspondence shows the difficulty attorneys experienced in obtaining convictions and the apparent indifference of the Washington office toward conditions in Georgia. The Federal Records Center at East Point, Georgia, provides additional information on peonage in Georgia.

In Georgia, the *Senate Journal* and *House Journal,* along with the *Acts and Resolutions of the General Assembly of Georgia (Georgia Laws),* are a chronicle of populist and progressive legislative proposals, including anti-black measures. Annual reports from various state agencies such as the Department of Education were helpful. The *Annual Report of the Prison Commission of Georgia* for the period 1897–1908 shows the discrepancy between the "official" view of conditions in convict camps and the actual state of the camps, described in "Report of the Convict Investigating Committee to the Extraordinary Session of the General Assembly," *Georgia Laws* (1908), 1059–1130. Voter registration lists on microfilm at the Georgia Archives document the decline of black voting both before and after disfranchisement.

Tax digests in a half-dozen selected counties were of assistance in determining the amount and relative value of black-owned farmland

and city property, and were used with city directories in the major urban areas to examine black middle-class housing patterns. City codes and municipal reports were also helpful in the study of black urban life.

Newspapers and Periodicals

Among newspapers examined, two black weeklies were essential: the Savannah *Tribune* (for the years 1899–1921) and the Atlanta *Independent* (1904–21). The *Tribune* gave better coverage of local and state black activities, while the *Independent* reflected the personal whims of editor Benjamin Davis. Unlike over a dozen other black Georgia weeklies, the *Tribune* and *Independent* were sound business operations and survived in the 1920s.

White dailies had good political coverage, but for the most part they limited racial news to lynchings, black crime, and "Sambo" stories. The Atlanta *Constitution* was politically conservative and at best paternalistic toward blacks; the Atlanta *Journal*, the voice of Hoke Smith, reflected that leader's views; the Atlanta *Georgian*, founded in 1906, was interested in reform, leading the fight for abolition of the convict lease system and for civic improvement. At the same time the *Georgian*'s racial views were the most reactionary of the three Atlanta dailies. The Columbus *Enquirer-Sun*, the Augusta *Chronicle*, the Macon *Telegraph*, and the Savannah *Morning News* all had unenlightened approaches to race relations during the progressive era, with the *Telegraph* and the *Chronicle* most conservative politically.

In addition to weekly newspapers, blacks published a number of periodicals, the best of which were the *Voice of the Negro* (1904–7) and the *Crisis: A Record of the Darker Races* (1910–). The two editors, Jesse Max Barber and W. E. B. Du Bois, shared the same radical philosophy, and their journals came out unequivocally for full equality for blacks. A national monthly, *Voice of the Negro* was published in Atlanta and carried much Georgia news. The *Crisis* was particularly useful for coverage of lynchings and other racial confrontations in the state. While teaching at Atlanta University, Du Bois published two small journals, the *Moon Illustrated Weekly* (1906) and the *Horizon: A Journal of the Color Line* (1907–10). The latter was the voice of the Niagara Movement, and gave Du Bois a forum to attack his critics, among them Washington and Ben Davis. Henry McNeal Turner's *Voice of Missions* (1893–1900) and *Voice of the People* (1901-c. 1907), both published in Atlanta, popularized the Bishop's dream of a national Back-to-Africa movement and exposed racial injustice in Georgia and

throughout the country. Also useful for this period is the annual publication, the *Negro Year Book, An Encyclopedia of the Negro* (for the
years 1912–19), edited at Tuskegee by Monroe Work. Unfortunately,
files of William J. White's *Georgia Baptist*, one of the most important
black periodicals, are not extant.

The Atlanta University Publications

The *Publications* are the product of original research by Atlanta Uni-
versity students and teachers into the condition of black Americans.
Most helpful for this account are W. E. B. Du Bois, ed., *The Negro
Common School* (No. 6, 1901); *The Negro Church* (No. 8, 1903);
Some Notes on Negro Crime, Particularly in Georgia (No. 9, 1904);
Economic Cooperation among Negro Americans (No. 12, 1907); *The
Negro American Family* (No. 13, 1908); also Du Bois and Augustus
Dill, eds., *The Common School and the Negro American* (No. 16, 1911);
The Negro American Artisan (No. 17, 1912); *Manners and Morals
among Negro Americans* (No. 18, 1913); and Thomas Brown, ed.,
Economic Cooperation among the Negroes of Georgia (No. 22, 1917).

The Phelps-Stokes Studies

The Phelps-Stokes Fellowships were established at the University of
Georgia for graduate students and professors to investigate aspects
of Negro life. By and large, the Phelps-Stokes Fellows held the racial
prejudices of most whites, and the *Studies* are often flawed by au-
thorial assumptions of Negro inferiority. The volumes are most useful
in their description of living and working conditions among Georgia
blacks. Works consulted are Thomas G. Woofter, *The Negroes of
Athens, Georgia* (No. 1, 1913); W. B. Hill, *Rural Survey of Clarke
County, Georgia, with Special Reference to Negroes* (No. 2, 1915);
Francis T. Long, *The Negroes of Clarke County, Georgia, During the
Great War* (No. 5, 1919); and Ruth Reed, *The Negro Women of
Gainesville, Georgia* (No. 6, 1921).

Autobiographies, Speeches

A number of blacks have written of their experiences living in Georgia.
James Weldon Johnson in *Along This Way* (New York, 1933) describes
his days as an Atlanta University undergraduate. Walter White was
born and educated in Atlanta, and *A Man Called White* (New York,
1948) includes his firsthand account of the Atlanta riot of 1906. Richard

R. Wright, Jr.'s *87 Years Behind the Black Curtain: An Autobiography*
(Philadelphia, 1965), contains sections dealing with the Wright fam-
ily's life in Savannah. One of Georgia's leading ministers, Henry Hugh
Proctor, discussed his work to bring the races together in *Between
Black and White* (Boston, 1925). Educator William H. Crogman
collected his earlier speeches in *Talks for the Times* (Atlanta, 1896).
The state's most famous black resident, W. E. B. Du Bois, recalled his
years as an Atlanta University professor in his autobiographies, *Dusk
of Dawn, An Essay Toward an Autobiography of a Race Concept*
(New York, 1940), and *The Autobiography of W. E. B. Du Bois* (New
York, 1968). His classic, *The Souls of Black Folk, Essays and Sketches*
(Chicago, 1903), contains autobiographical material as well as de-
tailed descriptions of life among rural blacks in south Georgia. In
The Reminiscences of W. E. B. Du Bois (1963) in the Oral History
Collection at Columbia University the scholar-activist candidly recalls
his Georgia experiences.

Interviews

Conversations with Georgia blacks who lived through the period of
this study were of inestimable value. Many of the men and women
interviewed were from the Atlanta area, some having migrated there
from rural sections of the state. Most were well educated and had
achieved positions of prominence in their communities. Mr. Henry
Williams spent a summer interviewing in south Georgia, near Albany.
His subjects were men and women from rural areas who had worked
as sharecroppers. The most interesting and informative conversations
were with the following persons: Dr. Miles Amos, Atlanta; Mr. J. B.
Blayton, Atlanta; Mr. Monroe Clark, Albany; Mrs. Ella M. Daniels,
Albany; Mr. Robert W. Gadsden, Savannah; Mrs. Grace Towns Hamil-
ton, Atlanta; Miss Louise Laney, Augusta; Mrs. H. S. Murphy, Atlanta;
Dr. Homer Nash, Atlanta; Mrs. Cecilia Carter Rogers, Atlanta; Mrs.
M. G. Wartman, Atlanta; Mrs. Ethel Wright, Newton.

SECONDARY ACCOUNTS

Biographies

Several Georgia blacks have been the subjects of biographies. Ridgely
Torrence has written a warm, fascinating account of a noted Georgia
educator in *The Story of John Hope* (New York, 1948). W. E. B. Du
Bois is the subject of two treatments: Francis L. Broderick, *W. E. B.*

Du Bois: Negro Leader in a Time of Crisis (Stanford, 1959), and
Elliott M. Rudwick, *W. E. B. Du Bois, A Study in Minority Group
Leadership* (Philadelphia, 1960). Elizabeth Ross Haynes has written
about the black educator, promoter, and businessman Richard R.
Wright, Sr., in *The Black Boy of Atlanta* (Boston, 1952). And John B.
Cade, in *Holsey, the Incomparable* (New York, 1964), traces the career
of the prominent Methodist bishop and racial separatist. Edwin S. Redkey's *Black Exodus, Black Nationalist and Back-to-Africa Movements,
1890–1910* (New Haven, 1969), devotes much attention to the life and
times of Bishop Henry McNeal Turner.

C. Vann Woodward's *Tom Watson, Agrarian Rebel* (New York,
1938) is an important study of a white leader who throughout his life
held contrasting views on the race question. Watson emerges as a
political realist willing to make alliances with blacks in the 1890s to
further his movement, and eager to disfranchise them in 1906 for the
same reason. Another Georgia politician, Hoke Smith, receives largely
favorable treatment from Dewey M. Grantham, Jr., in *Hoke Smith and
the Politics of the New South* (Baton Rouge, 1958). Grantham shows
that Smith was a racist who inflamed passions, but emphasizes his role
as a progressive leader. Convict lessee and peon-holder James M. Smith
is the subject of E. Merton Coulter's *James Monroe Smith, Georgia
Planter, Before Death and After* (Athens, Ga., 1961). Coulter treats
Smith sympathetically.

Monographs and Articles

RACE RELATIONS. For the period before 1900, two studies, Alan Conway,
The Reconstruction of Georgia (Minneapolis, 1966), and Alex M.
Arnett, *The Populist Movement in Georgia* (New York, 1922), discuss
race relations during their respective periods. A more recent study
which emphasizes black urban life in the late nineteenth century is
James Perdue, *The Negro in Savannah, 1865–1900* (New York, 1973).
Du Bois wrote extensively about black-white relations; two of his
articles, "The Relation of the Negroes to the Whites in the South,"
Annals of the American Academy for Political and Social Science, 18
(July, 1901), 121–40, and "The Negro South and North," *Bibliotheca
Sacra*, 62 (July, 1905), 499–513, relate directly to conditions in Georgia.
Ray Stannard Baker collected his impressions of the South in *Following
the Color Line* (New York, 1908), which deals extensively with white
southern attitudes toward blacks.

THE BLACK COMMUNITY. The Atlanta University *Publications* shed
much light on community and family life. See *The Negro Church; The*

Negro American Family; and *Manners and Morals among Negro Americans.* August Meier and David Lewis, "History of the Negro Upper Class in Atlanta, Georgia, 1890–1958," *Journal of Negro Education,* 28 (Spring, 1959), 130–39, was useful in examining the relationships among black socioeconomic groups.

Several studies of the development of black business relate to the problems faced by entrepreneurs in Georgia: John Henry Harmon, Arnett G. Lindsey, and Carter G. Woodson, *The Negro as a Business Man* (Washington, 1929); M. S. Stuart, *An Economic Detour: A History of Insurance in the Lives of American Negroes* (New York, 1940); and Walter B. Weare, *Black Business in the New South: A Social History of the North Carolina Mutual Life Insurance Company* (Urbana, 1973). The Atlanta University studies are important sources of information on black enterprise, particularly *Economic Cooperation among the Negroes of Georgia, Economic Cooperation among Negro Americans,* and *The Negro Artisan.* For blacks and the labor movement, the best general account is Sterling D. Spero and Abram L. Harris, *The Black Worker: The Negro and the Labor Movement* (New York, 1931). John Michael Matthews examines racism among white railroad workers in "The Georgia 'Race Strike' of 1909," *Journal of Southern History,* 40 (Nov., 1974), 613–30.

The black community developed under the ever-present shadow of Jim Crow. A good short account of segregation laws and practices is John Hammond Moore, "Jim Crow in Georgia," *South Atlantic Quarterly,* 66 (Fall, 1967), 554–65. Moore points out that Jim Crow statutes were not common before the 1890s and that a large number of segregation laws were being enacted in Georgia as late as the 1940s and 1950s. John Blassingame deals with the origins of residential segregation in "Before the Ghetto: The Making of the Black Community in Savannah, Georgia, 1865–1880," *Journal of Social History,* 6 (Summer, 1973), 463–86. Gilbert T. Stephenson examined "The Segregation of White and Negro Races in the Cities," *South Atlantic Quarterly,* 13 (Jan., 1914), 1–18, and Roger L. Rice discussed the court cases involving "Residential Segregation by Law, 1910–1917," *Journal of Southern History,* 34 (May, 1968), 179–89. One of the early black protests against Jim Crow laws is the subject of August Meier and Elliott Rudwick, "The Boycott Movement against Jim Crow Streetcars in the South, 1900–1906," *Journal of American History,* 55 (Mar., 1969), 756–75, reprinted in their *Along the Color Line: Explorations in the Black Experience* (Urbana, 1976), 267–89.

PEONAGE AND THE CONVICT LEASE SYSTEM. Literature on peonage in America is scarce, due in part to difficulty in obtaining hard evidence of the practice in the South. By far the best book on peonage is Pete Daniel, *The Shadow of Slavery: Peonage in the South, 1901–1969* (Urbana, 1972). Making extensive use of records in the Department of Justice, Daniel proves that the practice was widespread in the South long after 1920. T. H. Malone wrote a series of short articles for the *Voice of the Negro* in 1905–6, including "Peonage—Its Origins and Growth," 2 (Dec., 1905), 27–29, and "Peonage—The Remedy," 3 (June, 1906), 443–44. The celebrated *Alonzo Bailey* case received much attention, and Ray Stannard Baker listed the details in "A Pawn in the Struggle for Freedom," *American*, 72 (Sept., 1911), 608–10. See also Pete Daniel's "Up from Slavery and Down to Peonage: The Alonzo Bailey Case," *Journal of American History*, 57 (Dec., 1970), 654–70, which discusses Booker T. Washington's covert support of the anti-peonage campaign. Hugh M. Dorsey supplied evidence of Georgia peonage in *A Statement from Governor Hugh M. Dorsey as to the Negro in Georgia* (Atlanta, 1921).

More material is available on the convict lease system in Georgia, for public hearings and investigations have produced information about the practice. Fletcher M. Green, "Some Aspects of the Convict Lease System," in *Democracy in the Old South: The Essays of Fletcher Melvin Green* (Vanderbilt, 1969), is a good, brief account of convict leasing. Evils of the system in Georgia became known early, and were described by Rebecca Latimer Felton in "The Convict System of Georgia," *Forum*, 2 (Jan., 1887), 484–90, and George Washington Cable in "The Convict Lease System in the United States," *Century*, 27 (Feb., 1884), 582–95. A. Elizabeth Taylor has the best historical treatment of the convict lease system in Georgia in two *Georgia Historical Quarterly* articles: "The Origin and Development of the Convict Lease System in Georgia," 26 (June, 1942), 113–28; and "The Abolition of the Convict Lease System in Georgia," 26 (Dec., 1942), 273–87.

RACIAL POLITICS AND REFORM. Arthur S. Link was among the first to suggest that progressivism did not stop at the Mason-Dixon line in "The Progressive Movement in the South 1870–1914," *North Carolina Historical Review*, 23 (Apr., 1946), 172–95. In 1951 C. Vann Woodward wrote that progressivism was "for whites only" in *Origins of the New South, 1877–1913* (Baton Rouge, 1951), and Dewey Grantham reiterated the theme in "The Progressive Movement and the Negro," *South Atlantic Quarterly*, 54 (Oct., 1955), 461–77. Hugh C. Bailey, *Liberalism in the New South: Southern Social Reformers and the Progressive Movement* (Coral Gables, Fla., 1969), has good material on several movements, but his thesis that the South produced a number

of enlightened progressive reformers is not convincing. Jack Temple
Kirby, *Darkness at the Dawning: Race and Reform in the Progressive
South* (New York, 1972), should also be consulted. David W. Southern,
*The Malignant Heritage: Yankee Progressives and the Negro Question
1901–1914* (Chicago, 1968), shows that northern white progressives
had little interest in Negro problems.

For Georgia, both Woodward's *Tom Watson* and Grantham's *Hoke
Smith* discuss the links between racism and reform. Charles Crowe ex-
plores the similarities between violence and the reform spirit in "Racial
Violence and Social Reform—Origins of the Atlanta Riot of 1906,"
Journal of Negro History, 53 (July, 1968), 234–57. Clarence A. Bacote,
"The Negro in Atlanta Politics," *Phylon*, 16 (Fourth Quarter, 1955),
333–50, deals with the black response to political proscription; August
Meier, "The Negro and the Democratic Party, 1875–1915," *Phylon*, 17
(Second Quarter, 1956), 173–91, explains why Du Bois and other
disillusioned blacks turned their backs on the party of Lincoln; and
Arthur S. Link examines the importance of race in "The Democratic
Pre-Convention Campaign of 1912 in Georgia," *Georgia Historical
Quarterly*, 29 (June, 1945), 143–58. Also valuable for this study was
Willie M. Bolden, "The Atlanta Progressive Movement and Negro
Civil Rights, 1900–1914," a paper read before members of the Southern
Historical Association at its November, 1968, meeting in New Orleans.

RACE VIOLENCE. Lynching was the most obvious manifestation of white
violence in the South. Walter White, in *Rope and Faggot, A Biography
of Judge Lynch* (New York, 1929), describes a number of lynchings
which he investigated and analyzes the mentality of the mob. Arthur
F. Raper, *The Tragedy of Lynching* (Chapel Hill, 1933), is another
good account. The NAACP kept track of reported lynchings and issued
its findings in *Thirty Years of Lynching in the United States, 1889–1918*
(New York, 1919).

In addition to leading the nation in lynching, Georgia was the scene
of the Atlanta riot of 1906, the worst racial clash of the decade. Ray
Stannard Baker describes the riot in *Following the Color Line*, but by
far the best account is Charles Crowe, "Racial Massacre in Atlanta,
September 22, 1906," *Journal of Negro History*, 54 (Apr., 1969), 150–73.
A leading white progressive, Alexander J. McKelway, believed the riot
had some salutary effects. In "The Atlanta Riots I.—A Southern White
Point of View," *Outlook*, 84 (Nov. 3, 1906), 557–62, McKelway claimed
that Atlanta whites were breathing more freely after the riot because
the blacks had been taught a lesson. Blacks had fought back during
the riot, and they resisted white violence elsewhere. Elliott Rudwick

and August Meier, "Negro Retaliatory Violence in the Twentieth Century," in August Meier and Elliott Rudwick, *The Making of Black America, Essays in Negro Life and History,* II (New York, 1960), discusses this neglected aspect of black history.

BLACK EDUCATION. The best book on education in Georgia is Dorothy Orr, *A History of Education in Georgia* (Chapel Hill, 1950), a thorough account which includes sections on black education. Horace Mann Bond, *The Education of the Negro in the American Social Order* (New York, 1934), describes inequities between black and white schools, which are further documented in Louis R. Harlan, *Separate and Unequal, Public School Campaigns and Racism in the Southern Seaboard States, 1901–1915* (Chapel Hill, 1958). There are a number of good studies on higher education for Georgia blacks. Willard Range, *The Rise and Progress of Negro Colleges in Georgia, 1865–1943,* Phelps-Stokes Fellowship *Studies* No. 15 (Athens, Ga., 1951), is a perceptive account of the problems facing black colleges, including those of race relations on the campuses. Florence Matilda Reed, *The Story of Spelman College* (Princeton, 1961), is a personal account by a former Spelman president. Ridgely Torrence's *John Hope* provides insight into the early development of Morehouse under Hope. Clarence A. Bacote, *The Story of Atlanta University* (Atlanta, 1969), is a historical treatment of the most controversial of Georgia colleges. And Du Bois described what he called "The Cultural Mission of Atlanta University," *Phylon,* 3 (Second Quarter, 1942), 105–15, during the late nineteenth and early twentieth centuries. An excellent recent study which examines the origins and development of black colleges is James M. McPherson, *The Abolitionist Legacy: From Reconstruction to the NAACP* (Princeton, 1975).

BLACK THOUGHT. During the early twentieth century the black movement shifted from the accommodation of Booker T. Washington to a philosophy of protest symbolized by Du Bois and the NAACP. An excellent study of the forces bringing about this change is August Meier, *Negro Thought in America, 1880–1915, Racial Ideologies in the Age of Booker T. Washington* (Ann Arbor, 1963), which includes detailed discussion of black Georgia leaders and their programs. In *Black Exodus,* Edwin S. Redkey shows that there was much emigrationist sentiment among poor Georgia blacks near the turn of the century. Henry McNeal Turner and Bishop Lucius H. Holsey (who favored a black state in America) argued their cases in Willis B. Parks, ed., *The Possibilities of the Negro in Symposium* (Atlanta, 1904).

WORLD WAR I AND MIGRATION. The best of several articles on the effect of the Wilson presidency on black America is Morton Sosna, "The South in the Saddle: Racial Politics During the Wilson Years," *Wisconsin Magazine of History*, 54 (Autumn, 1970), 30–49. The migration of southern blacks to northern cities during the war years is treated in Emmett J. Scott, *Negro Migration During the War* (New York, 1921). Scott discusses migration in Georgia, which, although substantial, did not rival that of several southern states, particularly Mississippi. A more recent investigation is Dewey H. Palmer, "Moving North: Negro Migration During World War I," *Phylon*, 28 (Spring, 1967), 52–62. On forced labor during the war, see Walter White, " 'Work or Fight' in the South," *New Republic*, 18 (Mar. 1, 1919), 144–45. Of the books on the role of blacks during World War I, Emmett J. Scott, *Scott's Official History of the American Negro in the World War* (Washington, 1921), is probably the most comprehensive. A member of the Wilson administration, Scott has been accused of ignoring mistreatment of black soldiers, but he has described those injustices in some detail. What is questionable, given these facts, is Scott's optimistic conclusion that World War I had been a rewarding experience for black troops. Another firsthand account by Charles H. Williams, *Sidelights on Negro Soldiers* (Norwood, Mass., 1923), adds to the evidence that white officers and enlisted men regarded black soldiers about as highly as they did black civilians. For the postwar period, Robert T. Kerlin, ed., *The Voice of the Negro, 1919* (New York, 1920), is a collection of editorials from black newspapers reflecting the growing mood of militancy. Arthur I. Waskow, *From Race Riot to Sit-In, 1919 and the 1960s* (New York, 1966), tells of the Red Summer of 1919 and of attempts by the Justice Department to intimidate black leaders.

Dissertations and Theses

A number of doctoral dissertations and master's theses have been quite helpful in preparing this study. The dissertation of greatest assistance has been Clarence A. Bacote's "The Negro in Georgia Politics, 1880–1908" (University of Chicago, 1955), which provided both excellent background material and insight into the problems faced by Georgia blacks at the dawn of the century. Edward A. Gaston, "A History of the Negro Wage Earner in Georgia, 1890-1940" (Emory University, 1957), contains a wealth of statistical data on black farmers and workers. An excellent study of unions in Georgia which features material on race problems is Mercer G. Evans, "A History of the Organized Labor Movement in Georgia" (University of Chicago, 1929).

Other significant studies are Horace Calvin Wingo, "Race Relations in
Georgia, 1872–1908" (University of Georgia, 1969); John Michael
Matthews, "Studies in Race Relations in Georgia, 1890–1930" (Duke
University, 1970); Richard H. L. German, "The Queen City of the
Savannah: Augusta, Georgia, During the Urban Progressive Era, 1890–
1917" (University of Florida, 1971); Alton D. Jones, "Progressivism in
Georgia, 1898–1918" (Emory University, 1963); and Thomas M.
Deaton, "Atlanta During the Progressive Era" (University of Georgia,
1969). August Meier's massive dissertation, "Negro Racial Thought in
the Age of Booker T. Washington, Circa 1890–1915" (Columbia University, 1957), contains much important information about black
leaders in Georgia. Paul T. Murray, "Blacks and the Draft: An Analysis
of Institutional Racism, 1917–1971" (Florida State University, 1972),
has excellent material on abuses in the selective service system during
World War I.

Of master's theses relating to this period, Louie Davis Shivery, "The
History of Organized Social Work among Atlanta Negroes, 1890–1935"
(Atlanta University, 1936), contains material on self-help projects
among Atlanta blacks. Sidney Tobin's "Debates on Negro Problems in
Congress" (Howard University, 1961) is a fascinating study of race-
baiting in the nation's capital, and includes racist resolutions introduced
by Georgia congressmen. Comradge L. Henton, "Heman E. Perry:
Documentary Materials for the Life History of a Business Man" (Atlanta University, 1948), contains excellent source material on black
business in Atlanta.

General Studies

For an understanding of the South in the late nineteenth and twen-
tieth centuries three books are indispensable: C. Vann Woodward,
Origins of the New South, 1877–1913 (Baton Rouge, 1951); George B.
Tindall, *The Emergence of the New South, 1913–1945* (Baton Rouge,
1967); and Wilbur J. Cash, *The Mind of the South* (New York, 1941).
John Hope Franklin's *From Slavery to Freedom, A History of Negro
Americans,* 4th ed. (New York, 1974), remains the best black history
text. Although there are several histories of Georgia, they ignore black
Georgia and do not give adequate coverage to twentieth-century events.
Currently several scholars are at work on a multi-volume history of
Georgia which promises a more comprehensive treatment.

Index

Abbott, Robert S., 61, 187
African Methodist Episcopal Church: bishops file Pullman car suit, 19; membership figures, 53; prominent clergy, 53–54; founds Morris Brown College, 151, 155; mentioned, 137, 164, 175, 176. *See also* Churches, black; Morris Brown College; Turner, Henry McNeal
Afro-American Council, 169
Afro-American Life Insurance Company, 46
Age of consent, 119, 122
Agriculture, blacks in, 23–27, 191, 210. *See also* Peonage; Sharecroppers, black
Alabama: and peonage, 76–77
Albany: residential segregation, 14; and black migration, 187; mentioned, 25, 42
Albany *Herald*, 190
Alexander, Will W., 207
Allen, Peyton, 17
Allen, Richard, 53
A.M.E. Church Review, 53
American Baptist Home Mission Society, 151, 155
American Church Institute, 149
American Missionary Association, 149, 151
Americus: black voting in, 103; and black migration, 187–88
Amos, Miles, 42
Amos, Moses, 42, 101–2
Angier, E. A., 79

Anthony, Susan B., 120, 121
Appeal to Caesar, 168
Army Officer Training Corps, 194n
Arnall, Ellis: on Georgia penal system, 87
Artesian Drug Store (Albany), 42
Artisans, black, 29–32. *See also* Labor unions and blacks; *and individual occupations*
Athens: and peonage cases, 79–80; mentioned, 28, 43
Atkinson, W. Y.: opposes convict leasing, 84
Atlanta: segregation, 12–14, 15, 20–21; streetcar boycott, 16–17; blacks and labor relations, 32; and Board of Trade, 39; black banks, 44; black class structure, 59; and Neighborhood Union, 64–65; and Johnson-Jeffries fight, 70; high arrest rate, 88; conditions in stockade, 88–89; adopts white primary, 94; riot of 1906, 123–31; black schools, 146–48, 151; cultural life, 183; NAACP activities, 147–48, 206; and "work or fight" law, 199; Urban League activities, 206; NAACP convention, 207–8
Atlanta Baptist College: founding, 151; discussed, 158–59, 160. *See also* Colleges, black; Hope, John; Morehouse College
Atlanta Chamber of Commerce, 117
Atlanta *Constitution:* opposes peonage prosecutions, 80; on forced labor for blacks, 88; edited by Clark Howell,

225

Atlanta *Constitution* (*Cont.*)
97; on 1906 campaign, 98; on black migration, 190; racial philosophy, 215

Atlanta *Evening News:* and Atlanta riot, 124; calls for KKK revival, 130

Atlanta *Georgian:* opposes convict leasing, 85, 114; and Atlanta riot, 124; recommends castration for black rapists, 130; criticizes black voters, 148; racial views, 215

Atlanta *Independent:* on black clergy, 52; and lodge news, 57; and voter registration, 102; on reform, 111; black opposition to, 163–64

Atlanta *Journal:* for compulsory school attendance, 117; and Atlanta riot, 124, 129; on Statesboro lynchings, 135; reflects racial views of Hoke Smith, 215

Atlanta Mutual Life Insurance Company, 48–49. *See also* Herndon, Alonzo F.

Atlanta Normal and Industrial Institute, 159

Atlanta riot: and Prohibition law, 112; described, 123–31; and Max Barber, 166–67; interracial meetings following, 172; mentioned, 12, 100–101, 138, 140, 168, 205

Atlanta School of Social Service, 206n

Atlanta University: and black housing patterns, 13; hires white contractors, 43n; prestige, 60; neglects black music, 67–68; founding, 151; curriculum, 152; expels baseball players, 154–55; financial problems, 156–58; dramatics and music, 161; and Du Bois, 170–75, 178; and World War I, 194n; mentioned, 106, 142–62 *passim*. *See also* Colleges, black

Atlanta University Conference: on black business, 39; on black church, 52

Atlanta University *Publications,* 153, 180

Attorneys, black, 37

Augusta: black population, 9, 13; described, 11; residential segregation, 11–12, 14, 15; streetcar boycott,

16–17; and black churches, 50, 53; Negro aristocracy, 59; and white primary, 94n, 96; government, 110–11; and Haines Institute, 149–51; and W. J. White, 164–65; and C. T. Walker, 167–68; and film, *The Nigger,* 183–84; mentioned, 36, 43, 45, 69, 91, 180

Augusta *Chronicle:* on bribing white voters, 96; on W. J. White, 164–65

Back-to-Africa movement, 53, 164, 175–78. *See also* Turner, Henry McNeal

Bailey, Alonzo, 76–77

Bailey v. *Alabama,* 76–77

Bainbridge: and black migration, 187; and "work or fight" laws, 199

Baker, Newton B., 193

Baker County, 25

Baldwin, George Johnson, 18

"Ballad of Mary Phagan," 185

Ballou, C. C., 200

Banking, black, 44–45

Baptist Church, black: during American Revolution, 50; fundamentalist theology, 51; membership figures, 52; prominent ministers, 53; composition of membership, 60; mentioned, 167. *See also* Churches, black; Atlanta Baptist College; Morehouse College; Spelman College

Barber, Jesse Max: editor, 165–67; and Niagara Movement, 170; mentioned, 180

Barber family, 139

Barbers, black, 35, 37, 38. *See also* Herndon, Alonzo F.

Barnesville: cotton mill strike, 33

Barrie, James M., 1

Barrow, David C., 34

Baseball: black players and teams, 68–69, 154–55

Beach Institute (Savannah), 61, 149

Beck, Mrs. Lewis, 123

"Before Day Clubs," 135

Berkeley, 204

Bernhardt, Sarah, 183

Big Bethel A.M.E. Church (Atlanta), 53

Birmingham, Alabama: and Prohibition, 112
Birth of a Nation, The, 66, 185–86
Black belt: black population in, 2, 4; farming, 23–25
Black nationalism, 178–80
Blacksmiths, 29
Black studies, 152–53
Blakely, 204
Blassingame, John, 9
Blayton, J. B., 47
Blues, 67–68
Blum, Henry, 94
B'nai B'rith, 185
Board of Trade (Atlanta), 39
Boll weevil, 187, 210
Bolshevik Revolution, 203
Booker T. Washington High School, 148
Boston, Mass., 157–58
Boston *Guardian*, 157
Bowen, J. W. E.: and Pullman car protest, 19; efforts to be elected bishop, 54; arrested after Atlanta riot, 128; removed as president of Gammon, 160; and *Voice of the Negro*, 166; supports Booker T. Washington, 168; mentioned, 44, 180
Boxing, 69–71
Bradley, A. A., 5n
Brand, Charles H.: on lynchings, 139
Brantley, W. G., 74
Brawley, Benjamin: educator, 151, 153; and cultural nationalism, 178
Brick and stone masons, 29, 30
Brill, Edith V., 161
Brimmage, Henry, 72–73
Brimmage, Jeff, 73
Brookes County, 201
Brotherhood of Locomotive Firemen, 33. *See also* Georgia Railroad strike
Brown, John, 158, 172
Brown, Joseph E.: and convict leasing, 83
Brown, Joseph M., 56, 103
Brown University, 158
Brownsville, Texas affair, 104
Brownsville (Atlanta), 128–29
Broyles, Nash, 89
Brunswick, 149, 179, 192
Bryan, William Jennings, 6, 106

Buchanan v. *Warley*, 14
Buena Vista, 69
Bullock County, 132. *See also* Statesboro
Bumstead, Horace, 157
Bureau of Printing and Engraving: segregation, 181
Burroughs, 179
Burruss, G. S., 36
Bushnell, 179
Business, black: in Atlanta, 13; hackmen, 35; barbers, 35, 37, 38; contractors, 35, 43; ante-bellum, 37; grocers, 37, 41; and economic separatism, 38; growing dependence on black customers, 38, 41; factors retarding, 40; recreation, 41; pharmacists, 41–42; morticians, 43; real estate, 44; banking, 44–45; insurance, 45–49; growth, 210. *See also individual localities and types of enterprises*
Butler, H. R., 56
Buttrick, Wallace, 157

Cable, George Washington: on convict leasing, 84
Calvin Vagrancy Law, 115. *See also* Vagrancy laws
Camp Gordon, Ga., 194–96, 204
Camp Wheeler, Ga., 197
Candler, Allen D., 117, 142
Candler, Asa Griggs, 118, 193
Canton: segregation, 20
Carnegie, Andrew, 159n
Carpenters, black, 29, 30
Carrie Steele Orphanage, 64
Carter, E. R.: minister, 15n, 53, 63n
Caruso, Enrico, 183
Cato, Will, 133–35
Cement finishers, black, 29, 30
Central Avenue A.M.E. Church (Atlanta), 107
Central City College, 160
Chain gang: replaces convict lease system, 86–87; in Georgia cities, 88–89; mentioned, 68, 82, 195
Charleston, S.C., 9, 203
Chatham County. *See* Savannah

Chatham County Board of Education, 146

Chautauqua Circle, 60–61

Chicago, race riot, 203

Chicago *Defender*, 61, 187

Child labor: and reformers, 116; attempts to regulate, 118–19; and blacks, 210

Christian, Carrie, 87

Churches, black: ante-bellum history, 50; fundamentalist theology, 51; community influence, 52, 53–55; on college campuses, 154. *See also* Ministers, black; *and individual congregations, denominations, and localities*

Citizens and Southern Bank of Philadelphia (Pa.), 169

Civic organizations, black, 63–65. *See also individual civic groups*

Civil Service Commission, 181

Clansman, The, 66

Clark College: founding, 54, 151; prestige, 60; curriculum, 152; financing, 155; and racial problems, 160; mentioned, 127, 128, 168. *See also* Colleges, black

Clarke County: economic cooperation by blacks, 43

Class structure, black, 59–62. *See also* Lower class, black; Middle class, black; Upper class, black

Clay, R. M., 88

Cobb, J. M., 73

Colleges, black: enrollment, 148–49; founding, 151; curriculum, 152; discipline, 153–54; financial problems, 155–56; white control of, 159–61; social life, 161–62. *See also individual black colleges*

Color caste, 61–62

Colored Methodist Episcopal Church, 54, 151, 177. *See also* Churches, black; Holsey, Lucius H.; Paine College

Colored National Emigration Association, 176

Columbus, 108, 157

Columbus *Enquirer-Sun*, 70, 115

Comer, 78

Commission on Interracial Cooperation, 207–8

Committee on Compulsory Education, 117

Committee on Public Information, 193

Communities, all-black, 179–80

Congo Company, 175

Congregational Church, 55, 60, 149. *See also* Churches, black; First Congregational Church (Atlanta); Proctor, Henry Hugh

Conley, Sam, 136

Contract labor law, 76–77. *See also* Peonage

Contractors, black, 35, 43

Convict lease system: origins in Georgia, 82–83; mistreatment of convicts, 84–85; attempts to abolish, 84, 86, 114–15; replaced by chain gang, 86–87, 115; mentioned, 173

Convicts: felony, 83–87; misdemeanor, 87–89. *See also* Convict lease system

"Coon songs," 67

Cooperatives, economic, 43, 44

Cordele, 54, 135

Cornish, R. D., 179

Cotton mills: racial discrimination in, 32–33

Crawley, William F., 72–75

Crisis: "Close Ranks" editorial, 202; mentioned, 157, 167, 174, 180, 205. *See also* Du Bois, W. E. B.; National Association for the Advancement of Colored People

Crogman, William H.: on Atlanta riot, 127–28; racial views, 168; removed as president of Clark, 160

Crop lien system, 5, 24

Curtis, C. M., 196

Davis, Benjamin: and Board of Trade, 39; on Negro aristocracy, 61; Odd Fellows leader, 57, 58; attacks black political leaders, 93–94; says blacks disfranchised themselves, 102; opinions of Du Bois, 106, 173; racial views, 163–64; NAACP officer, 175; mentioned, 92n

Davis, Jefferson, 12

Dawson, 57

Democratic party (Ga.), 108–9, 110–
22 *passim*. *See also* Elections;
Gubernatorial campaign of 1906; *and
individual Democratic politicians*
Dentists, black, 35–36
Deveaux, John H.: family, 56; political
career, 91–94
Disfranchisement: early attempts,
94–96; and white primary, 95–97;
and campaign of 1906, 97–101;
achieved, 101–4; mentioned, 111,
122, 147
Dixon, Thomas, 66
Dobbs, John Wesley, 56
Domestic and personal services, blacks
in, 14–15, 26–27
Dorsey, Hugh M.: opposes peonage,
82; and lynchings, 137n; and black
migration, 189; reviews black troops,
193; role in *Leo Frank* case, 208;
attacks racial injustice, 208–9
Dougherty County: farming, 24–25;
chain gang, 86
Douglass, Frederick, 120, 172
Dowdy, John, 137
Dublin *Courier-Herald and Dispatch*:
on NAACP, 206
Du Bois, W. E. B.: on black Georgia,
3; on Atlanta housing patterns, 12;
protest activities in Georgia, 19, 21,
96, 143; on reasons for segregation,
22; on economic discrimination
against black farmers, 26; on
domestic service, 28; on black
business, 39; friendship with A. F.
Herndon, 49; on black church, 50;
on Theodore Roosevelt, 105–6; backs
Bryan in 1908, 106; on Woodrow
Wilson, 108–9, 181; on race violence,
123; and Atlanta riot, 127, 129; as
teacher, 151, 152, 153, 170–72; and
Atlanta University *Publications*, 153;
on student discipline, 154–55; and
industrial education, 156–57; conflict
with President Ware, 157;
correspondence with John Hope,
159n; and Niagara Movement,
169–70, 173–74; background and
philosophy, 170–71; breaks with
Booker T. Washington, 172; on

leaving Atlanta University, 174;
poem, 178; on World War I, 202,
205; gets Spingarn medal, 207; views
on Interracial Commission, 208;
mentioned, 92, 140, 163, 165, 168,
175, 179, 180, 210
Durham, J. J., 2
Durham, Lula, 73
Durham Coal and Coke Company:
and convict leasing, 85

Early County, 85
East St. Louis (Ill.) race riot, 201
Eastern Star, 55
Editors, black, 163–67. *See also
individual editors*
Education, black: law on taxing school
gifts, 115; efforts to divide school
fund, 116, 142–43; compulsory school
attendance law, 116–18, 122; black
schools in Georgia, 141–62. *See also*
Colleges, black; Teachers, black
Eighteenth Amendment. *See*
Prohibition
Elaine, Ark.: racial violence in, 203
Elections: of 1892, 6; of 1896, 6; of
1904, 104; of 1906, 97–101; of 1908,
106; of 1912, 107–9, 181–82; of
1920, 210
Elks, 56, 115
Emancipation Day: Savannah
celebration of, 1–2
Emigration to Africa, 164, 175–78. *See
also* Back-to-Africa movement;
Turner, Henry McNeal
Employment, black, 23–49. *See also*
Agriculture, blacks in; Business,
black; Labor unions and blacks;
Professions and professionals; *and
individual occupations*
English, James, 166
Episcopalians, 55, 60
Equal Rights Convention, 173–74, 180
Ervin, James, 200

Farrar, Geraldine, 183
Felton, Rebecca Latimer: on convict
lease system, 83; on compulsory
school attendance, 117; and women's
suffrage, 121

Fifteenth Amendment: Georgia refuses
to ratify, 5; Watson urges nullifica-
tion, 103; and women's suffrage, 120;
mentioned, 95, 182
Firemen, black, 32–34. *See also* Georgia
Railroad strike
First African Baptist Church
(Savannah), 53
First Baptist Church (Milledgeville),
205
First Congregational Church (Atlanta):
high prestige, 60; first black
institutional church, 63–64;
mentioned, 43, 167, 180
First World War. *See* World War I
Fisk, Harvey, 157
Fisk University, 152
539th Service Battalion, 195
Football: black teams, 69
Forsyth County: whitecappings, 26
Fort Des Moines, Ia., 193, 194n
Fort Oglethorpe, Ga., 194
Fort Valley, 168, 191
406th Reserve Labor Battalion, 195
Fourteenth Amendment, 182
France: reaction to black troops, 200
Frank, Leo M., 184–85, 208
Fraternal orders, black: and insurance
benefits, 45; development, 55–59. *See
also* Davis, Benjamin; *and individual
fraternal orders*
Fraternities, college, 61
Frazier, Lula, 72
Frazier, Nathan, 72
Freedman's Hospital (Washington,
D.C.), 99
Freedmen's Aid Society, 151, 155
Friendship Baptist Church (Atlanta),
15n, 53
Fulton Bag and Cotton Mill (Atlanta):
strike, 32
Fulton County: and Atlanta riot, 124,
131; selective service violations, 196.
See also Atlanta

Gaines, Wesley J., 53
Gammon Theological Seminary:
founding, 54, 151; and Atlanta riot,
128; racial problems, 160; mentioned,
168, 180. *See also* Colleges, black

Garvey, Marcus: compared with
Heman Perry, 48; and H. M. Turner,
175
Gate City Drug Store, 41–42
Gate City Free Kindergarten, 63
Gates, James T., 152n
General Education Board, 156, 157,
159n
General State Baptist Convention of
Georgia, 51
Georgia Baptist, 17, 164–65, 180. *See
also* White, William Jefferson
Georgia Baptist Association: on extent
of peonage in Georgia, 82
Georgia coast: black population, 2, 4
Georgia Federation of Labor: racial
attitudes, 30, 116. *See also* Labor
unions and blacks
Georgia Federation of Women's Clubs:
supports compulsory school
attendance, 116; condemns
lynching, 190
Georgia General Assembly: expels
black members, 5; streetcar
segregation law, 16; places black
lodges under bond, 56; bans
interracial fight films, 70; convict
lease law, 83; poll tax law, 94;
disfranchisement amendment, 102;
and reform legislation and blacks,
111–22 *passim;* education laws, 146;
licenses labor agents, 188; "work or
fight" law, 198
Georgia Prison Commission, 84, 85–86
Georgia Railroad strike, 33–34, 116
Georgia Senate Commission on the
Penitentiary, 84
Georgia State Industrial College: and
Taft visit, 107; funding, 155;
curriculum, 169; mentioned, 2
Georgia State Penitentiary, 84. *See also*
Convict lease system
Georgia Suffrage League, 102
Georgia White League, 107
Georgia Women's Suffrage Association,
120
German, Richard H. L., 111
Gibson, Josh, 69
Gordon, Asa: on black business, 40

Gordon, John B.: and convict leasing, 83

Grady, Henry, 12

Grady Hospital (Atlanta), 30

Grant, Ulysses S., 5

Graves, John Temple, 130

Griffith, David W., 185

Grimké, Archibald, 165

Grocers, black, 37, 41

Gubernatorial campaign of 1906, 97–101, 166. *See also* Smith, Hoke

Hackmen, black, 35, 38

Haines Institute, 149–51. *See also* Laney, Lucy Craft

Haiti: Marine occupation, 191

Hamilton, Alexander, 43

Hamilton, Grace Towns: on streetcar segregation, 17

Hampton Institute, 156, 159

Hancock County, 176

Handy, W. C., 68

Harding, Warren G., 210

Hardwick, Thomas M.: and 1899 disfranchisement bill, 96; supports Hoke Smith, 97; on 19th Amendment, 121; calls for repeal of 14th and 15th Amendments, 182; opposes U.S. involvement in World War I, 192n; on returning black veterans, 204; attacks Governor Dorsey, 209; elected governor, 210; mentioned, 53

Harlem Renaissance, 178

Harpers Ferry, W.Va., 158

Harris, Judia C.: starts economic cooperative, 43

Harris, Julian, 107–8

Harris, Nathaniel: on Prohibition, 113–14

Harris, Mr. and Mrs. Richard A., 123

Harrisburg, 179

Hart, George, 73

Harvard, John, 137

Harvard University, 152n

Health conditions, black: in cities, 10, 11, 13, 63; among soldiers, 195

Heard, James, 128, 130

Heard, William H., 176

Henderson, Fletcher, 68

Herndon, Adrienne, 171

Herndon, Alonzo F.: early life, 37–38; barber, 38; founds Atlanta Mutual Life Insurance Company, 48; contributions, 49; petitions legislature on disfranchisement, 101–2; and Niagara Movement, 170

Herndon, Norris, 49

Herne, Ben, 204

Hodges, H. H., 134

Hodges family, 132–33, 135. *See also* Statesboro

Hollinshead, C. S., 137

Holsey, Lucius H.: role in C.M.E. Church, 54; and racial separatism, 177

Holsey Normal and Industrial Academy, 54

Hoover, J. Edgar, 205

Hope, John: prominent Baptist, 60; petitions legislature, 96, 143; on lack of political influence, 97; teacher, 151; on student discipline, 155; background and philosophy, 158–59; appointed president of Atlanta Baptist College, 160; and Niagara Movement, 170; NAACP officer, 175; on establishing an all-black community, 179–80; member of Interracial Commission, 208; mentioned, 162, 168, 210

Hope, Lugenia: and Neighborhood Union, 64–65; organizes civic improvement committee, 147; activities during World War I, 196; mentioned, 210

Housing, black: in cities, 9–16; in Dougherty County, 24–25

Houston race riot, 200

Howard, David T.: mortician, 43; leading Methodist, 60; and Atlanta riot, 126, 129

Howard University, 36, 91, 152

Howell, Clark: and 1906 gubernatorial race, 97–100; and Theodore Roosevelt, 105; on black education, 142

Hughes, Charles Evans, 77

Humphries, Solomon, 37

Hunt, Henry A., 168, 191

Illiteracy, 141, 148, 210
Immigration Commission, 75–76
Industrial education, 29, 156–59
Industrial workers, black, 210n. *See also* Labor unions and blacks
Insurance, blacks in, 45–49. *See also* Perry, Heman; Herndon, Alonzo F.; *and individual insurance companies*
International Association of Machinists, 30. *See also* Labor unions and blacks
International Association of Plasterers and Cement Finishers, 31. *See also* Labor unions and blacks
Interracial Commission, 207–8
Interracial marriage, 8, 182
Irwin County, 176, 179

Jackson, Deal, 25
Jakin, 85
Jasper County, 81
Jeffries, Jim: and fight with Jack Johnson, 69–71
Jim Crow. *See* Segregation
Jockeys, black, 69
Johnson, Henry Lincoln, 37, 93–94
Johnson, Jack: and fight with Jim Jeffries, 69–71; marriage, 182
Johnson, James Weldon, 162
Johnson, Sol C.: Masonic leader, 56; and black protest, 163–64; opposes R. R. Wright, 169; and race pride, 179; on World War I, 192; mentioned, 180
Jones, Jackson, 120
Joplin, Scott, 67
Journal of Labor, 30
Juries: blacks serving on, 8

Kendrick, J. Z., 133–34
Kent, Fred, 85
Key, James L., 95
King, Martin Luther, Jr., 151
Kinnebrew, E. C., 80
Knights of Pythias, 55, 56, 115. *See also* Fraternal orders, black
Ku Klux Klan: terrorist activities in 1868, 5; and Standard Life Insurance Company, 47–48; *Evening News* calls for revival, 130; *ad hoc* group in

Augusta, 165; revival, 185–86; mentioned, 204

Labor unions and blacks: 28, 30–34. *See also individual unions and localities*
La Follette, Robert M., 110
Land ownership, black, 23, 25, 27, 191, 210
Laney, Louise, 150
Laney, Lucy: teacher, 149–50; educational philosophy, 150–51; starts NAACP chapter, 167; and voter registration, 206; mentioned, 158, 168, 210
Law enforcement. *See* Police and blacks
Lawyers. *See* Attorneys, black
Lee, M. O., 42
Legislature, Georgia. *See* Georgia General Assembly
Liberia, 175, 176, 177
Lincoln Guards (black troops), 115
Lipscomb, Mary Ann, 116
Literacy, black, 141, 148, 210
Little, Wilbur, 204
Lloyd, John ("Pop"), 69
Lodges. *See* Fraternal orders, black
Long, Jefferson, 92
Longshoremen, black, 28
Louisville *News,* 39
Love, E. K.: minister, 53; involved in political dispute, 93; attacks white control of black colleges, 160
Lower class, black: residential patterns in cities, 9–16; rural housing, 24–25; and employment, 27–28; and class structure, 59; and church and lodge membership, 59–60. *See also* Convict lease system; Lynching; Share-cropping, black; Violence, racial
Lowenstein, William J., 117
Lowndes County: peonage in, 72–75; mentioned, 25, 201
Lumber and turpentine industries, 28–29
Lynching: accounts of, 17, 133–35, 136, 137, 139, 164, 184–85, 201, 204; failure to legislate against, 116, 139; statistics, 131; motives for, 132; and

Lynching (*Cont.*)
law enforcement, 139; condemned by white Georgia women, 190; during World War I, 201; and Interracial Commission, 208; Governor Dorsey calls for legislation against, 209; mentioned, 206, 213

Lyons, Judson: political career, 91–94; petitions legislature on disfranchisement, 101–2; backs Progressive party in 1912, 107; mentioned, 37

McClellan, Thomas J., 72–75
McCollers, Emma, 137
McCrary, Rufus G., 198
McIntosh County: black land ownership in, 25; black political power, 98–99; mentioned, 101
McKelway, Alexander: and Prohibition, 112, 113; and child labor, 119
McKinley, William: and political patronage, 91
McLendon, Mary Latimer, 121
Macon: black Western Union employees fired, 32; black industry in, 44; orphans' home, 55; and Johnson-Jeffries fight, 69–70; adopts white primary, 94n; and Central City College, 160; and Equal Rights Convention, 173; and black migration, 188; and "work or fight" law, 199; Governor Dorsey denounced in, 209; mentioned, 37, 63, 68
Macon Acmes, 69
Macon *Telegraph*, 70, 209, 215
McRee, Edward, 72–75
McRee, Frank, 72–74
MacVicar Hospital, 161
Maddox, Lester, 197n
Madison, 135–36
Manhattan, Kansas racial incident, 200
Manning, Clyde, 81
Marietta, 185
Masons: fraternal order, 55–56; exclusiveness, 59–60. *See also* Fraternal orders, black
Medical Department, University of Georgia, 36
Meharry Medical School, 36

Mencken, H. L.: on lynchings, 132
Mercer, George A., 146
Merrick, John, 48
Messenger, 205
Methodists, black, 51, 60. *See also* African Methodist Episcopal Church; Colored Methodist Episcopal Church; Methodist Episcopal Church
Methodist Episcopal Church, 54–55, 160. *See also* Bowen, J. W. E.; Clark College; Gammon Theological Seminary
Metropolitan Opera: visits Atlanta, 183
Middle class, black: residential patterns, 10–11, 13, 15; defined, 15n; and status, 59–62. *See also* Business, black; Churches, black; Fraternal orders, black; Professions and professionals, black
Migration, black: to cities, 9, 12; during World War I, 186–91; black reaction to, 190–91; during the 1920s, 210
Milan: lynching in, 137
Milledgeville, 185, 197, 204–5
Millen, 204
Miller, Mr. and Mrs. James G., 123
Miller, Kelley, 165
Ministers, black: and streetcar boycott, 18–19; qualifications of, 51–52; leading Georgia clergy, 53–55; views, 167–68; and race pride, 179. *See also* Churches, black; *and individual congregations, denominations, and ministers*
Mississippi: and compulsory school attendance, 117
Monticello, 81
Morehouse College: prestige, 60; athletic program, 68; financing, 155; progress under John Hope, 159; and Benjamin Brawley, 178; Army Officer Training Corps established, 194n; school of social work, 206n; mentioned, 43, 151, 152, 153, 155. *See also* Atlanta Baptist College; Colleges, black; Hope, John
Morgan, John T., 176
Morgenthau, Henry, 181

Morrill Act, 155

Morris, E. H., 59

Morris Brown College: founding, 151; curriculum, 152; financing, 155; all-black faculty, 160; mentioned, 53, 99, 159. *See also* Colleges, black

Morrison, Jackson, 78–79

Morrison, Mentha, 78–79

Morticians, black, 43

Moultrie, 44

Mound Bayou, Miss., 179

Mount Olivet Baptist Church (N.Y.), 53

Movie theatres, black, 41

Mulatto. *See* Light-complexioned Negroes

Murphy, Mrs. H. S., 129, 171

Music, black, 67–68

Mutual Benefit Society, 43

Nash, Homer E., 25

National Association for the Advancement of Colored People (NAACP): in Atlanta, 81, 147–48, 192; compiles lynching statistics, 131–32; investigates lynchings, 137, 201; and Spelman College, 161; throughout Georgia, 163, 167–68, 175, 205–7; as successor of Niagara Movement, 173; and motion pictures, 183, 185–86; and "work or fight" laws, 199; national meeting in Atlanta, 207–8; and Dorsey statement, 209; mentioned, 61, 158, 164, 197, 210

National Association of Letter Carriers, 31. *See also* Labor unions and blacks

National Benefit Life Insurance Company, 49n

National Negro Business League: origin and growth, 39–40; Savannah chapter, 189, 192; mentioned, 169

National Urban League. *See* Urban League

Negro Artisan, The, 156

Negro Civic Improvement League, 63

Negro State Fair, 169, 183

Negroes, light-complexioned, 61–62, 93

Neighborhood Union: origin and development, 64–65; activities during World War I, 196; mentioned, 68, 178

Nelson, E. Johnson, 18

New Governor, The, 183

Newman, William T., 75

New York *World,* 166

Niagara Movement: and Alonzo F. Herndon, 49; on self-defense, 140; founding and platform, 169–70; opponents, 172–73; mentioned, 158, 180

Nigger, The, 183

Nineteenth Amendment. *See* Women's suffrage

92d Division, 200–201

North Carolina Mutual Life Insurance Company, 48

North Georgia Conference of Southern Methodist Women, 119

Odd Fellow City, 179

Odd Fellows: Georgia chapters, 57–58; mass appeal, 60; mentioned, 55. *See also* Fraternal orders, black

Odd Fellows Building (Atlanta), 43

Oglethorpe County: peonage in, 77–80

Organized Charities and Civic Settlement League, 63

Ovington, Mary White, 127

Pace, Harry, 46

Paine College: founding, 54, 151; financing, 155; racial problems, 160–61. *See also* Colleges, black

Palmer, A. Mitchell, 203, 205

Palmer, L. B., 170

Palmetto, 146

Peabody, George Foster, 152, 157

Peabody Fund, 156

Pekin Theatre (Savannah), 67

Pelham, 198

Peonage: cases, 72–82; defined, 74; federal law, 75; and contract labor law, 76–77; whites oppose law enforcement, 79–80; extent of in Georgia, 80–82; and black migration, 188; mentioned, 173, 209

Perdue, James, 61

Perry, Heman: real estate interests, 44;
   founds Standard Life Insurance
   Company, 46; background, 47;
   contributions evaluated, 48
Perry, William Augustine, 149
Pershing, John J., 200
Phagan, Mary, 184–85
Pharmacists, black, 41–42
Pharrow, R. E., 43
Philippine Islands, 176n
Physicians, black, 35–36
Piedmont: region described, 3–4;
   whitecapping, 26
Piedmont Hotel: and Atlanta riot, 125
Pierpont, W. L., 30
Pilgrim Health and Life Insurance
   Company (Augusta), 45
Plasterers, black, 29, 30
Pledger, William A., 90
Plessy v. *Ferguson*, 20, 142
Police and blacks: and Atlanta riot,
   125, 127, 128; background and racial
   attitudes of law enforcement
   officers, 138–39
Poll tax, 94, 96, 103, 147
Ponder, Willis, 85
Population, black: by section, in
   Georgia, 2–4; in Savannah, 10; in
   Atlanta, 12–13; farmers and farm
   workers, 23; in urban Georgia, 27;
   industrial workers, professionals,
   trade and transportation workers,
   210n. *See also* Migration, black; *and
   individual occupations*
Populism and Populists: in 1890, 5–7,
   90; party platform opposes convict
   leasing, 84; mentioned, 97. *See also*
   Elections; Watson, Tom
Porter, Mrs. Henry, 123
Powell, Bartow, 25
Presbyterian Church, 55, 150
Proctor, Henry Hugh: and Pullman car
   protest, 19; accused of elitism, 61,
   62; Yale graduate, 63; petitions
   legislature on disfranchisement,
   101–2; on Prohibition, 112; role as
   mediator, 167; mentioned, 179, 180
Professions and professionals, black:
   34–35, 210; physicians, 35–36;

dentists, 35–36; attorneys, 37. *See
   also* Ministers, black; Teachers, black
Progressive era: and blacks, xi
Progressive movement: in Georgia,
   110–22
Progressive party: and 1912 campaign,
   107–9
Prohibition: in Georgia, 111–14, 122
Putney, F. F., 24

Ragtime: black opposition, 67, 68
Railroads: and black workers, 28;
   regulation, 110. *See also* Georgia
   Railroad strike
Randolph, A. Philip, 205
Realtors, black, 44
Reconstruction: in Georgia, 3, 5
Recreation, 64-71 *passim*
Red Cross: discrimination against
   blacks, 196n
Red Scare, 203
Red Summer, 203–5
Reed, Paul, 133–35
Renfroe, Amy, 145
Republican party (Ga.): and
   cooperation with Populists, 90;
   racial makeup, 90–91; influential
   blacks in, 91–92; intra-party dis-
   putes, 92–93; weaknesses, 104;
   mentioned, 167
Residential segregation, 9–16. *See also*
   Segregation
Restaurants, black, 41
Rockefeller, John D., 155, 156, 167
Roddenbery, Seaborn A., 182
Rogers, Cecilia Carter: on residential
   segregation, 15
Rogers, William H.: opposes dis-
   franchisement, 101
Rome: streetcar boycott, 16–17; cotton
   mill strike, 33; gubernatorial debate,
   98; protest against convict leasing,
   114; interracial meetings, 191
Roosevelt, Franklin D., 193
Roosevelt, Theodore: claims decline in
   peonage, 80–81; early relations with
   blacks, 104; attitude toward blacks,
   105–6; and election of 1912, 107–9;
   mentioned, 130, 166n, 167
Root, Elihu, 176n

Ross, Mrs. Edgar A., 117
Rucker, Henry L.: accused of elitism, 61, 62; political career, 91–94; petitions legislature on disfranchisement, 101–2; backs Progressive party in 1912, 107
Russell, Charles W., 76
Russell, Richard, Sr.: 1906 gubernatorial candidate, 100
Russell Sage Foundation: investigates Atlanta public schools, 146–47
Rutherford, Mildred, 120

St. Athanasius School (Brunswick), 149
St. Stephen's Episcopal Church (Savannah), 60, 61
Sanitation workers, 32
Savannah: and Emancipation Day celebration, 1–2; segregation, 9–11, 20; and streetcar boycott, 16–19; black workers, 28, 29; and National Negro Business League, 39, 189; black realtors, 44; black banking capital, 44, 45; Negro aristocracy, 59; Urban League, 63, 206; and Johnson-Jeffries fight, 69; adopts white primary, 94n; black private schools, 149; racial incident in bank, 169; and African emigration, 175; and *Birth of a Nation*, 186; and black migration, 187, 189; and local NAACP, 206; mentioned, 13, 50, 53, 63, 68, 91, 107, 133, 183
Savannah Electric Company, 18
Savannah *Press*, 18, 69, 215
Savannah Trades and Labor Assembly, 30. *See also* Labor unions and blacks
Savannah *Tribune*: critical of black ministers, 52; founding, 91; on 1906 governor's race, 100; opposes R. R. Wright, 169; advertising policies, 179; on black migration, 190–91; on World War I, 191, 200; mentioned, 163, 180, 189
School attendance, compulsory, 116–18, 122, 142
Schools, black: public, 141–48; private, 148–62. *See also* Colleges, black; Education, black

Scott, Emmett J.: letter from Alonzo Herndon, 49; reprimands Henry Rucker, 92; and *Voice of the Negro*, 165; and World War I, 193, 194, 197, 223
Segregation: 8–22 *passim;* in Savannah, 9–11, 14; in Augusta, 11–12; in Atlanta, 12–14, 20–21; Atlanta housing law, 13; in Albany, 14; of public transportation, 16–19, 115; in theaters, 22, 26; local laws, 110; of convicts, 114, 115; unsuccessful attempts to legislate, 115–16; in Washington, D.C., 181; after 1912 election, 182; in U.S. Army, 193–95, 200
Selective Service Act, 193, 198
Service Realty Company, 47. *See also* Perry, Heman
Sharecroppers, black: working and living conditions, 23–25, 27; and peonage, 76; and racial violence, 136; during World War I, 191. *See also* Agriculture, blacks in
Sheldon, Edward, 183
Simmons, William J., 185
Sims, Willie, 69
Slater Fund, 156, 159n
Slaton, John, 184
Slaton, William, 147
Slavery, 37, 56, 66, 135. *See also* Peonage
Smith, Charles Spencer, 55
Smith, David, 72–73
Smith, Hoke: and Georgia Railroad strike, 34; 1906 campaign for governor, 97–101; opposes blacks voting, 98–99; reputation as racial moderate, 99; elected governor, 100–101; loses Watson's support, 103; as governor, 111–15, 122; filibusters against women's suffrage, 120; opposes U.S. involvement in World War I, 192n; mentioned, 53, 173
Smith, James Monroe: violates peonage laws, 77–80; candidate for governor, 100
Smithonia, 78–79

Social Darwinism, 16

"Song of the Smoke, The," 178

Souls of Black Folk, The, 156, 170, 172, 180

Southern Bank of Savannah: segregates deposit windows, 20

Southern Education Board, 156

Southwest Georgia Conference of the A.M.E. Church, 187

Speer, Emory: presides in peonage trials, 74; on peonage, 80

Spelman College: founding, 53, 151, 153; prestige, 60; daily routine of students, 154; financing, 155, 159*n*; and white control, 160; conservative policies, 161. *See also* Colleges, black

Spingarn, Joel E. (medal), 207

Spivak, John L., 86–87

Sports, blacks in, 68–69, 183. *See also* Johnson, Jack

Spratling, George, 202*n*

Standard Life Insurance Company: founding, 46; expansion of operations, 47; reasons for failure, 47–48; mentioned, 58, 198. *See also* Perry, Heman

Statement from Governor Hugh M. Dorsey as to the Negro in Georgia, A, 208–9

Statesboro: Hodges murders, 132–33; lynchings, 133–35

Stinson, Richard D., 159

Stone Mountain, 185

Stowe, Harriet Beecher, 79

Streetcar boycotts, 16–19, 164

Suffrage, black: during Reconstruction, 3, 5; in 1890s, 6–7; in early 1900s, 94, 97; after disfranchisement, 103–4; and Niagara platform, 169. *See also* Disfranchisement; Elections; White primary

Sumter County: black voting in, 103

Sunday, Billy, 184

Tabernacle Baptist Church (Augusta), 53

Taft, William Howard: policies toward blacks, 106; racial attitudes, 107

Tapley, Lucy Hale, 161

Tate, James, 37

Teachers, black: pay and training, 143–44; in Atlanta, 147; support Booker T. Washington, 168–69

Telfair County, 137

Terrell, Joseph M.: and black troops, 115; and Atlanta riot, 126, 166

Terrell, Mary Church, 165

Terrell County, 97

"Terri" (Augusta), 11, 110–11

Theaters, black, 67

Thirteenth Amendment, 76, 77

Thomas, Jesse O., 205–6

Thomasville: and black migration, 187; interracial meetings, 190; NAACP chapter, 206–7

Thompson, R. F., 196

Tiedman, George W., 10

Tifton *Gazette,* 190

Tillman, Benjamin, 101

Toomer family, 56

Towns, George A.: boycotts streetcars, 17; petitions legislature on disfranchisement, 101–2; supports Monroe Trotter, 157–58; honors W. H. Crogman, 168; and Niagara Movement, 170; NAACP officer, 175; mentioned, 162

Tri-State Medical Association, 62

Trotter, Monroe: disrupts Booker T. Washington meeting, 157; meets with Woodrow Wilson, 181; mentioned, 92

Turner, Hayes, 201

Turner, Henry McNeal: protests removal as state senator, 5; and Pullman car protest, 19; on black clergy, 52; role in A.M.E. Church, 53–54; influential Mason, 56; and Johnson-Jeffries fight, 69; recommends Hoke Smith, 99; opposes Smith in 1906 race, 100; portrait in Georgia capitol, 151; as editor, 164; comments on America, 174; and Back-to-Africa movement, 175–78; evaluation of, 177; and race pride, 179; death, 179; mentioned, 163, 178, 180, 210

Turner, John, 176*n*

Turner, Mary, 201
Turpentine camps: peonage in, 77
Tuskegee Institute, 156, 159, 205. *See also* Washington, Booker T.
Twiggs County, 145

Uncle Remus's Home Magazine, 107
Uncle Tom's Cabin, 79, 185
Undertakers, black, 43
Underwood, Oscar: and 1912 campaign, 108
Union Development Company, 44
University of Georgia, 156
Upper class, black: definition, 15n; and social status, 55, 56, 59–62. *See also* Ministers, black; Professions and professionals, black; Teachers, black
Urban League: in Georgia, 189, 205–6, 210

Vagrancy laws, 87–88, 115
Valdosta: and peonage, 72–75; and lynching attempt, 139n
Van Renssalear, Mrs. Fleming, 123
Vardaman, James K., 101
Vaudeville theaters, black, 41, 67
Venereal disease: among black soldiers, 195
Vienna, 73
Vining, D. M., 88
Vinson, Carl, 182
Violence, racial: during Reconstruction, 5; on streetcars, 16–17; in Augusta, 17; whitecapping, 26; in Early County, 57; black retaliatory, 126–30, 136–40, 204; during World War I, 201–2; after World War I, 203–5. *See also* Atlanta riot; Lynchings
Voice: and Atlanta riot, 129. *See also Voice of the Negro*
Voice of Missions, 164
Voice of the Negro: and 1906 gubernatorial campaign, 100; and Atlanta riot, 129; founding and history, 165–67; mentioned, 180
Voice of the People, 164

Wage Earner's Savings Bank (Savannah), 45, 189
Walker, Alex, 128n

Walker, Charles T.: minister, 53; views, 167–68; as Booker T. Washington informant, 173n
Walker, T. W., 137
Ware, Edward T.: expels baseball players, 154–55; conflict with Du Bois, 157
Ware County: and peonage, 72–73
Washington, Berry, 137
Washington, Booker T.: and Pullman car protest, 19; founds National Negro Business League, 39; influence in Georgia, 45, 92–93, 163–80 *passim;* lobbies against disfranchisement bill, 96; dines with Roosevelt, 104; on Prohibition, 112; addresses Boston meeting, 157; and industrial education, 156–57; letter to J. W. E. Bowen, 166; opposes NAACP, 174–75; death, 180; mentioned, 27, 42, 53, 109, 140, 146, 159
Washington (D.C.), race riot, 203
Washington *Bee,* 17, 92
Washington, Ga., 43
Watson, Tom: Populist candidate, 5–6; attacks convict lease system, 84; opposes blacks voting, 97; supports Smith in 1906, 97; racist rhetoric, 101, 122; supports Brown in 1908, 103; opposes Wilson in 1912, 108; and *Leo Frank* case, 184–85; calls for KKK revival, 185; against U.S. involvement in World War I, 192n; elected to U.S. Senate, 210; mentioned, 96, 173
Waycross: black industry in, 44; and peonage, 72; interracial meetings, 190; mentioned, 87
Weekly Jeffersonian, 184–85
West Indies, 179
West Point, 192
White, Julius St. George, 137
White, Walter: on upper-class blacks, 61; and Atlanta riot, 126–27; investigates Turner lynchings, 201; on postwar racial climate, 205; mentioned, 162
White, William Jefferson: lynch threats against, 17; political activity, 93; background, 164; threatened by

White, William Jefferson (*Cont.*)
  KKK, 165; and Equal Rights
  Convention, 173; mentioned, 180
White primary, 94–97, 103
Whitecapping, 26, 209
Williams, J. B., 139
Williams, John, 81
Williams, L. E., 189
Wilmington (N.C.) race riot, 100
Wilson, Woodrow: and 1912 campaign
  in Georgia, 108–9; segregates federal
  agencies, 181; on *Birth of a Nation*,
  186n; has black support of foreign
  policy, 191–93; dismisses Fulton
  County draft board, 196; opposes
  lynching, 201n
Winter, Lovick P., 112
Wiregrass section: black population,
  3–4
Wister, Owen, 105
Women, black: in Georgia cities, 27n;
  in churches, 52; and women's
  suffrage, 120–22. *See also*
  Chautauqua Circle; Hope, Lugenia;
  Laney, Lucy; Neighborhood Union;
  Teachers, black

Women's Christian Temperance Union,
  119
Women's suffrage, 120–22
Woodward, James: and mayoral
  elections, 95; and Atlanta riot, 124,
  131
Work, Monroe: on black business, 40;
  and Niagara Movement, 170
"Work or fight" laws, 198–99
World War I: black business in, 40;
  black response, 192–93, 199–202;
  training of black troops, 193–96;
  selective service and blacks, 196–97;
  and "bounty hunting," 197–98; and
  "work or fight" laws, 198–99; black
  soldiers, 200–201
Wright, Richard R., Sr.: political
  activities, 93; educator and
  businessman, 168–69; mentioned,
  183
Wrightsville: and "work or fight" laws,
  199

Young Women's Christian Association
  (Phillis Wheatley branch), 196